Painting at School

If the essential experience of the world of color is not nurtured in our time, children will be born who will no longer have an organ with which to experience color. Life becomes visible through color. However, humanity will no longer be able to see colors, much as it is no longer able to experience elemental beings. The world will become bleak and grey.

– From a conversation between Rudolf Steiner and
Margarita Woloschin during the construction of the
first Goetheanum, 1914–1917

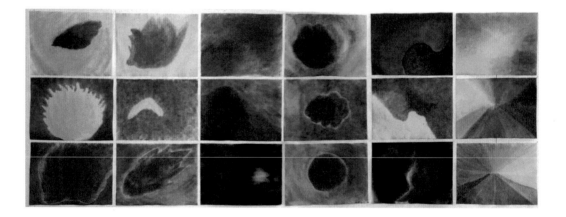

Dick Bruin and Attie Lichthart

Painting at School

A handbook for elementary
and secondary education in Waldorf schools

Special thanks to:

> Hildegard Berthold-Andrae, Fritz Weitmann and Margrit Jünemann,
> our inspiring teachers
>
> Peter Schiefer for his steadfast color research
>
> Filip and Carine Desmet from Belgium, for making their students' work
> available to us
>
> Bas Bijker for taking care of the digitalization of the pictures
>
> Tiny and Spiros, our spouses, for their loving support while we worked
> on this colorful project
>
> All our painting students and colleagues for their wonderful
> contributions

Printed with support from the Waldorf Curriculum Fund

Published by:

Waldorf Publications at the
Research Institute for Waldorf Education
351 Fairview Avenue, Unit 625
Hudson, NY 12534

Title: *Painting at School*
Authors: Dick Bruin and Attie Lichthart
Translator: Barbara Mees
Copyeditor: Melissa Merkling
Proofreader: Ruth Riegel
Layout: Ann Erwin

ISBN# 978-1-943582-13-6
Copyright ©2018 Waldorf Publications

Originally published in Dutch by Christofoor uitgeverij (Publishing House),
The Netherlands, with the title: *Schilderen op School. Een werkboek voor primair,
voortgezet en beroepsonderwijs, ontwikkeld vanuit de vrieschoolpedagogie*
Translated and printed with permission from the publisher.

Contents

Part 4   Grades 7–8 curriculum

Part 5   The high school curriculum

Foreword

Writing a curriculum is an adventure, because it's difficult to pin down an education that is alive. A curriculum can become too set: "It must be done this way!" That is the last thing we intend to do. The outlines in this book are there only to give the reader direction. It is not enough for teachers to prepare and teach painting lessons relating to all the different subjects; we must also keep our eye on the bigger picture over the years. Through our own painting experiences and our understanding of the art of painting, we can develop wonderful insights into the workings of color. It is why this book contains so much information about color. We also give concrete lesson examples:

- basic exercises for the teacher;
- a general introduction for each grade;
- sample lessons for each grade.

If you are looking for painting exercises for a specific grade, be sure to look for them in the chapters on earlier grades as well. You can use them as introductory lessons, especially for students who have not yet mastered all the exercises for a particular grade.

More challenging exercises, which can be reused in later grades, are also given for every grade. It is therefore highly recommended that you read the chapters on earlier grades.

Not all grade-school teachers are natural painters. Painting is a talent, just like the talent for sculpting or music that we find in our colleagues. Nevertheless, it is preferable for painting to be taught by the class teacher in the elementary grades. The extra energy we invest in our own development can be felt by our students and influences our work with them. A number of basic painting exercises for teachers are included in Part 2 of this book.

Painting classes should also not be seen as isolated events, but should be integrated as much as possible into the program of the day or week, in both content and rhythm. If the student-teacher relationship is based on

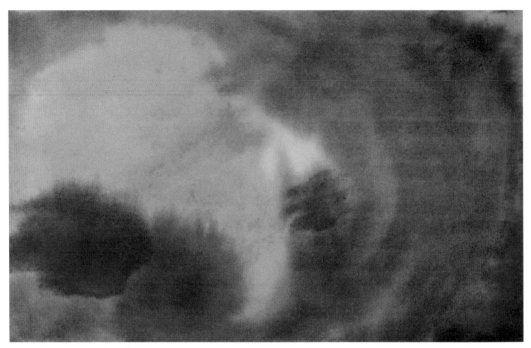

Color exercise. (Student, age 6)

trust and safety, painting classes can be a valuable pedagogical space for experimentation and experiencing the joys of color and art in general.

To make the text more readable, sources are not cited extensively, but are included at the end of the book. The bibliography gives an abundance of background reading material so that interested readers can focus on what interests them. A chronological overview of Rudolf Steiner's quotes on painting at school can be found on pages 438 and 439 of his book *Farbenerkenntnis (Colour)*.

We hope the explanations and examples in this book will be an inspiration for painting lessons and that the children will enjoy their discovery of the world of color.

Part 1

Painting in education

1 An introduction

1. The child's colorful world

> When you look
> Around you
> You'll see that
> Everything has color.
> *K. Schippers*

Children are constantly surrounded by color. Colors disappear into the night; daylight allows them to reappear. The colors in nature undergo major changes over the course of the year, every year. The grey, somber winter blossoms into spring colors: first a fresh spring green, then colorful flowers and a pink glow in the budding beech forest. When spring gives way to summer, the greens around us become heavier and darker. Children pick wildflowers that grow along roadsides and cover the meadows. Gardens become a profusion of color experiences, and every child has a preference for a particular color or flower. When autumn comes, things become even more interesting. Bright, warm new colors glow on trees and bushes. Before the leaves fall and the plants yield to the earth, they display the fruit of the warm summer sun once again in yellows, reds, oranges and browns.

Life, which until now was found in profusion above ground, moves inward into the soil, into the earth itself. In winter the colors withdraw as well and become much more subtle. Bare branches show up sharply against the chilly autumn sky. Everyone takes refuge inside. Children now experience the color impressions of the home's interior. Today we see the most fantastic colors in furnishings, on walls and floors, from soft pastel hues to bright, vividly dyed fabrics.

Colors are present everywhere we look, indoors and outdoors. Children's fashions feature lively, flowery or striped designs bursting with color. Prints from all over the world appear on dresses, blouses and pants. Patterns and

17

colors can be mixed and matched every which way. It's a wonderful time for children when color is so present in clothes, in the home and in the environment.

The day has its own color nuances: a red or orange sunrise, pitch-black threatening thunderclouds, or the bright blue of a cloudless sky. What child doesn't admire a glowing sunrise, or hope to find a pot of gold at the end of a rainbow shining against dark clouds? In the evening we gaze silently at the moon, casting its pale, slightly mysterious light onto houses and landscapes.

Children love to play with light. Where there's light, there are shadows. Shadow tag, with shadows long and short cast by friends, is a favorite game. Older children will notice that shadows can also be colored. As children grow, new color experiences continually beckon, particularly during trips to new regions or countries.

Wherever a big sky is visible because of a flat landscape or seascape, the sky's light sets the mood in a big way; different possibilities abound, including dramatic changes. In coastal areas, clouds, rain and fog play a constantly shifting game with sea winds and light, giving rise to fresh, lively colors. Consciously or not, children internalize this play of color and want to work with it. For all the children in the world, playing with color is a favorite game. At school, daily experiences with color are provided and expressed, and learning becomes playful. Both parent and teacher provide helping hands in this process. This workbook has been written for them.

2. Colors and their effects on us

Everything around us has color: blue sky, golden-yellow corn, grey buildings, pink blossoms. The younger the child, the more transparent the skin separating the outer and inner worlds. Colors affect our emotional life. Whether or not we want them to, colors get to us and permeate us by way of our observations, our senses. Colors can greatly influence or "color" our moods. On the other hand, we express ourselves with the colors we choose in clothes, interiors or works of art, setting up a lively dialogue with the outside world through color.

The painter Wassily Kandinsky (1866-1944) was inspired not by the reality of visible nature, but by his inner feelings, which led him to "Seelengemälde" (soul paintings), a type of abstract expressionism. He said the following about color:

In general, in this way, color is a means of directly influencing the soul. Color is the key. The eye is the hammer. The soul is the many stringed grand piano. The artist is the hand playing this or that key consciously causing the vibration of the human soul.[1]

3. The child

Children are more susceptible than adults in general, so they are also more sensitive to colors. For example, seeing an overcast grey sky when opening the bedroom curtains can sometimes set the mood for the rest of the day. Or in a lush, colorful summer meadow, a child may be inspired to run wild with joy. These are extreme examples, but they show the obvious, powerful effects of color in any environment. The youngest children will pick up the most brightly colored toy; in a way, they become one with the color. Inwardly they "color" themselves constantly to match their surroundings. One child may feel comfortable with a particular color while another is adversely affected by it. The child's environment has a direct effect on the working and shaping of the body. Color influences the way the body absorbs experiences.

In adults these forces are less strong; we are less open to this phenomenon in our daily lives and can close ourselves off to a degree. Adults have thicker skins.

Rudolf Steiner pointed out that even our metabolism can be stimulated by correct development of the sight organs through color and light.[2] We know that our appetite is influenced by the colors of food. Who really likes blue pudding? Thus a link is revealed between health, food and color. Color therapy is the subject of serious research, development and applications. Rudolf Steiner tells us about the effects of color on the child at the change of teeth:

> An excited child, referred to as a nervous child, should be treated
> differently with regard to his environment than a lethargic,
> inactive child. Here everything should be considered, from the
> colors of the room and its contents to the clothes the child
> wears. An excited child should be surrounded by red or orange
> colors and dressed in these colors. Conversely, a passive child
> should have blue and blue-green colors in his environment. These
> contrasting colors are important, because they are awakened
> internally. The complementary color of red is green, of blue

orange-yellow. These complementary colors are reproduced by the physical organs of the child and create a structure in accordance with the color that is necessary for the child.[3]

After the ninth year, as children become more distant from their outer environment and develop their inner world further, the influence of color will acquire a different character. The complementary effect diminishes and, as in adults, direct color observation becomes stronger: Red will activate and green will bring peace. Those of us who work with children know for sure that color works strongly on the inner self. But how does it do that? This is knowledge that requires the schooling of observation, as child and educator travel the road together.

4. The art of raising children

Our fast-paced world increasingly places new demands on us. The minute we feel we've mastered one new development, another shows up. Many technological innovations are all but incomprehensible to the layman; we may feel we are constantly, hopelessly trying to catch up, with the result that we're tempted to give up and close our eyes to it all. It's not easy to deal with the constant barrage of external impressions and the inner reactions they provoke. The extremes are far apart these days and can create great tension in us: How can I find a balance? We can all recognize this dilemma. Could the art of raising children provide the answer?

5. Head, heart and hands

As individuals we are built up of polar forces. On one hand we are part of the realm of nature—the animal, plant and mineral worlds—with our bodies; on the other hand, our ideals, wishes and expectations come from a world in which our spiritual origins lie. The soul, an inner space, is nourished both by the thoughts that live as ideals in our imagination and by the creative force that comes from our will. (Schiller calls these areas "Form- und Stofftrieb.") Our soul also lives in the opposition created by these two areas. The center, where balance is created, is the location of our emotional life. Physically this is expressed through rhythmic breathing, which constantly links our inside and outside. The heart and blood circulation also connect these opposites. We can concretely apply an idea, which has been formed into a clear image by our thinking, through our enthusiasm (warming to something), by means of our will (i.e., our hands). On the other hand, by performing an action (at first unconsciously), we can become enthusiastic; this can eventually lead to an idea or thought. Many a notion enters our thinking life this way and can then be dealt with consciously. Two areas are always involved: the essentially different qualities of thinking and acting. The feeling life is the bridge between them.

The soul world, in which the three soul qualities of thinking, feeling and willing function independently yet together, expands as it processes new experiences. The soul matures through new actions, feelings and thoughts. In thinking and willing, there is tension between one-time events and recurring events, between spontaneous creativity and repetitive training. If these natural, lively interactions in the soul are halted, causing the three soul qualities to become isolated from one another, stress and fear will take possession of the soul. In a manner of speaking, the head will no longer know what the hand or foot is doing. Ideas will remain unrealized ideals; feelings will be suppressed or bottled up. An individual may become unreachable and apathetic. The distance between inner life and the world increases, and the soul is no longer capable of providing a connection. In contrast, healthy soul development is constantly creating a unity within which we can develop the capability to answer questions—external questions as well as those in which our intentions and inspirations live. To guide these developmental processes in growing children is a real art.

6. Working as an artist

Soul development is stimulated and supported by artistic activity. The three abovementioned soul qualities are appealed to by creativity. By doing, we become enthusiastic and can thus develop new ideas. When we have thought of something we want to develop, we first go through a process of consideration, of discernment. This takes place in the area of feeling. Eventually we can take the necessary actions to realize our original idea. The process of painting, particularly painting with transparent paints, is especially suitable for experiencing the artistic process. Head and hands are continuously in communication with each other when appealed to by feeling.

Two-dimensional painting. (Attie Lichthart)

7. Painting

When we paint we enter the two-dimensional world. The illusion of depth is created only by the effects of color: Some will fall back, some come forward. Thus, they create space, not through the interplay of light and darkness, but purely through their effects, through so-called "color perspective." A certain training of the eye is required to recognize this in a painting; we are too used to seeing the successful results of classical linear perspective, in which the illusion of space is created by lines and the use of light and dark. Many examples of color perspective can be found in works by early 20th-century painters. They rejected the old traditions and fought for a new way of thinking. Paintings became "flatter," and as a result color interplay became more prominent. The almost physically palpable spaces of classical painting gave way to new, alternative representations of reality. Vanishing points and fixed elements of composition no longer applied. The artist Cézanne shows us how painted objects free themselves from their environment through the use of color. They seem to free themselves from gravity, thus creating a new reality in another dimension.

Steiner identifies another tendency in art as follows:

Deeper insight into colors has somehow dissipated and the artistic approach nowadays has given way to a falsified sculptural approach. Nowadays we prefer to paint three-dimensional people onto the canvas. With that aim, spatial perspective was developed (which actually emerged in the fifth post-Atlantean epoch)[4] which, with the perspective line, tells us that one aspect is more in the background and the other more in the foreground, meaning it wants to conjure spatial relationships onto the canvas. This rejects at the outset the most important material the artist has, for he does not create in space, he creates on a flat surface and it is quite ridiculous to want to experience the thing spatially when one's basic material is flat.[5]

23

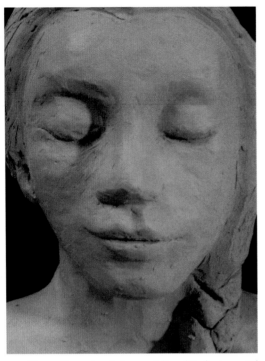

Three-dimensional clay modeling. (Student, age 16)   One-dimensional form drawing. (Student, age 9)

8. Sculpture and modeling

One art that genuinely requires three-dimensional physical space is sculpture. Objects created by clay modeling or sculpture have a front and back, right and left sides, top and bottom. Sculpture explores space, lends itself to space. We can observe a sculpture from different angles.

9. Form drawing

The primary goal of form drawing is to capture a movement, small or large, made in space by a hand, a foot or the whole body. A movement expressed in a line is the essence of form drawing. The line becomes solidified movement, the movement's trace. This play of lines exists in the one-dimensional world. The line becomes clearly visible on paper, contrasting with the background. Dark shades of crayon or pencil are preferable for form drawing. Color plays no part here. The eye must be given the chance to follow the movement, the gesture of the line, without interruption. We prefer to describe this subject with verbs, rather than nouns that anchor the movement excessively and often call up fixed images. For example, terms such as "falling asleep" or "waking up" give the student more space than "spiral" when describing a movement that goes in and then out again. Verbs stress the process more, the path that must be traveled in time.

10. Three paths in the curriculum

In the Waldorf curriculum we see that to work with these three different ways of dealing with space—through lines, color and image—three separate courses of study have been developed: the curricula for form drawing, painting and sculptural modeling. In the upper grades and high school these directions can, of course, intersect in many ways. In the first few years, however, it is important for the teacher to alternate the three areas.

In addition to painting, modeling with beeswax or clay and form drawing are also important for the child's diverse artistic development in the first years of school. They each appeal to different parts of the developing human being. When these three fields are clearly and separately addressed, students will be less inclined to fill in areas with color during form drawing, or to start drawing with a paintbrush.

2   The painting lesson

1. Preparation

Preparing for painting lessons involves several essential elements. An indication by Steiner immediately points to one of the most important: One should be able to think equally well in colors and forms as one can in concepts, in thoughts,[6] a task that naturally goes beyond just one painting lesson. The foundation for the necessary skill of "thinking in color" is years of working with color in all its facets. Study and self-motivation, observation and the practice of teaching itself will help us work responsibly and consciously as we create painting assignments. Each small step inspires the next. The need to connect theory and practice should encourage us to undertake further study and research. Through practice, the teacher walks the path together with the children.

   The more experienced the teacher, the shorter the preparation time needed. By painting an assignment yourself prior to teaching the lesson, you gain experience and become better able to set the stage and give the right directions to the children. Sometimes several practice sessions are needed to achieve the proper result. The assignment should always align with previous and future exercises and fit the children's experience and potential. Once the assignment is clear to us, we need to ask ourselves an important question: Should this be a painting or a drawing? We need to be able to recognize the considerable difference between color area and line. By working with (two-dimensional) color areas we address the feeling world; the (one-dimensional) line appeals more to consciousness (see Part 1, sections 7, 8 and 9).

2. The lesson

After the paints have been prepared (Basic exercise 1 for the teacher, see page 74), the actual lesson can start. In the early grades, the paints and water jars are shared by pairs of children. Each student has his or her own painting board, paper, sponge, brush and perhaps a painting apron or smock. Preparing and passing out the materials can be done in several ways, provided the sequence is well thought out and organized. During a previous break the children can take turns getting everything ready, or it can also be done by the whole class. Supplies are handed out row by row and collected the same way at the end of the lesson. Even the youngest children can distribute most of the materials together. Order and quiet are important; it will help if we follow the exact same well-planned sequence of distributing and collecting every time.

To let paintings dry slowly after class, a convenient method is to leave them on the boards and store the boards horizontally in a painting cupboard (see pages 63–64). One can also leave them to dry on the floor at the front or back of the classroom or on the desks if the classroom will be empty for the next period. Each class will find its own practical solution.

Painting at the same time each week also supports the teacher. Rhythm is healthy for both student and teacher. Another advantage of a fixed day for painting (preferably not the last day of the week) is that the teacher will be better able to observe painting's aftereffects. Letting color work on the child during the night's sleep is important. Working in the two-dimensional sphere, painting has its specific effect in the etheric-astral realm. Steiner frequently stresses the importance of learning to breathe correctly and of healthy sleep in connection with learning.[7]

3. What can we see in a student's work?

The painting lesson lets us peek into the inner world of the child. The soul still expresses itself directly and purely in painting. All children do this, even if overshadowed by life circumstances: They "show their true colors." If we can learn to observe this expression, we can use it for further pedagogical work. How does the child paint? How does she understand the assignment; how does she get started? How does she deal with the equipment; how does she hold the brush? Which movements stand out; which colors and

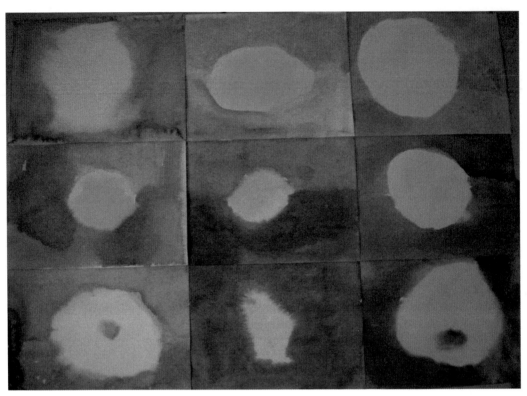

Nine paintings by 6-years-olds, arranged according to color and form.

forms are emphasized? Does the child crawl into the paper with her tongue sticking out, or does she sit back and work in a slightly detached way? Is the brush pushed through the paper, or does it slide inaudibly across the surface? Is the work dry or wet? Are her cheeks red from the effort? Are her hands sweaty?

Asking ourselves these kinds of questions and listening for the answers are meaningful when we want to know more about a child. These observations are also important for working with the four temperaments in the class. Each child is inclined toward a certain temperament. Is the student predominantly choleric, melancholic, sanguine or phlegmatic, or a mixture? Observations throughout various lessons, and throughout the different seasons, can give clues to help the teacher get started. This will be discussed later in the book.

Exhibition at a teachers' college in Ireland.

4. Displaying student work

Before hanging paintings on the wall, let's look at the work of the class as a whole. The teacher must first create some order in the colorful "chaos." The paintings can usually be divided into four categories (not the temperaments!): paintings with strong colors; paintings with light, thin colors; paintings with distinct forms and strong boundaries; and paintings with soft, fluid colors. Imagine grouping the work in this way. (If a painting doesn't fall obviously into one of these categories, we can put it in the middle, between the extremes.)

We could hang the lighter paintings at the top right and those with more powerful colors at the bottom left. Paintings with softer forms (fluid, without defined edges) could go to the right and the more strongly formed paintings to the left. In this way we create an initial order, and the eye (sense of movement) can slide from right to left, bottom to top, to meet the transitions in color and form. This sequence is pleasing to the eye and evokes a feeling of pleasure (sense of life), especially in the children. In a class of twenty-plus students, all these types will be amply represented.

Or does the class as a whole have a certain tendency? Often a certain balance appears, which would hardly be discernible if we look at a random collection of paintings on a wall.

By adopting a specific plan or order in displaying the paintings (many others are possible, of course), each individual child's achievement is seen as part of the whole. This contrasts with discussing and showing each painting separately, which takes much time and emphasizes individual achievement. A child will not be able find his own work on the wall too quickly; once found, it is seen as part of the whole.

5. Class discussions

The following day or later in the week, we can hold a class discussion. First we review the assignment that the paintings strove to fulfill. Some of the children will talk immediately; others will chime in. We now look to see in which paintings the assignment can be clearly identified. The children look and whisper among themselves; give them time to figure it out. "Where is blue looking forward to the arrival of yellow?" "Where is red putting a spell on yellow?" "Can anyone see orange sitting in a corner?" From these questions and the ensuing conversation, both teacher and students will develop a new color language, a new vocabulary as they learn to describe without judging. The contributions by the children are important. During the conversation, the teacher encourages the children: "What do you think of this?" or "Did you choose that one too?" Colors can manifest in the most diverse ways: in strength and dynamics, in composition, in relation to each other, in tone, in light and darkness, and so on. In the lower grades a color language develops; in the upper grades we can refer to natural phenomena: "Why do you think this is a night mood?"

Class discussions are also appropriate for other subjects. A listening attitude is built, which is why it is important that a degree of discipline be kept. The teacher holds back and guides where necessary. She continually tries to lead the class back to the phenomena themselves, because even a discussion about red and yellow can turn into a chat about the neighbor's dog. Furthermore, a new painting assignment can arise from what is seen and talked about during the discussion.

Left: Mohammed, age 6, wets the paper with a natural sponge.
Right: Brilliant yellow in the center.

6. Evaluation and self-reflection

Evaluation and assessment are part of learning. Evaluation can take many forms. Nowadays methods have been developed in which children assess their own work and become the owners of each new step. We can use these methods because they help children learn to value their work through observation and reflection.

For example, in fifth grade, a teacher wants to call attention to painting techniques: brushwork, the wet/dry relationship, working with the paints, and so forth. Together with the students, the teacher creates a list of points that will be given extra attention in the next painting lessons. After two lessons, the students examine their own work with the list of points in mind (self-assessment). They write down what went well and what could be better. A few lessons later the work is reviewed again. Now another student or group of students looks at the work (peer assessment), each writing an assessment. Once a period of painting on a specific theme is finished, the work can be taken home, accompanied by a number of questions that the children have thought up for the parents. At home, the work is shown and the parents answer the questions. In this way students, parents and teacher(s) form a pedagogical unity in which they are all involved in the creative process of developing an image or picture of the child. This process can be repeated at another time in the school year, with new points of interest. These written reflections form part of the student's portfolio and can be included in year-end reports.

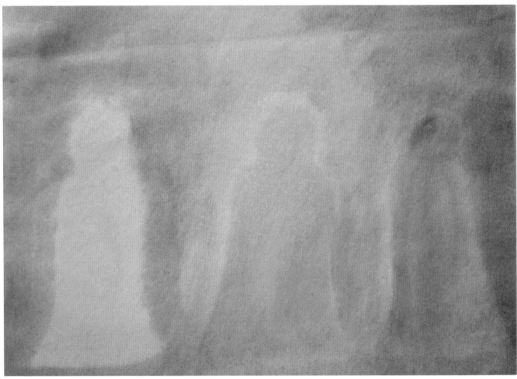

Four paintings by 9-year-old children in which the four temperaments can be observed.

7. Recognizing temperaments

For a more elaborate description of the four temperaments, we refer you to the many lectures on the subject by Rudolf Steiner.[8] Basically, we can distinguish four fundamental moods of soul in the temperaments. These moods are created from two different tendencies, like green from yellow and blue: the soul-spirit being and the physical body, which is also strongly determined by heredity. The way these tendencies interweave is a determining factor in the "temperament color" of the child. It is up to the educator to observe and recognize them and, through education, work with the one-sidedness so that there can be harmony among the qualities of all four temperaments. This is the ideal situation. In her book *Formenzeichnen*[9] *(Form Drawing)*, Hildegard Berthold-Andrae makes clear connections of the temperaments to form drawing. The paintings of the four temperaments in the book *Education Towards Freedom* by Frans Carlgren come from her practice (see Bibliography).

In many ways understanding the temperament is the real key to recognizing and addressing the extreme one-sidedness of a child. The temperament is expressed in the child's paintings through the choice and composition of the colors, in the way color areas spread, and in either strong or vague forms. There is no ready-made recipe; we can, however, give guidelines to help with the teacher's research.

The *choleric* child is often inclined to use strong colors; the areas are formed, but not always sharply contrasted. The painting is a dynamic whole in which inner dynamics stand out.

The *phlegmatic* is often a master of color transitions. Use of color can be strong here too. The unity of the painting stands out.

The *melancholic* child usually wants to handle the colors very carefully. His work is usually translucent, thin and often a little dry with strong edges. It does not flow. Strong colors are sometimes present, like lead on the paper.

Mobility in color form and gesture often characterize the work of the *sanguine* child. She tends toward too much moisture and an unformed quality, but may produce surprising color nuances.

No child has one temperament exclusively, but one often dominates. However, good educators will not label a child. We must weigh and balance, observe again, and have discussions with ourselves and our colleagues. There are many moments throughout the school years when expressions of temperament come to the fore. The painting lesson is one such moment because, when they paint, children reveal themselves naturally in color and form.

The teacher leads and lets go at the same time. Experience bridges this seeming paradox as we learn to do both together. When talking about painting, Steiner did not have childlike art in mind; he refers to elements directly inspired by and connected to "great art." A weekly drop in the child's colorful "bowl of the soul" contributes to a healthy upbringing.

8. Therapeutic and pedagogical painting – the difference

The classroom door opens and the art therapist beckons to a child. The other students carry on with their work. This child will be given undivided attention for a short time. He paints. What he paints can vary considerably. How he paints matters a great deal: delicate or strong colors, from wet to dry or vice versa, small or large areas, with what kind of brush strokes, etc. The therapist's choice of words and his relationship with colors and materials are carefully thought out: respectful, loving. The child has the opportunity to express himself while painting. The therapist is there to guide each step. He observes intensely and leads the process.

In collaboration with a doctor, the art therapist chooses a medium for the child: sculptural modeling, form drawing, painting, or a combination. Each artistic activity works in a certain way in the feeling area. From the soul the essence of humanity is nourished and healed. Working with color and water generally has a liberating, loosening effect. How we fall asleep and awaken is influenced by the images that keep on working in the soul through our thoughts. Painting brings an enrichment of the world of images. Dealing with color strengthens the senses and a sensitivity to qualities. Atmosphere, mood, gesture and/or tone become part of reality. If a certain rigidity appears in feeling, painting can make one more receptive.

What the art therapist does through painting during therapy must be seen as a support to medical treatment. Consultation with a doctor is therefore imperative. Diagnosis and pre- and post-therapy discussions usually include the class teacher.

Painting as described in this book (for whole classes) also has a certain therapeutic value for each student. However, therapy in the sense of art therapy is out of the question when it comes to the class as a whole. By emphasizing the therapeutic aspect too strongly, one could think of, and use, painting like a healing bath or a remedy; that is certainly not its primary function.

In schools today, including Waldorf schools, it is right and necessary to encourage painting, but not for its therapeutic value. Painting as a subject in the curriculum serves a pedagogical purpose. Together with the other subjects, it forms the complete human being. In school in general, and in painting with the class, we are concerned with the healthy teaching of subject matter; the healthy incarnation of the young human being is our goal.

Painting at school is different from painting as therapy. One cannot simply translate the "what" and "how" of art therapy into a pedagogical situation. However, certain ways of working in art therapy, such as handling materials with respect, painting certain forms or creating specific color moods or techniques, can also be good for certain classes. A firm, step-by-step procedure, or even painting specific images (the sun, the grass, etc.), as is done in therapeutic pedagogy, can also be used as an educational means. Yet what is appropriate in therapy is not automatically appropriate in the classroom. The child-therapist, therapist-child relationship is the therapeutic basis on which all sorts of activities become "therapy."

The teacher aims for a different, pedagogical goal. She makes choices as to content and method with the children's phase of development in mind. She builds on what has gone before and prepares new material. She makes sure that assignments are in keeping with the framework of the curriculum as a whole. Class or group one-sidedness and individual differences between children are taken into account in the series of assignments and variations in method which painting offers. The teacher provides developmental material that moves the healthy child, including those with a tendency to one-sidedness.

The therapist may draw from this curriculum, but she does so with "healing" in mind as she seeks the best approach. The "how" and "what" as well as the essence of painting therapy are different from pedagogical painting as done in the classroom. Collaboration between the teacher and therapist benefits both, and thus benefits the child. A chronological overview of therapy and painting as discussed by Steiner can be found in the book *Farbenerkenntnis (Colour)*, pages 452–456.

In relation to the above, we would like to discuss two color-form assignments that Steiner described during a lecture in Oxford. In the lecture he describes the one-sidedness of "everything that remains in the head" and how "subject matter doesn't stick."[10] From this example, both the teacher and the therapist will be able to take what is relevant to them.

We must first put Steiner's indications in the right context. He describes how the teacher, through a long-term relationship with the child, approaches the artistic-pedagogical process layer by layer via the temperament and nature (e.g., Is this a "thinking" or "doing" child?), finally arriving at the individuality. In a subject such as painting, this could mean, for example, that the teacher does not have all the children paint the same thing, but that a child who seems to "remain in his head" is encouraged to begin with yellow and lilac at the center and place colors next to each other.

The second assignment takes a different approach for a child in whom impressions flow directly away from the head into the rest of the organism. The colors are more mixed in this case, and a drawing element is used in the brush strokes; from the center between violet and yellow, the violet flows away, dissolves, fans out upward. The colors fade and the line becomes important.

Steiner says this exercise should be done in watercolor. He continues with the example of how these two differently-natured children should be approached in physical education classes, with tasks that go beyond the subject. He not only pleads for the class teacher to be involved in the artistic pedagogical process, but also gives an example of how this becomes an individual task. Each child should paint independently. "A closed form arises which starts to shine within itself." The fanning-out shape can be seen as the learned subject matter flowing out of the head: The head becomes "like a sieve." The child's actions emphasize movement and line. Thus, we connect our teaching to what the child "is," and create a personalized assignment using color, form and direction based on our observations of the child during other classes. (For more information, please see the complete lecture.)

Below is the translation of the above exercises as Rudolf Steiner described them in Oxford. In the first exercise, we start from yellow-blue-red (purple) while the colors remain next to each other. In the second painting, we again use yellow-blue-red next to each other, and then let the blue-violet fan out upwards with long brush strokes; likewise the red.

It concerns the contact between teacher and child veritably being immersed in an artistic element. This will often cause the teacher to know intuitively, instinctively, how he should deal in relation to the individual child at a given moment. Let us, in order to clarify this, imagine the matter as concretely as possible.

Imagine, we have a child before us with learning difficulties. We notice: The images we offer, the feelings we wish to awaken, the ideas we wish to give the child—all this produces such a strong blood circulation and such a nerve impulse in the head, that the thing I want to impart to the child cannot, as it were, penetrate from the head into his remaining organism. The physical organization of the head becomes partially melancholic in a manner of speaking. The child has difficulty sending on messages from perceived images or what she experiences. What has been learned somehow gets trapped in the head. It cannot permeate the rest of the organism.

Specifically all artistic elements in upbringing and education will be entirely instinctively tuned to this, when guiding such a child with an artistic feeling. To a child such as this I will impart the painting, working with color, entirely differently from other children. And it is important to point out that this is why painting has been part of the Waldorf education from the outset. After all, I have told you how writing is developed from painting. In painting we can approach each child individually, because the child has to do everything herself.

Imagine I have a child before me, the way I have just described her. I let her paint. Then, if there is a proper artistic contact between teacher and pupil, something will appear on that sheet of paper the child is filling with color that is completely different from another child.

Let me show you roughly, schematically, what should appear on the paper of such a child, where the impressions, the ideas get more or less stuck in the head. More or less the following should appear. A color patch [yellow] will appear, then this type of color patch [purple] because it is about the harmony of the colors. Then there will be here a transition area [orange] which will stretch a little further and the whole will be closed off on the outside [blue]. This is how the sheet will look with a child whose ideas remain stuck in the head, as it were.

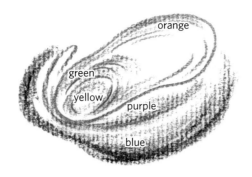

Imagine now, I have another child, where the ideas do not at all remain stuck in the head, but leak through it as it were, like through a sieve. Everything sags into the body, the child cannot hold anything because his head is a sieve. There are holes in it, everything seeps through. You should be able to experience that the condition of this child is such that the circulatory system wants to absorb everything from the rest of the body.

Then you instinctively, intuitively want this child to follow directions and cause something entirely different to appear. With such a child you are likely to see the following appear on paper. You will see that the colors take on less closed off, less rounded shapes. You will see them elongate more and the painting turn into drawing, with loops appearing that take on more of the character of drawing. You will also notice that the colors are not so differentiated: In the first drawing they are strongly differentiated, but here [see the second drawing below] they are to a lesser degree.

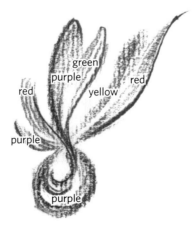

When we paint with proper colors—not with that awkward chalk, which does not allow one to show this properly—we will be able to have a curative and healing effect on those properties of the children we have discussed; on the one hand through pure color, on the other colorful forms.[11]

There is no direct indication as to the student's age, but in view of the other subjects discussed in this lecture and considering the skills necessary to execute this exercise technically, we estimate the age to be that of a second- to fourth-grade student. Whether and how often the exercises should be repeated is not mentioned, and therefore depends on the insight of the teacher who knows the children.

Steiner's description shows us a class with individual students and groups, all painting, with both therapeutic and pedagogical effects.

9. High school

Most of Steiner's recommendations for high school will be discussed in the chapters describing the curriculum for those classes. His so-called school sketches as examples of subject matter, and how they should be developed starting from the color, are discussed at length starting on page 274. He points to the riches that Dürer's etchings offer in the way of developmental material for the high school student. "Start again and again with the simplest" is one of his mottoes, which stays valid over the years, but does not mean "always do the same thing." It is important for the high school teacher to continuously shape the elementary aspects that Steiner mentions into new work forms and themes adjusted for the student and class, to pursue topical interests, and to build on the rich technical experience the students bring with them from elementary school.

The teacher will use class and individual discussions to help the students with assignments. As in elementary school, judgments and especially preconceptions must be avoided. By asking questions the teacher can make sure that students learn to observe, contemplate and judge their own work—not in a detached way, but with the goal of learning, changing and doing.

In high school, students' work can also be viewed as an open fan of possibilities all emerging from a common theme. However, the 14- to 18-

year-old is strongly focused on achievement. More variety can be seen in the assignments and creation of work than in elementary school.

The teacher must keep discussions from becoming long, deep-digging sessions. At the same time, high school students will not accept superficiality and will benefit much more from honesty. In each lesson, at any time and in any manner, moments of contemplation can be scheduled that will have a stimulating effect for the next assignments. For example, one project is discussed, or two projects are compared to clarify a point. The work of all the students can be hung up or laid out on the floor. The students can observe silently or, with a direct question in mind, observe and consider together.

It is important for the student to be aware that the teacher is familiar with her work and development. This is why students' folders should be perused regularly (one never knows when a certain helpful hint can be given to the student; though sometimes it is even better to keep quiet). The developing individual is still vulnerable in her newly released astral body.

In elementary school the temperaments become visible in painting. In high school it is also the task of the art teacher to collect material to be discussed during a faculty meeting, for example, or to point out various tendencies to the student that he sees in her work. This will help the teacher identify particular qualities or directions that will shed light on the student's development and personality.

We have already mentioned Steiner's recommendations to create pairs of painting assignments. This way of working requires an investigative research attitude, especially in high school. Art and science complement each other in such transformation assignments. On the other hand, art connects with daily life through design. This is important in high school and through all the years of schooling. In art class we are dealing not just with the talented artists but with all the students, including potential scientists and craftspeople. All dispositions can be accommodated in applied arts classes by working specifically on two aspects of each assignment: research and design (for example, making picture books or posters). In the case of the visual arts this also includes the finishing touch (a frame) and the location within a space/ room (which painting should go where?).

3 A journey through the color wheel

1. Light and darkness

Johann Wolfgang von Goethe (1749–1832) was a philosopher and naturalist who studied the processes of metamorphosis in living things. About the eye and its relation to the perception of color, he said:

> Color is an elementary natural phenomenon intended for the sense of sight, which manifests itself, just like all others, through separation and contrast, through mingling and unification, through intensification and division and is best observed and understood in relation to these general natural formulae.[12]

Goethe saw that the world of color originates from the "deeds and sufferings," the actions of and obstructions to, light. In doing so he constructs an entire world of light, darkness and turbidity: a threefold world. Between light and darkness, color comes into being. In Goethe's physics we constantly find the concepts of metamorphosis, polarity and intensification (Steigerung), by which he describes processes that happen beyond the visible world of color. These processes eventually determine the appearance of color.

2. Blue and yellow

Goethe identified only two pure colors: blue and yellow. They are diametrically opposed, meaning that it is impossible for blue to be present in pure yellow and vice versa. This discovery results from observing what happens when a turbid medium moves in front of light, or a light medium in front of darkness. When clouding occurs *in front of* the light, a yellow-red color appears. When light comes *in front of* darkness, a bluish-violet color appears. We see this blue color every day in the atmosphere: the blue of the sky, when the earth's atmosphere, lit by the sun, passes in front of the black universe. We see the yellow-red in the sun, when the light of sunrise and sunset, the one weak and the other strong, is made turbid by the atmosphere. Yellow, orange and red appear as an activity of light in darkness, blue as a working of darkness in light.

These two elementary phenomena are the principles of Goethe's theory of color. Through the intensification of both processes, yellow-red and blue-red come into being. When these two shine onto each other, purple appears. When blue and yellow are mixed, green is formed, thus closing the circle. Thus this color circle arises from processes and is an expression of living forces. Goethe assumes that darkness is as great a reality as light in the emergence of color.

3. The balance between light and darkness

In the ancient phenomena that Goethe discovered, Steiner saw confirmation that principles in nature as well as in humanity can be in opposition. All living things have an opposite; between these opposites, a balance must continually be found. Steiner goes further by describing darkness, colors and light as spiritual beings that lie at the foundation of all aspects of the physical life, soul life and spiritual life of humanity. Thus there are three separate forces that work in the above order: light, darkness and the creation of balance. Light dominates over darkness in yellow-red. Darkness dominates over light in blue-violet. In green, both are in balance. Aristotle already mentions this threefold notion, and Goethe observes that "My theory of color is as old as the world itself." Rudolf Steiner adds that this insight into nature explains corresponding processes in humanity and nature, and that this forms a bridge that connects self-knowledge and world-knowledge.

4. Phenomenology

The method that Goethe used to make his observations, to allow them to mature in his soul and come to conclusions, is what we call phenomenology. Through these carefully observed phenomena, he developed a new approach. He plunged wholeheartedly into reality and did not approach it with concepts, as Newton had done. Newton understood colors to be a fan-

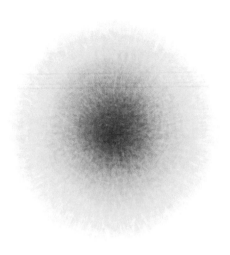

Left: Yellow, painted to emphasize its character. (Julius Hebing)
Right: Blue, painted to emphasize its character. (Julius Hebing)

shaped refraction of light in which all hues had equal value and only differed from each other quantitatively, by wavelength. Goethe opened the way to a scientific, but not materialistic, observation and treatment of color. His theory of color forms the essential foundation of painting.

5. Color qualities

Colors arranged in a wheel can be a source of inspiration for painting lessons. The circle is created when two opposite color forces, yellow and blue, are united through intensification (red) and mixing (green). The closed circular band of color is a representation of rising and falling processes that take place in nature, calling forth the greatest possible range of colors. It is an inexhaustible source. When your eye passes along all the different color qualities, images and experiences arise. They can evoke different times of day, different seasons. Randomness disappears and only the essence of things is expressed. One's own imaginations and experiences do the rest; as we paint, we arrive at an understanding of the language of colors. As educators we must learn to speak this language as fluently as possible to guide the students in the painting process.

The color circle is a world of its own. If you allow this world to take you in, you feel absorbed into its harmony. Goethe refers to this impression,

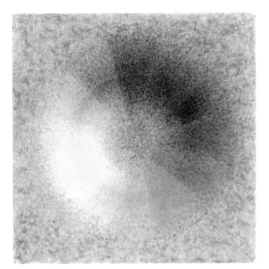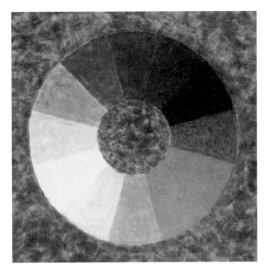

Left: Continuous color circle, with grey inner and outer areas. (Julius Hebing)
Right: Twelve-part color circle according to Goethe, with grey inner and outer areas. (Julius Hebing)

which goes beyond the mere senses, as the sensorial-moral working of color, in this case the working of colors inside and opposite one another. Viewing his organic color arrangement, Goethe said:

> Once you have really understood the opposite positions of yellow and blue, and have taken on the intensification to red, making the opposites come together and uniting itself to a third principle, the special thought will come to you, that these separate and opposite beings could have a spiritual significance. Then when you see how they create green below and red above, you can only think of, on the one hand, the earthly and on the other, the heavenly children of Elohim.[13]

Goethe did not touch on the sensorial-moral workings of color until the end of his writings on the theory of color. He probably sensed that he had discovered a special field. We can now enter the color circle, the color space. What we call the third dimension in physical space, creating front and back, near and far, is the expression of the qualities of colors in this color space. Red comes toward us. Blue moves away from us. We can experience the warm red pole going through us, while the cool blue pole is endlessly far away. In this way I participate in the color circle. As I go through it, I experience a great deal; soon I can no longer distinguish myself from the colors, I am living in them. Yellow-red always comes toward me and appeals to me, radiating warmth and life. Blue pulls me along but gives me space, and I can come to myself. Thus we find ourselves between these opposite trends, which make a clear impression on our soul. We are absorbed by the color circle and move along with the changing impressions of colors.

6. Colors and emotion

We can try to describe our impressions as we "walk" through the color circle. Each color has several aspects, positive as well as negative. In addition, there are many nuances within each color. Through experience, in other words through our activity, we can create a list of characteristics, moods and properties of the different colors that can continually be expanded and improved upon. Whoever carries this dictionary of color qualities within can draw richly from it for painting assignments. However, one condition is that the whole should remain in motion. Taking part in a process demands mobility, flexibility and room for self-development, as well as conscious awareness of new experiences. Goethe's work is a base from which we can start, complemented by other experiences. It is important to describe each color in the circle with a range of feelings. Below are some examples.

white: The brightest shadow of light. Peripheral and ever-expanding, it breaks through barriers and is objective and cool. White quickly loses its purity.

black: The darkest shadow of light. Related to darkness. Searching for the center. Hermetically sealed. It forms and limits itself. It pulls one inward.

yellow: The color closest to the light. In its purest form, yellow is bright, cheerful and brisk. It expands and enlivens the heart. It is a beaming color that does not want to be restricted. Depending on its movement toward red or green, it exudes a jocular, teasing, reckless or quick-witted mood. In a slightly impure state, yellow can have an unpleasant influence. It becomes a color of shame, evoking disgust and displeasure.

orange: This color can enchant us, even to the point of becoming aggressive. In addition it makes us strong; we feel strong. It gives us enthusiasm, joy and warmth. Orange is also festive. It invites us forth.

The rainbow with Noah's ark. Class illustration painted by a teacher.

red: Leads us into the center of life, into the lively element. It can also be solemn, splendid and bombastic. Strong and therefore also serious. Warm, proud, wrathful or angry.

pink: A light shade of red. Mild and beguiling. Memory of our eternal youth and our incarnation. Fragile, soft and familiar.

lilac: Fragile, just like pink. However, it can also be coquettish and vain. Or serious. Leading toward blue, it leads us to the inner depth of our being.

violet/purple: Leading toward red, it can have quite a disturbing effect. It takes us along, forcefully. It can also be lively, but without cheerfulness. Modest and reserved to a feeling of cosmic holiness and detachment in blue-violet.

blue: Not only quiet and enveloping, but also cold and aloof. Closed off to the outside. Easily forms contours and outlines. It can emanate peace. Sometimes yields to us and creates space. Also has a receptive and calming mood.

indigo: Brings us to darkness. Closes. Meditative, listening.

green: Spreads peace and contentment. It has a harmonizing effect and is good for tranquility. It can also be dull.

These qualities can be summarized in the following poem:

The Rainbow

Red advances
Orange dances
Yellow shines
Green reclines
Blue surrounds
Indigo frowns
Violet slows
Purple glows

We could also search for colors to fit soul moods. We could paint a color circle and put together a series of moods such as joy, sadness, shyness, slyness, caution, etc. Where do these moods belong in the circle? If we try to classify them, we need to decide carefully whether a certain mood fits a specific color or not. We can thus gradually build up a "soul moods color chart," a color circle that can become a focal point for painting lessons. In the first three grades, when the children are mainly painting soul moods, this preliminary work on the teacher's part can be a good support.

For example: In an animal fable, a sly animal and a very courteous, innocent animal meet. This is a meeting between two completely different soul moods. Which colors should we pick? Should a color from the cool side of the spectrum meet one from the warm side? Should we look for a color that is introverted or one that shines out on all sides? Such considerations are necessary to arrive at a good color dialogue.

Colors are important in their own right. Children will start to recognize the color elements in a story and learn to distinguish between various qualities. Thus we can arrive at a series of moods, characters and feelings that each have a place in the color circle, using words like vain, mystical, flirtatious, courteous, refined, philosophical, thoughtful, humble, introverted, receptive, pure, sad, detached, passive, calm, shy, timid, quiet, dull, confident, annoyed, sly, malicious, cunning, fresh, clever, happy, cheerful, light-hearted, enthusiastic, beaming, pleased, surprised, elated, sharp, fanatical, active, pushy, enraged, angry, reckless, impetuous, overpowering, forceful, brave, proud, dignified, regal, and so forth.

Everyone will be able to come up with a person or an image from a story to match a word on this list. The more adjectives (color tones) we use when we tell a story, the more alive the images and color richness that will be evoked in the children. These are the foundations on which the teacher and student can develop an organ for colors within and around us.

While speaking with the painter Margarita Woloschin, Steiner said the following about the development of a lively concept of color in children:

> To the young child inner and outer world are only moderately separate from each other. With the outer impression the child also receives the quality of the individual color, something of its own character, and instinctively the child is still aware of the actual essence of red, of blue, of yellow and of other colors. This is lost as a child grows older. School children ultimately experience colors as properties of objects (the blue ball, the red roof, and so forth). This however causes the ability in the soul to be paralyzed, which impedes the further development of the soul's eye. Children often learn at an early stage that red and yellow are warm colors and green and blue cold, but in their experiences they can sense this less and less. In this way these judgments easily become an abstract and lifeless knowledge. If the true experience of colors is not nurtured in our time and the mechanical theories about the nature of color live on in humanity, children will be born on this earth no longer having an organ for the observation of colors.[14]

This is why we try to guide the children into the world of colors as early as possible in the Waldorf schools.

7. Painting and the senses

The senses are our gateways to the world. They enable us to observe the world around us. Our senses develop throughout the different stages of our lives. Senses such as sight, hearing and touch are generally well known; Rudolf Steiner opened new paths in the field of the senses. He divided everything that is available in sense impressions and experiences into twelve areas. They are clearly distinguishable, but are also inwardly related. They are so strongly interlinked that you cannot actually describe one single sense without simultaneously knowing the others. The whole forms one composition: a unity formed by twelve senses. They can be divided into three groups of four that indicate the relationship of humanity to the world in three layers: the will, feeling and thinking. Because the development of the senses is closely linked to the development of artistic abilities, a look at these twelve areas in relation to painting and color is appropriate. The senses can be characterized as follows.[15]

The physical senses
- touch
- life
- movement
- balance

The outer senses
- smell
- taste
- sight
- warmth/temperature

The spirit senses
- hearing
- speech
- thinking
- the "I"

The physical senses

The first group of senses includes the senses of *touch, life, movement* and *balance*.

We experience the *sense of touch* mainly with our skin, mostly with our fingers and hands. We are constantly exploring the world. Is it hard, soft, rough, wet or dry? Everything gives us a particular impression. These impressions are perceived inwardly through our sense of touch. When we explore the type of paper, stroke the brush on the back of our hand, handle the sponge, dampen the paper and blot it, our sense of touch is activated. It lets us comprehend the painting materials and sets the condition for working with colors. It provides us with plenty of experiences: wetting the paper and observing how it responds to moisture; feeling the children's cold or warm hands; and so on. Many factors are involved in the exploration of the painting materials, which is why it is best to let young children do as much by themselves as they can.

With the *sense of life,* we observe the condition of our living body, particularly when it is out of balance due to fatigue, hunger or thirst. Working with color evokes reactions in our life body. The child reacts to this work with her life sense. A good variety of moods during the lessons will stimulate the sense of life: calm and quiet, activity and enthusiasm. One impediment to the development of the sense of life is demanding too much from the students, for example having the painting class last too long, or working too monotonously with particular colors.

The *sense of movement* concerns not our ability to move as such, but our perception of our own movements; it tells us whether our bodies are at rest or in motion. We can sense inwardly that we are moving; we don't need to look at our feet to know whether they are in motion. Many traditional children's games and folk dances include movements that stimulate the development of this sense. They are often rhythmic movements, alternating between fast and slow, activity and rest. In repetition and in moving together, and by observing the movements around us, we are constantly involved with our sense of movement. We explore with our eyes the shapes that arise in a painting: This is the work of the sense of movement. The movement of our eyes follows the outlines. Over time we learn to describe the forms and movements we see in painting: waves, stripes, strokes. From a pedagogical point of view it is important to follow the brush (the painting hand) with the eye. In form drawing the sense of movement plays an even larger role.

With the *sense of balance,* we first observe our own sense of being in balance. In painting we deal with right and left, upper and lower, diagonals. In the working of color and color perspective, we talk about before and behind, spatial directions that we explore with our sense of balance. This results in an awareness of composition.

These four senses are distinctly inwardly directed. They are primarily focused on our own physical condition and are therefore called the physical senses. They connect us to our bodies. The young child in particular must develop these senses to be able to take her first steps into the world—literally and figuratively. However, stimulating this sense at the beginning of elementary school is also of great importance as a foundation for intellectual and emotional development.

The outer senses

The second group of four senses—*smell, taste, sight and warmth/temperature*—is related to the human soul, the world of feeling and perception. These could be called the soul senses. They are unmistakably "feeling senses." Their impressions always involve contrasts: for the sense of sight, beautiful or ugly; for the sense of warmth, warm or cold; for the sense of smell, pleasant or foul-smelling; for the sense of taste, salty, sweet, bitter or sour.

In painting we don't activate only the *sense of sight*; the *sense of warmth* and the *sense of smell* are also involved. The fact that certain colors can evoke a smell or taste (earth tones, for example) shows that the perception of color in many, if not all, sense areas evokes a strong reaction. Not only paints (particularly plant-based ones) and damp paper, but moldy sponges and fermenting fixing agents, too, can be memorable experiences during the painting lesson!

Of course the most important sense activated by painting is the *sense of sight*. Whatever we do is immediately visible: how the color spreads on the paper, how it relates to other colors, what images appear in it. We observe, we compare. The eye is a very active sense organ: More than three quarters of all impressions enter us via the sense of sight. This is why it is important that the painting lesson not last too long. We all know how we feel when we spend too much time in a museum: The first few paintings are the ones we peruse most intently. This is the moment to take advantage of in painting lessons. Preparations should not take too long, so the children can still be fresh while observing the colors. Older children can work for longer periods and take in more.

Aside from observing the visible colors attached to the things we see, we also meet the so-called afterimage, the complementary color, through the eye. Complementary colors appear on our retina from within.

The eye owes its existence to the light. From undifferentiated animal organs, the light calls forth an organ to correspond to itself, and thus the eye is formed by the light for the light, so that the inner light can approach the outer light.[16]

Goethe summarized this poetically:

Wär nicht das Auge sonnenhaft,
Wie könnten wir das Licht erblicken?
Lebt' nicht in uns des Gottes eigene Kraft,
Wie könnt' uns göttliches entzücken?

If the eye were not sun-like,
How could we see the light?
If God's power did not live in us,
How could the godly enrapture us?

Goethe continued:

No one will deny the direct relationship between light and the eye, but to see the two as one and the same is more difficult. A still light lives within the eye that is awakened by the slightest stimulation from within or from without. We can see the clearest images in our mind's eye even when we are in total darkness. We can experience the faintest beam of light from outside.

With Goethe's remarks about the eye and the light we come to a greater understanding of other senses and realize how intensely we take in, and are formed by, the outside world.

The blind Jacques Lusseyran, French author and political activist (mid-1900s), uniquely pictures the inner observation of colors in his book *The World Begins Today:*

The eyes create the colors. Not the physical eyes of course, the object of ophthalmology. The two tender organs positioned in the front of the head which are not the true reality are merely mirrors. Broken mirrors, but they keep on living. The essential eyes, to which I am referring, function deep within us. Seeing is an extremely essential deed in life; seeing is an indestructibly strong act, independent of the physical instruments used for this purpose. For seeing derives from a life source, even before objects are seen, even before something presents itself outwardly in a certain form. One sees inwardly. If that inner light and consequently color (light's small change) had not first been given to you, we could not have admired the colors in the world. All this I know now, after twenty-five years of blindness.

The sense of warmth. Experiencing warmth or cold is only possible if an environment or object has a different temperature from our body; otherwise we feel nothing. The sense of touch helps us, but tells us nothing about temperature. Steiner calls this the first sense of humanity. It is an elementary sense, present in all other senses. Our language has all sorts of expressions relating to our sense of temperature: "to warm" to something, to leave someone "out in the cold." The activity of painting and the experience of color have a profound influence on the child's warmth organism. The child is aware of this. Thus, we can say that the sense of warmth is also called upon in painting.

The spirit senses

The third group of senses—*hearing, speech, thought* and the *"I"*— is related to the *sense of imagination.* Through these senses we direct ourselves more toward the outside world: We have to exert ourselves to meet what is outside of us. We know the expression "to put one's ear to the ground"; if we truly wish to meet someone, we must leave our little house and go out to meet the other. Developing these senses depends on developing the other senses. In painting we particularly address these senses during the introduction and review of the painting. We initially look and see, then "listen" and "let speak," and eventually learn to enjoy and relate to art.

8. The kindergartner and the elementary school child

If we look at the development of the senses through painting, there is a clear distinction between the kindergartner and the elementary school child. In his last series of public lectures, Steiner said that the senses do not start to become independent until around the seventh year.[17] From this time onward the child can do the assignments independently.

With younger children all sense impressions melt together into one whole impression. There are no clear distinctions yet. The observations themselves are not yet conscious. Thus, we cannot speak of "observation, understanding and merging into an image." The young child still gives himself up entirely to all the senses.

Not until the child goes to school does an interest in the usefulness, meaning or benefit of a certain impression come to the fore. The young child's thinking world is still bound to time and place. After the seventh year, elements from the past can be properly linked to the present. The free imaginative faculty, linked to the growing ability to remember, is what makes the child able to reproduce a thought or an image. Children in the first years of elementary school remember visual images better than aural images. The structure of the outside world becomes more interesting after the seventh year. Children seem to take hold of the outside world with the forces they used for physical development before the seventh year. The ability to distinguish between light and dark, for example, develops strongly. Observing differences in color increases by ninety percent after the seventh year; distinguishing pitch improves fivefold between the sixth and tenth years. Thus, from the sixth or seventh year, the child develops his own independent soul space in which to work and paints from this soul space. The younger child actually still paints from within.

During this phase, painting can reactivate the senses, appeal to them and allow them to continue their development, helping in the process to bring about healthy respiration, circulation and digestion.

Well-developed senses enrich our lives. They are of vital importance. It is to them that we owe a healthy understanding of the world around us. In the field of education, stimulating and activating the senses is essential. For the children we try to open the senses as "gates to the world." Art education in particular contributes much to this.

4   Painting techniques and materials

An abundance of painting materials is available to us. In this chapter we will discuss these materials and painting techniques, as well as ways of using them during painting lessons.

1. Watercolors

Through color, the soul of the world expresses itself. Color also gives expression to our experiences. Consciously or subconsciously, we experience color in our souls. This applies to both our inner image or experience and our perception of what goes on outside of us. A sunny day puts people in a different mood than a cloudy, grey day. We feel differently when we receive bad news than when we look forward to a festive occasion. Thus, on the one hand, moods in nature are soul moods, and on the other, soul life can express itself in color. Inwardly it is an impression; outwardly it is an expression. We are constantly moving in color and color is constantly moving us: It is a flowing process.

The transparent medium of watercolor lends itself best to this purpose. With watercolor both elements—color and motion—can be expressed. This is why we work mainly with watercolors in school and use lively, energetic techniques such as wet-on-wet and veiling.

For the developing child, watercolor is the ideal method for experiencing color and form. The child still has a great deal of creative, imaginative forces and wants to use them. With color and water we can start to connect these creative forces with the fixed, crystallized world in which the child must learn to live. Time and again, with each painting, the children experience the wet, fluid paint slowly drying to become fixed color forms. The colors mix on the paper. It is the process of becoming that is the most important. In this the children can experience the working of color most intensely and give expression to their creative imagination.

2. Transparency

The purest form of painting—if it were possible—would be painting with light. At sunrise or sunset we can experience a feeling of movement in the changing light. The rainbow, for which we will gladly interrupt our lessons to let the children look outside, appears on a curtain of rain. Nature allows colors to appear magically in the atmosphere, colors that the Impressionists attempted to capture in their paintings. Color dances vividly in stripes, dots and patches across the sky, water and landscape. Next to light and air (also known as the "shadow of light"[18]), water is the next-densest medium that can retain color. Mixed with as transparent a pigment and binding agent as possible, water makes "light color" into a manageable color with which we can paint. Water has a living nature of its own: It is pre-eminently the giver of life, transparent and colorless.

Painting materials
on a teacher's desk.

57

3. Color and water

Rudolf Steiner describes how the origin of colors naturally relates to the element of water. In earlier stages, during the development of the earth, the element of water came into existence through the workings of spiritual beings. Steiner refers to these as beings of the third hierarchy: archai, archangeloi and angeloi. The angeloi-beings become mediators, as it were, between light and darkness. From this activity colors arise. In the air and shadowlike darkness, all colors of the rainbow begin to glisten. In his scientific writings Aristotle already described how the third hierarchy was involved in the creation of colors. This knowledge was lost over the course of the centuries.

When color sprays itself across the airy element, the fluid, watery element comes into being. Steiner says that it can be compared to a process in which, under certain conditions, pressure causes counter-pressure: "As air is the shadow of light, in cosmic thought, so water is the reflection, the creation of the element of color in the cosmos."[19]

4. Moist on moist

Through the ages painters have used the bond of moist (water) paint and a moist (absorbent) foundation for their work. Think of fresco painters who painted on damp limestone walls.

In works by William Turner (1775-1851), the pre-eminent landscape painter, we see not only examples of atmospheric, color-rich paintings, but also the mood of a landscape revealed through his excellent use of water, color and light (paper). Paul Cézanne's (1839-1906) use of watercolor was a turning point in the history of the medium. His work initiated a new phase of modern art. Later Paul Klee (1879-1940) said: "Color has me [...] the color and I are one." Wassily Kandinsky's (1866-1944) first image-free painting was a watercolor. Shining, vibrant watercolors were suited to the task of finding new experiences of color. Emil Nolde (1867-1956), Oskar Kokoschka (1886-1980) and many others followed.

5. The domes of the first Goetheanum

Rudolf Steiner initiated another new development in the use of watercolor at the beginning of the 20th century. This technique was used in the painting of the domes of the first Goetheanum, the school for spiritual science in Dornach, near Basel in Switzerland. The painting foundation was a mixture of paste-like white casein, wax and balsam with paper cellulose. It was applied in several layers onto cork sheets. Thus Steiner actually painted on a kind of liquid paper layer. In doing so, he developed a new kind of fresco technique, but without the restrictions. He created immense floating areas of color that seemed to move with great color intensity in the domes above the viewers. Special plant dyes were developed for this purpose by dissolving vegetable pigments in water, an intensive and time-consuming process at the time. Unfortunately none of this work remains because of the fire that burned the building down, but many people have developed this technique further.

6. Vegetable-based paints

Paint made from plants has been manufactured and used on a large scale since the 1960s. The intensity of this type of paint is remarkable. The colors harmonize well. Their use in the classroom offers a special experience. It also becomes a pleasant-smelling exercise through the method of preparation and by mixing the paint with etheric oils. By adding a binding agent that includes beeswax and resin, everyone becomes involved through the scent. Carefully stirring small amounts brings a quietly questioning, inquiring and festive mood to the classroom. First the pigment is pulverized with a mortar and pestle, then the binding agent and finally water are added and carefully stirred, and the paints are distributed to the children.

Botany lessons in fifth grade can be a starting point for painting with vegetable paints. The dandelion can be painted wet-on-wet: white root, pink stalk and yellow corolla, and one white ball of fluff where the paper is left to shine through. Delicate vegetable indigo meets warm Reseda yellow; together they create a mild green that harmonizes with Krapp or Madder red. The children notice that red does not flow as easily. Blue changes when it comes into contact with water. All in all, there is much to experience in the different pigment qualities.

Make sure you warn the class that one layer of vegetable paint will not create a strong color, but does give a special brilliance. Vegetable pigments are prepared in a wax and resin emulsion. They are expensive, but painting with them is an intense experience. Artemis vegetable watercolors are also available as liquid ready-to-use paints.

7. Wet-on-wet technique

The term "wet-on-wet" is a little misleading: The paper should not be so wet that the paint puddles and runs in all directions. "Moist-on-moist" would be a better description. After the paper has been wetted on both sides, it is blotted with a sponge to achieve a subdued matte surface. Wherever it is still too shiny, it needs to be dabbed drier; air bubbles will disappear if the paper is carefully lifted and put back down evenly. In this way one can paint on a flat sheet of white paper, enabling the students to apply the colors transparently, to easily extend color areas, and even to remove paint from the paper with a squeezed-out brush. Water around the paper should be removed with the sponge. When the painting is finished, it should be allowed to dry slowly and evenly on the painting board.

8. Veiling: layer by layer

The veiling technique affords many new and valuable experiences. It builds upon the children's experience with wet-on-wet painting and can be started in sixth grade, provided that the class has the necessary skills. Prerequisites are being able to distance oneself from one's work while painting; understanding how colors are built up; handling the brush correctly; and using the proper amount of water with the paint. Many students will have acquired these skills unnoticed. The need to give the colors more intensity and depth will result in students' taking the necessary care while working and having the patience to let the layers dry between classes. (Ideas on how to structure the lesson can be found in the sixth grade curriculum, later in this book.)

First of all, one needs paper with a strong, resilient surface. It must be able to withstand being wetted again and again without crumbling or disintegrating and to absorb sufficient water; otherwise it will not accept more than three or four layers of paint.

The paper is wetted on both sides and placed on a water-resistant or synthetic white board. It will expand considerably when wet, which becomes evident if we wet only one side: The sheet will roll up as the fibers lengthen on that side. Excess water is then removed by dabbing with a sponge. Once the paper lies flat on the board, it is taped down on all sides. While drying, it will contract into a smooth, white base, ready for the first veils.

Veiling can be done in various ways. The absolute rule of thumb is: The brush may go over a spot only once, or else it will remove the already-applied paint. The paint is thoroughly diluted so that only a very light layer is applied to the paper. As more veils are applied, the intensity of the color can be strengthened.

Veiling creates an intense color quality. Colors can be mixed and painted in any shade. As we paint, we can look for shapes; figures and images arise from the color areas. The work comes into being over time—a little more each day—and is a new and intriguing process for students used to the relatively fast wet-on-wet technique. It can be compared to the gradual processes of nature. We recreate nature while painting: sky, water, the outlines of a crystal. The final painting becomes visible only at the end of the process.

If this technique is learned carefully, the students will meet the color world in a whole new way. Whoever is after quick results will get a nasty surprise or at least an unexpected result, because veiling is a process of holding back or accelerating, learning about moderation. The process forces you to confront yourself and your way of working. If you persist and succeed, the light and the white paper will work together in such a way that the color comes alive.

9. Papers, sponges and painting boards

Many types of paper are available, but it is not always easy to find a kind that works for both wet-on-wet painting and veiling. In both cases the paper needs to be able to absorb a lot of moisture without breaking down or crumbling. Apart from the quality, price is also a consideration; weekly painting classes use a lot of supplies. A thick newsprint, although not pure white, can give good results, is affordable, and works well for wet-on-wet painting. Wet both sides, leave to absorb and dab dry with a sponge or cloth.

A heavier type of paper is needed for veiling, preferably pure white so the light can shine through several layers of paint. Always let the students test the wetness of the paper with their fingertips; be careful that their fingers are not greasy. In more expensive papers, the two sides of the sheet have different textures; we recommend always paint on the rougher side. The children can also feel the weight.

Each type of paper has advantages and limitations. Try out as many as possible; classroom experience will tell you which is best for which age group. In third grade crafts, one could make one's own paper, giving the children a new understanding of the material. This can be further explored in the upper grades.

Natural sponges are recommended for wetting the paper. Their different shapes and densities provide an extra experience for the senses. Although natural sponges are expensive, they last longer: all six elementary school years. They grow deep under water at the bottom of the sea and require careful handling. They easily absorb lots of water, and each sponge is different. Synthetic sponges could also be used; they can be cut in half to fit small hands. Sponges cut from a foam mattress also work fine.

Painting boards should be white, as the board color can be seen through the wet paper and can affect color perception.

10. Paints

Many types of watercolors are available: Stockmar, Talens, Winsor & Newton, etc., as well as vegetable paints. The choice depends on personal experience, quality and cost. Stockmar is a good value for school use.

Try them out and see for yourself how the primary colors (red, yellow, blue) relate to each other, how they mix, and whether a harmonious color circle can be painted with a particular brand. Working with the paint, its brilliance, purity, strength and intensity will become apparent. There will be many differences. Ultimately, the choice rests with the teacher, the experiences of other teachers, the culture of the school, and the reactions of the students. Watercolor paints should be prepared the day before they are to be used so they will be completely dissolved and can be stirred before pouring into the smaller jars. A wooden board with holes in which the jars sit is very practical when handing them out, to minimize the risk of upsetting the jars.

Working with dried paints that one dissolves with a wet brush is not recommended. The young child moves with the water and color more easily when using liquid paints. Dried paints may be easier to work with (less mess, less waste) but tend to draw our attention to dry vs. wet areas, thick vs. thin application, etc. Liquid paints let us get straight into the colors and how they relate to one another. Steiner says the following on this subject:

> It is necessary to learn to live with the colors and not to paint
> from the color palette, but to use a jar of dissolved color. The child
> will then develop a feeling for how the colors can live adjacent
> to each other and a feeling of inner harmony and the inner
> experience of color. [...] It is always about the colors adjacent and
> across from each other. The child empathizes with the color, and
> eventually a shape will emerge from the color.[20]

11. Brushes and the painting cupboard

Wide, flat brushes of about 3/4" to 1" made with strong boar bristles are preferable. This encourages the painting of color areas; thinner brushes encourage drawing with paint.

Even broader brushes can be used for veiling. The width of the brush is also determined by the size of the paper. The hairs should be able to absorb a lot of water and release it easily. Brushes that are too hard will damage the paper; if too soft, they will not provide enough grip. Brushes are best stored with the bristles facing down. Telling the students about the origins of the wood, bristles and casing of the brushes will awaken their interest for the people who made them. The way the teacher treats the supplies, with care and respect, will contribute to a good work attitude and a mood suitable for painting.

For grades 2 and up, it is efficient and effective to store painting materials in a special cupboard on wheels. As an example: The topmost shelf could contain jar holders, each with six colors (lemon yellow, golden yellow, vermilion, carmine red, ultramarine and Prussian blue). The paper and a box of sponges are on the shelf below, and on the bottom shelf the water jars and a box of brushes.

Painting cupboard with paint jars, sponges, paper, brushes and water jars.

If grades share a cupboard, they should agree who keeps it in order. By working with fewer sets of supplies you will save space, especially in the upper grades, and the paints can be centrally prepared and distributed. The schedule can be arranged so that different grades also share painting boards.

5   Color in other lessons and in the school building

1. Drawing, form drawing and crafts

In painting, learning takes place by way of color. For aesthetic, functional and pedagogical reasons, color also plays an important role in other aspects of education.

We will first mention imaginative or "free" drawing. The choice of colors in free drawings should be left completely open. The teacher can encourage the use of color, but should leave the choice of color to the child. Generally, the child will choose vivid colors for drawings. Black is needed too, if only to make the dots on a ladybug's back.

From third grade onward, when drawings can start to become a bit drab, the children can be encouraged to enrich their work by including more color. We can do this by creating a drawing together, built up of color areas, but more strongly than in painting. We call this "painted drawing." It is also important that blackboard drawings (in the lower grades) be made this way, with lots of color, many color areas and as few outlines as possible.

In form drawing, the line—the fixed movement—is the means of expression; color is of secondary importance. In certain exercises (think temperaments), color can be used to support the form. Thus we don't just use color to make a form drawing more beautiful, but to emphasize the character of the drawing.[21]

Needlework in all the grades awakens the sense of color. What is created during these lessons, no matter how simple, results in a useful end product. This makes crafts a subject in which we learn from a young age how an object's function is revealed by color in the shape. Think of designs on hats and bags, or a slipper's matching inside and outside, for example.[22] This is especially important in bookbinding lessons, when deciding on the covers and inside pages of the book.

2. Making transparencies

Making transparencies is a remarkable way of working with light and color. With this technique, a certain mood can be brought into the classroom by covering a window with tissue paper of various colors, to highlight a seasonal festival or other theme. The layers can be torn or cut and overlapped. Take care that it doesn't become too gaudy. Transparencies are made by overlapping the layers so that the colors relate to each other and light and dark areas are balanced. When applying this technique to making lanterns or shadow-puppet scenery, the teacher should provide the same insight regarding the character of the colors as was discussed in painting. How do the colors fit in with, for example, the mood of a scene in a puppet play?

For kindergartners and children in the lower grades, using beeswax is extremely gratifying; they love to give form to their imagination with this material. They should be given full freedom in choosing the color. Badly separated, mixed or greyish colors are much less popular than those with a definite identity. Therefore, we should keep the colors in separate jars so we can use them again and again. In the upper grades, colored modeling wax can be used to make transparencies on glass plates.

3. Drama

In a play, colored lighting helps support the content to add dramatic insight; in addition, identifying, choosing and coordinating the colors of costumes, props and scenery bring unity and impact to the stage and intensify the audience's experience. Color is extremely important, and it is therefore essential that the teacher acquire at least an elementary understanding of this phenomenon.

4. Blackboards and main lesson books

In general we tend to use color to make something stand out. The choice of color can be significant in its own right. We should try to use color advantageously, for example on the blackboard or in main lesson books. An excess of color restricts function; lack of color emphasizes intellectualism, lessens interest and enthusiasm, and extinguishes emotion. When well balanced, color, shape and function bring beauty to daily things. In the design of individual reports, in main lesson books, and in all other written work, students are encouraged to create beauty. The teacher stimulates and gives advice; the student discovers, acts and learns.

5. Rudolf Steiner's color recommendations for school buildings

Waldorf schools try to guide and support student development by making certain color choices for the classrooms, hallways and other spaces in which artistic and pedagogical considerations play a large part.

The various areas of education are supported: The students move around in an artistically formed environment, education in its entirety is practiced in an artistic fashion, and attention is given in the lessons to creating and enjoying (artistically). Thus aesthetics mediates between the spiritual and physical, and art forms the link between processes of the spirit-soul and the physical-material realm.

Such thoughts are expressed and developed in Schiller's *Letters on the Aesthetic Education of Mankind*. They are also the foundation for Waldorf pedagogy. Schiller saw the realm of the arts as a haven for and of human freedom, because humanity creates and delights in the arts, forging a bond between material and form. Besides being "creator" and "user" of his consciously created environment, the human being is also the "enjoyer." It is most certainly not immaterial how the environment is formed and what colors are used.

Together with the architecture of the school building, color forms an essential part of the environment, in service to the education of young people. In Part 1 of this book, we talked about the effects of color. How can we use these ideas without having them become rigid principles and constantly test them in practice? How do we employ this knowledge so we surround the students with colorful and appropriate environments? After all, they spend a great deal of time in the school building.

When designing the interior of the first Waldorf school, Steiner gave a series of directions for the colors of the classroom walls. He aimed for transparent colors, colors with a lively character, not thickly plastered walls painted a solid color, but walls that could "breathe."[23] An artistically developed colored environment has a harmonizing and even healing effect.

Suitable materials were not easily available at the time; these were developed during the construction of the first Goetheanum. Steiner said:

> We should succeed again in not just watching the colors and applying them here and there as an external feature, but we must live with the colors, be part of the inner life force of color. We cannot reach this aim by just studying how one or another color acts while we are painting. We can only do this by submerging our souls in the direct flow, of how, for example, red and blue flow: experiencing the flow of colors vividly in our minds.[24]

A wall painted in transparent colors does not feel as confining as a wall painted a solid color. With veil-painted walls, the room has an atmospheric effect. It becomes wider, larger and more spacious—different with each color. Spaces painted in this way do not have a direct effect on the imagination but leave us free. The veiling technique can include many nuances in color intensities, and color transitions can easily be achieved.

Steiner advised painting the classrooms all one color: warm, enveloping colors for the young children and cooler, receding shades for the upper grades. He developed four color schemes for three different locations in Europe, taking into consideration the climate, landscape and natural character of the students in southern and northern Germany and in England. To activate the feeling world of the students in northern Germany, Steiner chose warm red-orange colors for kindergarten and the first six grades.

In the colors given for the school in London, we notice that yellow does not appear between orange and green, as we might expect. The English child, by nature more sensitive and active, needs bluish tones in order to concentrate better, thus supporting the thought process.

In the wooden barracks in Stuttgart where the first Waldorf school started, a single color was chosen for the first eight years: bluish lilac. Wherever possible, the furniture was also painted this color. The curtains were a lighter shade of the same color. Thus a unified color impression was created for the students.

These indications are used throughout Waldorf schools worldwide. Each country creates its own use of color, materials and techniques, fitting the natural character of the people. Using this information artistically means that everyone considers, tests and observes the effect of the color palette on the children. Simply applying it without understanding contradicts the method Steiner advocates.

> The "lazure" or veiling technique is a watercolor technique usually applied on a white foundation. The original color of the foundation is covered, but the structure remains visible. If stronger colors are desired, a lightly colored foundation can be used, as it is technically very difficult to apply veils regularly with a lot of color. Each new layer must be a thin, weak layer of paint that gives the wall only a small bit of color. The working of the color is thus intensified and differentiated. When only one color is used, the wall can become too dominant. A painter's secret is to paint the final one or two thin layers on the wall in a complementary color, subduing the brilliance of the color so that it does not force itself on the viewer. For example, a yellow wall can be given some lilac or purple veils creating a very special color effect. Everyone must try this for themselves. Only through observation can the complementary colors be chosen. They will then have to be applied with the utmost care to achieve the desired result.

The importance of a good choice of color, to fit a certain age group and support the development of the child is clearly signaled in Ernst Weissert's *Erziehungskunst (Education as an Art)* from June 1952:

> The question about the children's environment, how the spaces in which they spend their school hours are formed, is even more important today than before. Nowadays a number of visual impressions force themselves onto the young child. A speedy development of observation is encouraged. Questions which occupied Steiner from the pedagogical and medical points of view are turned into actual assignments: to address the child's needs by having a suitable design of class space and by painting transparent colors that have a calming or an activating effect on the child.

Following are the color schemes recommended by Steiner:

Goethe School in Hamburg (1925):

Grades 1, 2 and 3	– red, gradually reduced in strength per class
Grades 4, 5 and 6	– orange, gradually reduced in strength per class
Seventh grade	– yellow
Eighth grade	– green
Ninth grade	– lighter green
Tenth grade	– blue
Eleventh grade	– blue tending toward violet
Twelfth grade	– violet
Eurythmy hall	– violet
Physics classroom	– green
Music classroom	– lilac

The Stuttgart barracks; the second color listed was for the new building in Stuttgart (1922–1923):

First grade	– bluish lilac, red
Second grade	– bluish lilac, orange
Third grade	– bluish lilac, yellow
Fourth grade	– bluish lilac, light green
Fifth grade	– bluish lilac, green tending toward blue
Sixth grade	– bluish lilac, blue
Seventh grade	– bluish lilac, indigo
Eighth grade	– bluish lilac, violet
Ninth grade	– bluish lilac, violet
Tenth grade	– bluish lilac, lilac
Eleventh grade	– bluish lilac, lilac
Eurythmy hall	– bluish lilac, mallow
Physics classroom	– bluish lilac, blue
Corridors	– yellow, reddish lilac
Music hall	– indigo, bluish lilac
Gym hall	– bluish lilac, reddish lilac
Doctor's room	– bluish lilac, orange
Handicraft room	– bluish lilac, orange
Needlework room	– bluish lilac, light violet changing to red

London (1925)

Kindergarten	– red-yellow
First grade	– orange
Second grade	– green
Third grade	– green, darker
Fourth grade	– blue-green
Fifth grade	– light blue
Sixth grade	– blue, darker
Eurythmy hall	– light violet
Corridors	– yellow

Above: Teachers in Israel.
Below: Complementary colors.

Part 2

Basic exercises for the teacher

The following exercises form a type of action plan for teacher self-education. They are related to the curriculum. You do not have to do them all, but by doing them, you the teacher walk once again the path of the students. The exercises also involve different aspects of art and artistry, such as experiencing the richness and limitations of the pigments, respecting the independent nature of colors, gaining skill in mixing them, identifying the qualities of a color, playing with color, and giving form to themes from the curriculum.

These are all experiences that should be part of teacher-training courses. Students in the lower grades follow the achievements of the teacher. In the upper grades, teachers are often so well trained that they know all the forms of modern artistic expression through personal experience. The technical know-how may be there, but the ability to translate it for a specific age group and curriculum and create enthusiasm in the students must still be developed. During teacher-training courses these exercises have proven useful and rewarding.

Basic exercise 1
Choosing colors

Objective: Assembling the three primary colors for painting in the kindergarten and first grade. This age group is given the three colors with which all other colors can be created.

For painting with the young child we select lemon yellow and golden yellow, carmine red and vermilion, Prussian blue and ultramarine blue. Other blues such as cobalt, cerulean and indigo are set aside because of their cool, distant character.

Of these six colors—two yellows, two reds, two blues—one shade emphasizes the color's coolness, the other its warmth.

Lemon yellow tends toward blue and is a cooler yellow; it readily creates green. *Golden yellow* tends toward orange-red; thus it is a warm yellow.

We need to mix a neutral yellow for the children to work with. Put lemon yellow into a jar and add a bit of golden yellow. Now add water, 4 parts water to 1 part paint. Stir well and paint several strokes on a moistened paper. The yellow should be strong and brilliant, but still transparent.

We then do the same with the two blues. *Prussian blue* is a cool blue. *Ultramarine* is a warmer color and tends toward violet. Ultramarine needs to be stirred well, as the binding agent tends to settle.

Take Prussian blue, add about an equal amount of ultramarine blue and enough water to give it some transparency. Stir well and try it out next to the yellow on the paper.

And now the reds. *Vermilion*, almost orange, is the more active red. *Carmine red* is a royal color expressing self-possession, stateliness.

Start with carmine red and add a small amount of vermilion and enough water to give it some transparency. Paint it next to the yellow and blue on the paper. It is best to mix the paints the day before the lesson so they will be well dissolved.

In the next exercise we'll see whether these colors combine well and form a balanced color circle. Through such mixing and experimentation, the teacher arrives at satisfying color shades while simultaneously training the senses. Explore different options, observe intently, step back and try again until you find the right color. You will develop a definite inner feeling for the right red, yellow and blue, as well as skill in mixing them.

Basic exercise 2
Mixing colors

Objective: Painting a color circle in which all the colors are well mixed and in the right relationship with each other. This will provide the young child with a rich palette based on the primary colors.

After mixing the three primaries and diluting them with water, we look at how well they fit together, how harmonious they are. How do they relate to each other? Does one stand out? How strong is the yellow when compared to the blue? Blue can sometimes dominate. To discover the answers to these questions it is good to paint a continuous color circle. Yellow and blue make green, blue and red make purple, and red and yellow make orange. Try to put yellow directly across from purple, green across from red, and blue across from orange. The circle is now complete: yellow, orange, red, purple, blue, and green next to yellow. If we look at the whole, we can see whether the colors are well balanced. Does the cool side dominate? Does one color jump

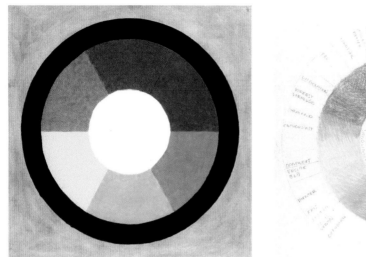

Above: Six-part color circle according to Goethe. (Julius Hebing)
Right: Color circle with moods written in. (Dick Bruin)

out? Let your eyes pass around the color circle, and decide for yourself if it is a harmonious whole.

The "painting a color circle" exercise should not be done by younger children. It is not easy and is not introduced before sixth grade. Only then are the children ready to paint such a circle with color areas and to work with color instead of playing with it. Before then, color circles can be painted in a variety of ways; see, for example, the first lesson for the third grade on page 123.

Basic exercise 3
Naming color moods

Objective: Naming the moods of the colors. We should have a vast trove of words at our disposal to express the qualities of the colors. Through your work you will develop the ability to express moods in colors when telling a story or creating an image. This forms the foundation for an inspiring painting lesson.

Paint a large color circle. Try to let many different colors appear, a large variety of mixed colors. Now look at a small part of the circle, focusing on one color, and decide what mood it expresses. Write the mood in the space outside the circle, next to the color. A ring of words will thus slowly be built up. Sometimes the moods of different colors can be quite similar: Green, for example, can be sly, peaceful or boring, depending on its position compared to yellow and blue. This exercise is not meant to rigidly or dogmatically pin colors down to a fixed mood, but to enrich your own vocabulary with regard to color quality and to let the moods of the color circle move you. Where would you put pride, grief, anger, humility, stubbornness? The next day new words might come up. The main thing is for you to work with it. The color circle is like a living circle in which colors appear and change. It is fertile ground for the development of a young child's soul. Always keep the color circle with all your discoveries close at hand.

Basic exercise 4
Experiencing color

Objective: Experiencing the interactions between colors, to discover tendencies toward form and movement. This will help you learn to work with various color combinations.

The paintings we will now describe are based on three examples given by Steiner during his first lecture for artists[1]

First paint green on a paper; within the green, paint red. Two or three areas of red, surrounded by green. Next, do the same on a new sheet of paper, using light pink instead of red. Steiner called this color "peach-blossom." Do this a third time using blue, creating a blue-green color scheme.

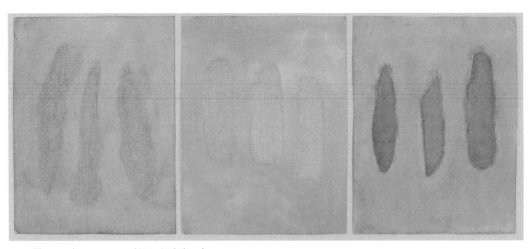

Three colors in green. (Attie Lichthart)

We have now painted three different colors surrounded by green. A certain amount of skill is needed to paint the color areas with firm boundaries in the green. The green can best be created by mixing lemon yellow and Prussian blue. We are actually practicing painting with a complementary color (green-red), a neighboring color (blue-green), and a color that harmonizes well with green: peach-blossom. These combinations summon three different reactions from the viewer. Steiner summarizes the different impressions as follows:

> Imagine you would see this: Across a green field red people are walking, or across a green field peach-blossom colored people are walking, or even blue people are walking across that field. In all three cases a completely different range of experiences. On seeing the first scene, you will say, those red people I see in the green, in the green field, they bring that entire green field to life. That field becomes even greener by having red people walking in it. The green becomes even more saturated, even livelier, because of those red people. And when I watch these red people the way they just stand there, it makes me furious. Then I say, actually it is senseless, it cannot be this way. I should really paint these red people like flashes of lightning, they should be moving. Because quiet red figures in a green field cause tension because of their peace—they are already moving due to their red color, they cause something in that field which actually cannot possibly remain at

peace. So out of necessity I end with a complex experience if I really wish to establish such an idea.[2]

This is a typical reaction to complementary colors. (Another exercise: Paint red and green in such a way that red's character becomes evident through its form. Paint red as a moving area. Seek a balance in the relationship between red and green.)

Now let's look at Steiner's description of peach-blossom on green:

This is quite possible. People like these, with their peach-blossom color, can stay there quite peacefully; even if they stand there for hours, it won't bother me. My feeling tells me that these peach-blossom colored people do not actually have a special relationship with that field, they do not cause any tension in that field, they do not make it greener than it already is, they are completely neutral in relation to this field. They could stand wherever they please, they do not bother me there. They fit in anywhere. They have no inner bond with the green field.[3]

The exercise for the teacher is to paint the peach-blossom areas in rounded, curved forms, seeking the greatest possible peace and harmony with regard to its surroundings.

I now go to the third example and I watch those blue people in that green field. That, you see, cannot even persevere, cannot endure at all. Because the blue in the green suppresses the entire green field. The green of that field becomes dull. That field does not stay green at all. Try to imagine: In a green field blue people or whatever creatures they are, are wandering about—they could be blue spirits haunting the field—just try to picture it. The field ceases to be green; it even takes on a bluish hue, it stops being green. And if those blue people were to remain long on that green, it would all slip away from me. Then I would imagine an abyss there somewhere and find myself thinking that the blue people are trying to carry off the field and dispose of it in some deep abyss. A green field cannot stay as it is if there are blue people in it; they take it up and make off with it.

Look, this is experiencing color. You must be able to experience color, otherwise you will not be let into that which the world of color actually is. If you want to get to know a phenomenon that has its most beautiful, its most important use in the imagination, then you must dare to experiment in the realm of the imagination.[4]

This experiment teaches us that blue seems to absorb green. It is as if green disappears into a deep hole. Try to paint the blue in such a way that it drags green into the deep.

This is how we learn how color works: trying out three colors in comparison with green. In the class assignments we will encounter a multitude of possibilities in this area.

Basic exercise 5
Color nuances

Objective: Experiencing the boundaries between the primary colors (red, yellow and blue) and the secondary colors (green, orange and purple). This exercise will train the observation of color nuances and the skill to create nuances within the colors.

On a prepared sheet of paper, paint yellow over the entire surface. Now try to create as many different shades of yellow as possible without losing the yellow mood, even if the color breaks down into borderline areas of green or orange. On one side the yellow will tend toward greenish yellow, on the other toward orange. If you study the sheet intensely, you will see more and more shades of yellow.

Now repeat this exercise with red as the base color, tending toward purple and orange at the edges. We could add yellow and vermilion on one side and Prussian and/or ultramarine blue on the other.

The third exercise, using blue, will result in greenish and reddish blues.

Now repeat this exercise using green, orange and purple as base colors.

Lay the finished paintings in a circle and you will have created a marvelous color circle. This exercise can be done as a group exercise with parents during a parent evening, to let them experience the unity in color movement and to experience painting.

Six exercises that make up a color wheel.
Basic exercise 5. (Attie Lichthart)

Basic exercise 6
Heavenly colors become earthly colors

Objective: Using the six main colors, we create brown and grey/black: earth tones, shadow colors or tertiary colors. This will allow us to paint realistic subjects from nature, among others.

Paint equal areas of red, yellow and blue on a sheet of paper: at the top, at the lower right and lower left. The colors should touch each other.

Now paint the yellow (using the paint already on the paper) into the red (rinse your brush), the blue into the yellow (rinse again) and, taking red from the jar (because the red has turned orange by mixing with yellow on the paper), paint red into the blue. All three primary colors have now moved into the next color, creating green, orange and purple.

We now shift the colors again, at first without dipping the brush into new paint. We paint part of the green into part of the orange, the rest of the orange into part of the purple, and the rest of the purple into the rest of the green. If there is too little paint on the paper, add more from one of the jars, but try to use the paint on the paper as much as possible.

81

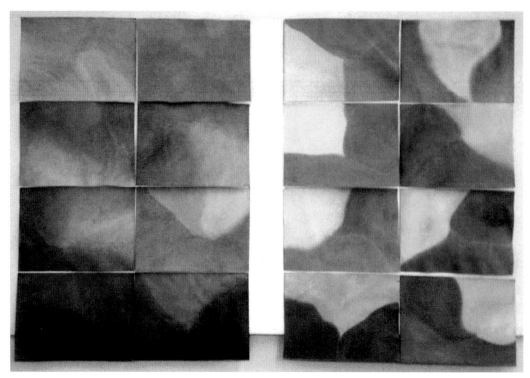

From heaven to earth colors paintings created at a teacher training school England.

We have now created the tertiary colors (fall colors): the browns and greys. In theory only one color should have been created, since they all started from the same red, yellow and blue. But those colors have now disappeared. Practice shows that by changing the order of application in a lively painting process, we can create a wealth of new colors. These earth tones may not be immediately appreciated by everyone; after our experiences with bright, pure rainbow colors, the "muddy" hues don't always come across as pleasant. But by working with them, we can distinguish more and more subtle nuances, and it will become apparent that the tertiary colors make the others shine. It just takes time to appreciate them and find them beautiful.

Landscapes created at a teacher training school England.

Basic exercise 7
From soul mood to nature mood

Objective: Connecting color qualities with the four elements of earth, water, air and fire. We will develop the ability to make the elements visible when painting nature scenes.

In this exercise we will use two elements from the Norse creation story: Muspelheim and Niflheim. Muspelheim is the world of fire, of heat. Niflheim is the land of ice and cold. Two totally different worlds adjacent to each other, with opposing qualities: a wonderful point of departure for painting landscapes.

It is obvious that we should choose different colors for each landscape, for example blue and red. But in this exercise we will limit ourselves to nuances of warmth and cold within the same color: shades of yellow, red and blue.

Holding the paper vertically, cut it into three equal horizontal pieces and lay them horizontally, one above the other.

For each color we will use two shades. For the first sheet lemon and golden yellow, for the second vermilion and carmine red, and for the bottom

83

sheet ultramarine and Prussian blue. Each sheet will display a warmer and cooler shade of the same color.

We now paint one of the two shades on the top half of each horizontal sheet and the other shade on the bottom half. Because the paper is horizontal, a horizon will automatically appear where the two shades meet. It will show up in different ways.

Basically, it doesn't matter whether you start with lemon or golden yellow at the top—try both options. Once the six colors have been applied to the three sheets, choose one sheet to work on further. Add small color areas to form mountains, clouds, lakes, trees, etc., making sure the two initial colors remain dominant.

When all three landscapes are finished, they will be completely different. The goal of this exercise is to experience how different colors can express moods of nature. Or, how a warmer or cooler base color can determine the mood of a landscape. Which painting looks more airy, watery, earthy or fiery?

This exercise can also be done with two greens, two oranges or two purples. Various other combinations are also possible. As a final step, try giving the landscape you have just painted a name.

These exercises encourage us to look at the color circle not only from the soul-mood angle, but also to connect colors to the four elements and move from soul moods to nature moods.

Paint the color circle again, now giving the four elements each a location in the circle. We can also connect certain colors to the four compass directions and their associated climates, depending on where we live. South might lie between yellow and red; north, between blue and green. Based on your local geography, which colors would best represent east and west? Where in the circle would the four elements go: heat, wetness, air/light, and earth/dryness? Warm and cold, wet and dry could be across from each other. The color circle can thus help us discover moods and qualities in nature and landscapes, useful in the upper elementary grades.

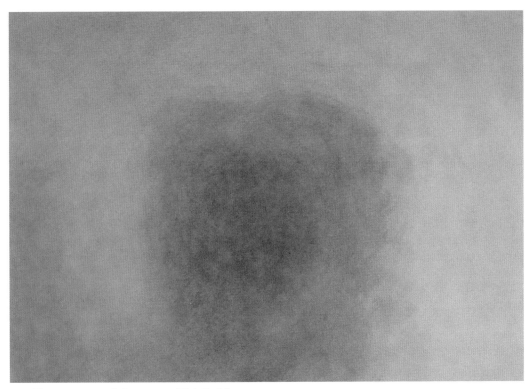

The emergence of plant green. (Dick Bruin)

Basic exercise 8
Plant green: from luster color to image color

Objective: Clearly experiencing the difference between a green created by mixing blue and yellow and a plant green.

Paint the middle of the bottom part of a sheet with soft carmine red, letting it become slightly stronger as you go down. Now paint one side of the sheet yellow and the other blue. In the middle, from top to bottom, green will appear as a mixture of the yellow and blue. At the bottom, where red was used as a base color, a different green will emerge. This green is deeper, darker. By adding more carmine red, we can make the contrast with the above green even stronger. The "image color" green is the one with red in it; the top green is what Steiner calls a "luster" color.

We will now go one step further. To experience it fully, the above exercise should really be done with veiling rather than wet-on-wet. Once the "image color" green has been created, it looks rather lifeless. Steiner says

85

green is the lifeless image of life. In order to give it a living character, which is necessary since nature is alive, yellow-white should be painted over the bottom green (just a few veils). Now the image color will regain a "luster image" quality, becoming an animated plant green.

Summary: The luster colors yellow and blue give green a luster character. Red darkens green into a shadow color, an image color. With the help of the luster quality of yellow-white, an animated green appears: a "luster image."

We will now use plant green to paint plants.

To paint plants, we can start by covering the whole sheet with soft carmine red. Steiner describes this as the color of warmth, which is the foundation of life connected to the Saturn epoch, a number of epochs before the current earth phase.[5] We now paint yellow and blue over this thin layer of red, allowing green to appear. Thus we connect the element of light/air with the elements of earth and water. In this first exercise, the underlying red works evenly through the yellow, green and blue.

In a next exercise, we can add accents to the underlying carmine red, for example by painting the lower half more strongly red than the top half, creating a warmer shade at the bottom. We thus create a season in which the earth is warmer than the air. We could also paint the middle or top of the sheet with a stronger red. In the first case the plant green acquires a warmer shade and a stronger brownish-green color. By using more red in the light-warmth area, the heavens are given a glow. Other color combinations remind us of autumn or late afternoon. Changing the placement of the stronger red changes the mood: time of year or day, type of landscape, etc.

If we want to continue this study, we could change the foundation to blue or yellow, varying in strength. Painting from top to bottom, blue above and yellow below with plant green in the middle, produces a surprising effect and a unique mood.

The above exercises, as yet nonspecific with regard to plant types, are a good start for Botany main lessons in fifth grade. The plant is at one with its surroundings. A new world is created with red, yellow and blue, depending on the strength and placement of the color. Developing a feeling for the unity of nature is a prerequisite for learning about different types of plants and their parts. Botany lessons are thus easily combined with color exercises, which can also be done with wax crayons or blackboard chalk.

Basic exercise 9
Light, color and darkness

Objective: Practicing letting a subject appear out of color areas and developing the courage to explore the extremes of light and darkness. Working with indigo blue and mirror images.

We take a vertical sheet of paper and mentally divide it into three equal vertical strips. We start painting Prussian blue in the upper left of the first strip, becoming fainter as we go down, ending up very light in the lower left-hand corner. On the middle strip we also paint a transition from dark to light Prussian blue, but this time the darkest part is at the bottom. On the right-hand strip we repeat what we did on the first strip: dark above and light below.

It is important that the borders between the strips be indistinct. The color differences should be clearly visible, but the borders should not be definite lines.

Out of these dynamics between light and dark, we now let a steam locomotive come toward us. From the darkness of the middle strip (bottom part) we paint the cowcatcher, the rounded front of the boiler, the chimney above and behind it the cabin. These details are painted in the faded blue section of the middle strip. The lighter parts of the painting (top middle and bottom left and right) suggest smoke and/or steam.

In order not to let the light run off the page, we close off these lighter areas by painting dark Prussian blue along the edges of the paper. This gives the impression of a puff of smoke coming from the chimney and clouds of steam escaping at the bottom, next to the train. Next we paint over the whole thing, carefully, with a pale vermilion wash. This will change the Prussian blue to a shade of indigo, almost black.

Reddish-brown shades will appear where a lot of red is added. Finally a little yellow can be added to create a few accents, for example the lights of the train: Remove a bit of indigo with a dry brush and add light yellow in its place.

Locomotive. (Student, age 13)　　　　　　Locomotive in charcoal. (Student, age 13)

For the second exercise, we lay the sheet horizontally. The subject is an industrial zone. Once again we mentally divide the sheet into three strips, but this time they are one above the other.

Starting at the left side of the top strip, we paint Prussian blue in a gradual transition from dark to light toward the middle of the strip and back to dark on the right side. We repeat this, in reverse, on the center strip: light at the edges and dark in the middle. The bottom strip reproduces the top strip. We can now see a strong interplay of dark and light on the paper.

In the dark area in the middle of the sheet, we now develop an industrial zone: factories, chimneys, roofs, buildings perhaps with windows, anything that looks right. For the most part the lighter areas stay in the upper and lower strips. As in the previous exercise, we close these off with dark blue around the edges, suggesting plumes or clouds of smoke above the landscape. By enclosing the light at the bottom in darkness, we emphasize the ominous, sinister atmosphere. The factories could also be reflected in the lighter area at the bottom, suggesting a lake or river. We could transform some of the blue into indigo by adding vermilion and experiment with other colors to accentuate the theme.

These paintings can also be done in black and white with charcoal, as illustrated above.

Part 3

Kindergarten and grades 1–6 curriculum

1 Painting in kindergarten
Play and imitation

Fleur turned four years old yesterday. Today she is allowed to go to kindergarten for the very first time. A painting activity is in process; first she watches the teacher to see how it's done. Then she picks up her brush and with a huge smile dips it into the water, strokes it against the rim of the jar, and dips it into the jar of red paint. She paints a red circle and softly whispers, "I'm going to make a flower." The petals are a challenge because it is still hard for her to hold her brush. The brush goes from one hand to the other, first vertical, then almost horizontal. This is not a problem for the flower; she continues painting it yellow, and it shines out at her. Then Fleur paints the whole sheet yellow and red and sighs, "Painting smells so good!"

Painting in kindergarten is a weekly treat. The rhythms of the day, week and year form a large part of the kindergarten curriculum. Every day the children play, sing, listen to stories and eat together. The rhythm of the week follows a set pattern: Monday might be drawing day, Tuesday bread-baking, and so on, at the same time every week. This gives the children security in what the new day will bring; they always know what will happen next. The daily and weekly rhythms also provide a healthy alternation between more active and relaxing activities.

Kindergartners have a natural need to express themselves, to busy themselves with color. They look forward to playing with color and are surprised at the way new colors come into being on the paper. All the objects in the world around them are a definite color, but on the wet paper colors appear and disappear. What an amazing experience!

Kindergartners learn through imitation. They follow the teacher's lead in painting. Because they love and identify with their teacher, they want to imitate her.

Above: Kindergarten. "Yay! It's painting day!" Christopher, the class gnome, is wearing his smock. He begins with care, wetting his brush, stroking it against the rim of the water jar, choosing a color... and painting. The children watch attentively.

Below: Now Christopher whispers in Lanielle's ear, "Would you like to try it?" Yes, she would. Christopher watches her paint.

Above: Kindergarten. As soon as Lanielle is finished, Christopher the gnome asks Henry to continue. Below: Victor finishes the painting, and Christopher looks happy with the colorful painting they have all created together. Now the children get to work on their own paintings, using the materials set out for them.

When the kindergarten teacher arrives in the morning, she gets everything ready and then sits down to paint. She is painting as the children come into the classroom. As they take off their coats, they see their teacher at work. While greeting the children, she continues to paint as much as possible. The children are all standing around her now, watching. They see everything she does: the way she handles the paints, water, brush and paper, the attention she gives to the colors, and the way new colors appear on the paper and sometimes disappear. There is something magical about it, like out of a fairy tale.

It whets their appetites. "I want to paint too!" "Me too!" The teacher finishes her work and together they prepare for painting. This is how they begin: by imitating the teacher. It is important to leave the children the option of joining in or simply watching. Becoming absorbed in watching the interplay of color is enough for some children.

Not all teachers follow the above procedure; in some kindergartens painting has become more of an actual lesson, with supplies set out first and the whole class painting together.

Kindergartners like to help with the preparations: stirring and pouring the paints, filling the water jars, arranging the tables and chairs, and so on. The oldest children know the routine by heart. The teacher's mood and manner set the example: the way she does everything, the respect that she exudes.

Experiencing and imitating the meaningful actions of a craft are important for the young child. Thus we could invite an artist into the classroom to paint in the midst of the children, in the same way that a bicycle repairman, blacksmith or baker could be at work in the class during free-play time. The children follow with great interest all the craftsman's actions and preparations and the way he approaches his work. They observe the artist's dedication and enthusiasm. "Yes, I want to be a painter just like him when I grow up," one child tells the teacher.

What the kindergartners paint is entirely up to them—no assignments are given. The play of color on the paper and in the water jar is a constant adventure of discovery. The children often comment excitedly while painting. After school, many a parent is pulled into the classroom by a child to be shown the day's creation. The painting may not yet be completely dry and is therefore still very "alive." Never ask a kindergartner, "What is that?" if she doesn't volunteer the information. The main thing is for the children to paint, to have the experience of painting.

What colors do we use in kindergarten? We use the primary colors, red, yellow and blue, because they have the potential to create all the other colors. If one color is missing, we limit the children's ability to express themselves. The "right" color to use is the one we feel is best; this will vary depending on the child. Make sure all the colors are vibrant and pure, not too watery. Kindergartners need strong colors to paint with, however they must also retain their transparency. For children four years and older, we start with lemon yellow, Prussian blue and carmine red and mix them with a little golden yellow, ultramarine blue and vermilion respectively, to end up with a neutral yellow, blue and red suitable for kindergarten use. (Mixing these colors is described in Basic exercise 1 for the teacher.)

2 Painting in first grade
   ## Exploring the world of color

Tommy looks around with excitement in his eyes. "Painting," he thinks. "This will be fun." The materials are passed out, row by row. "You really need a lot of stuff for painting." The teacher has just repeated what everybody will need: one, a painting board; two, a brush; three, a sponge; four, paper; five, a water jar; six, paint jars; seven ... really looking forward to starting! Tommy dips his hand in the water. It's nice and cool and fun to play with. Time to wet the paper. This is fun. The sponge goes into the water (what a weird natural sponge—did it really grow at the bottom of the sea?). Squeeze the water out onto the paper. Wow, a little pond! But then the water starts flowing all over the place... watch out that it doesn't run off the desk! Quick, dab it dry. Now make sure the whole paper is wet, then turn it over, wet the sponge, squeeze the water out over the sheet and blot it dry again. This is great, playing with water in class! It's a good thing that the teacher comes around and dries the papers off a little more, so that the class can start painting. Otherwise Tommy's colors would flow right into the classroom.

The children have crossed the bridge from kindergarten to first grade. We are now in elementary school.[1] The colors were discovered and explored in kindergarten, and the children already know their names. Each of the exercises will now fit into a larger context. Step by step, brush stroke by brush stroke, the will children discover the "land of colors" with all its rules and opportunities. Each year the teacher will draw back her bow and the students will experience, more or less consciously, the goals she aims to reach with her arrows.

A final brushstroke. (Student, age 6)

1. The first step

Steiner gives a clear starting point for the first lesson. In an exercise with the students, he immediately shows the way two colors work side by side. He says to the children: "I now want to tell you something that you will not understand yet, but one day you will. What we just did (painting yellow next to blue) is more beautiful than what we did below, painting green next to yellow." Many teachers find it strange to state that one color combination is "more beautiful" than another. Here is an explanation.

Yellow, the first color that appears when light is obscured by darkness, and blue, the first color that appears when light shines into darkness, are polar opposites. Together they create green, which is therefore related to both and contains both. Goethe calls yellow-green and blue-green "monotone" and yellow-blue "characteristic." Thus, by saying "more beautiful," Steiner is agreeing with Goethe. Other ways of describing this might include "more interesting," "more exciting" or "more adventurous."

The children often come up with the best descriptions themselves. The main objective is for it to become obvious that yellow and blue have more possibilities for development than the "monotone" color combinations yellow-green and blue-green. Yellow-green and blue-green are more like brother and sister; they flow into each other. They are less exciting, less pure, less bright next to each other. After all, each secondary color is slightly obscured, subduing its intensity and strength. By intensifying yellow and blue, we can even create red (or purple, according to Goethe). Thus light and darkness, active and passive, extroversion and introversion are the foundation for this first indication by Steiner. It can be seen as the first attempt to have the children assess the interactions of colors for themselves, rather than learning a fixed viewpoint about what is or is not beautiful in the world.

2. Two colors

The second point we can derive from these indications is that we always start painting with two colors: with opposites, with colors that create tension. In form drawing, this is found in the straight and curved line, and in music, in experiencing the intervals. Working with two different qualities creates alertness in the children. There are no painting exercises using only one color. Two (or more) colors create a healthy tension in the soul, a feeling that stirs and stimulates the children to get to work. The first brush stroke creates enthusiasm for the next. The six- to seven-year-old child can thus exchange trusted imitative forces for his own imagination. He learns to move from one color mood to another. Before the seventh year, the child experiences the world in a more dreamlike, instinctive way; from first grade onward we encourage the children to be more observant of the qualitative differences in colors. They already have a feeling for this from listening to fairy tales. They feel for the prince, the little girl in the dark forest, or the king mourning the loss of his bewitched daughter. Each mood is related to a color, and the teacher must master this color dictionary. Each color exercise becomes part of the development of the growing child's inner life. She is learning to decide for herself: Which color, where and how?

3. Colors represent emotions

During the painting lesson, we do not connect colors to objects around us (as yellow as the sun, as blue as the sky, as green as grass). These are, of course, true comparisons, but they do not yet supply nourishment or inspiration for painting lessons in the first two grades.

In the lower grades, we connect colors to moods and qualities using adverbs, adjectives and verbs, not nouns. Cheerful and happy, sad and afraid, enthusiastic and passionate, stately and dignified, vain and regal: We try to find the basic moods of the images in fairy tales. When reading a fairy tale we can visualize the images in a particular mood of color, as if we were wearing constantly changing colored glasses. This connection between a subject's image and color mood is an important source of inspiration for the teacher. However, the children don't always need to be told what fairy tale is the basis for a painting exercise; in their soul they unconsciously recognize its color mood. There is power in the unspoken word. The colors, water, paper and brush are enough. To prevent more graphic, figurative elements from interfering with the pure experience of color moods, we paint with large color areas right from the start. This is why we use broad brushes.

4. Composition

Where the colors go on the paper should be left to the children as much as possible. A child's soul does not have a right, left, below or above as far as mood is concerned. Since a young child sees herself as the center of the world, she will usually begin intuitively in the middle of the paper and paint from and around this starting point. The teacher should also be aware of other possibilities and incorporate them into the lesson. Such variations often appear spontaneously if a color's movement is emphasized. Colors can move from top to bottom or vice versa, from right to left, left to right, or diagonally across the paper. If the children get stuck in one type of movement, we can encourage them to try other directions. The main thing is for the teacher to keep connecting with the children, with their experiments and experiences. Freedom should be encouraged wherever possible.

It is fun to experiment with color movement during a parent evening. Parents hardly ever begin painting in the middle of the paper; adults usually begin at the edge.

5. Three colors: all the possibilities together

The totality of the color circle is hidden in the three primary colors. If we offer all three colors in the lesson—yellow, red and blue—then we have all the possibilities. The teacher needs to know all the color mood combinations that are possible. And interestingly, even though the same color mood will ultimately result, changing the order in which the colors are added will create a new, different exercise every time. If red comes after yellow, we add an element of warmth, courage, nerve, strength. If red comes first and yellow is added, the color brightens, becomes cheerful, makes everything radiant. This applies to all the color sequences. One color emphasizes aspects of the other in a certain way, and that makes it exciting. Blue obscures yellow to become green; yellow lightens blue to become the same green. But these two experiences have totally different foundations.

6. More exercises

Steiner points out how important it is to let the colors trade places. If yellow is in the middle and red is painted around it in one exercise, let red be in the middle and paint yellow around it the next time. These *Austausch-übungen* (exchange exercises)[2] are very productive, as they require great flexibility from the child's soul. Steiner describes this as follows:

> In art education it is like this—the most differing things can be done in the most differing manners. It is not possible to say: that is definitely right or definitely wrong. We let the children express colors in such a way that they paint only from the elementary color imagination. One can say to them, for example: "Here you have in the middle of your sheet a yellow patch. Now paint a blue patch on a different sheet. Now finish it in such a way that all other colors change along with it." Thus, a deeper knowledge of color is needed if the children change a color and completely focus everything else on that color.[3]

Another aspect of painting in first grade is learning to paint with and without sharp edges. We can paint colors with definite borders between them, so they are next to but independent of each other. An edge will be clearly visible where the colors meet. Or we can paint colors that flow together with no border, just a gradual transition from one color into the next, sometimes barely discernable. "Paint the colors so that you can't tell where one ends and the other begins." Painting with borders has a strong formative character. The colors vary in ability: Red "forms" differently from yellow. Each color has its own form signature. The children discover this through playing with colors. "Does yellow feel it has been pushed into a corner? Doesn't it want to shine?"

But when the colors come together and transform each other, "The colors put a spell on each other—look what suddenly happens!" To describe these processes the teacher needs to have many suitable verbs at her disposal: to transform, to sweep along, to overpower, to give in, to swallow up, to harmonize, to absorb.... The student will then use this same rich vocabulary to describe what is happening on the paper. To prevent one-sidedness, painting with and without borders should alternate regularly.

7. The lesson

The painting lesson is all about painting. It sounds logical, but let's think about that for a moment. An exciting fifteen-minute introduction that results in five minutes of painting will miss the point entirely. What is painting class really about? Many aspects have already been mentioned. It's about the moments that the child connects, identifies and dives into color, the moment the brush is dipped into the paint. While painting, the children need quiet without distractions so they can express themselves and identify with the color mood. This is an intense experience and can be exhausting for many children after about ten minutes. To work with color in this way is the weekly soul nourishment we can give a child. Of course, painting twice or more per week is also possible. This drop of color will support the children's development, even though they are only painting for a short while compared to set-up and clean-up time.

Assignments can be given in quite a matter-of-fact manner, often following directly from the previous lesson. The most important thing is to state the task clearly and briefly, using a strong image. Each teacher will develop her own style, and each must determine the mood of the colors for herself. She should also have an idea of the desired size (how big) and composition (where) of color areas. She does not need to tell the students everything. The situation, school, class, age group, time of year and day, etc., will determine the assignment. Doing and describing the assignment first in front of the children can actually detract from their experience. It will attract their attention outward onto your own painting, instead of letting the world of color speak to them itself. We want to achieve the opposite: We want the colors, supported by the teacher's words, to connect with the children's soul mood. At this age, the children want to follow the teacher and imitate her, but they must get to know this new world of moods and color themselves. The boundaries the children need will be provided in the way the assignment is worded. The children will also understand the assignment if it is built up logically from the start. In the upper grades a colored chalk sketch of a few areas or lines, or more words, may be necessary.

The technical aspects of painting should sometimes be demonstrated, perhaps accompanied by songs or poems, and can be left to each teacher's imagination. How to hold the brush often needs to be shown: It should lie freely in the hand, not too tight. The children can feel the brush by stroking it on the back of their hand, at a slight angle; it should feel soft. If the brush is pressed hard, it will be damaged.

Wet paper is delicate. Painting strokes should not be rushed or mechanical: "We are not sweeping the floor or painting a door." In the first years it is especially exciting to see how dry or wet the paper needs to be for the paint not to flow off it, making the child into a mere spectator of the colors' antics. The other extreme is painting too dry, so that the colors become fixed and there is no movement. Steiner puts it concisely:

> An inner sense of color build-up should be developed in the children so that they acquire a feeling for the color world in experiencing fairy tales. When they let the imagination work, shapes will also arise, letting the forms grow out of the color. In the world of color you can speak with the children.[4]

Children can be taught to look at their paintings correctly if we carefully hang their work on the wall the following day. One of the possibilities is to hang the paintings with softer shades on top and those with stronger colors underneath, paintings with little tendency to form on the left and those with stronger forms on the right. The paintings with the greatest differences are now displayed at the upper left and lower right. (See Part 2.4, pp. 29–30, for a review and more information.)

8. Lesson examples from first grade

1 A story in colors

Letting color arrangements appear step by step through a narrative during painting.

a   "Radiant yellow asks red to come for a visit. They are very happy together and invite blue to come too. Blue thinks this is a bit scary and almost doesn't dare come, but once he's there, he is happy he came to visit with yellow and red."

b   What color will sit way over there in the corner today? Choose a color that you think wants to be there. And who will show up next, in the other corner? Now the third color can't be left behind. Here he comes, covering all the empty spots. During such an exercise, a child once remarked when red was the last color to arrive, that red was pretty jealous of the other two. "Well, that makes sense, because red is jealousy!"

2 Color transformations

Colors can transform one another, accomplishing amazing things.

a   "Red and yellow are taking a walk, happy and brave. Here comes blue, and he stops them." Or "Yellow is happily on her way. Every place red touches gets more excited (orange). My goodness, let's ask blue to calm things down a bit." Blue is painted next to orange; we could also let it change yellow and red.

b   Many fairy tales speak of spells and enchantments, for example "Jorinda and Joringel" by the Brothers Grimm. We don't have to introduce this exercise by way of a fairy tale, but it can help stimulate discussion. In this story, an old witch changes Jorinda into a nightingale and puts her in a cage. The class could discuss what colors might work for this. Before Jorinda was enchanted, she and Joringel were very sad. What colors can magically enchant each other? Two colors meet and—abracadabra—one transforms the other: Something new appears. A secondary color emerges, either purple or orange or green. The most surprising discovery for the children is that this always happens when two colors meet; they always give each other something, always transform each other. It is most challenging for them to paint a gradual transition from one color to the other. Don't expect that yet at this age; it requires talent and practice. Not until second or third grade will you see children start to master this technique.

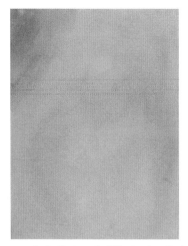

Left: First grade: What color sits in the corner today? (Student, age 6)
Right: Colors enchant each other. (Student, age 6)

This exercise can also free colors from enchantment! A new color appears: Was it there before? Amazement and astonishment are important moods when working with this theme. Something so everyday and self-evident for us can be a small wonder for many children. And it all happens right there on the paper in front of you. It is important to give the experience a name. This will validate their feeling, their world and the reality in which they live and experience everything. Rich language, rich images, rich color experience! Red is stamping its feet, yellow flies like a butterfly, blue is sleeping in the corner!

3 Color combinations

Give short, concise directions for the following exercise: color mood as starting point.

a   Sad blue is carried by red. How shall we tackle this today? Where should we start? How do you paint a sad blue? And red, should it be a strong or a weak color? You need to be pretty strong to carry blue. It's a good thing red is nice and warm. It's sweet of red to help blue, don't you think? It is always about questions, answers and a conversation that involves the children. It is important for the class atmosphere to be engaging and upbeat. Discussions on color can also include gestures.

b   Brilliant yellow shines through blue! Should we begin with blue or yellow? Let's start with blue today, but make sure to leave room for yellow

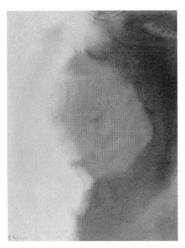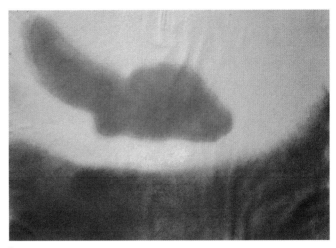

Left: Red carries blue. (Student, age 6)
Right: Brilliant yellow surrounds blue and is carried by red. (Student, age 6)

so it can shine through blue. Next time we'll start with yellow and see how that works; then blue will protect yellow more. The children can also decide for themselves which color they want to begin with. If they are allowed to choose, it is interesting to see who chooses what color. The final result is the same, but the process is completely different.

4 Color moods in fairy tales

Take, for example, the fairy tale "The Frog Prince."

a   Start with a discussion about the princess and the golden ball. With the experiences she goes through, the princess feels at least three obvious moods. Let's first look at her happiness when she receives a golden ball and plays with it in the garden. The scene can be re-enacted in the classroom.

Let us see how happy you are with the ball. What would you do with it? Have you ever gotten something that made you so happy? We have three colors: yellow, red and blue. Which one of these do you think is happiest if you look at all three next to each other? Many children will choose yellow; pay attention to those who choose blue or red. Acknowledge the color the child chooses: You'll paint blue today, perfect. Don't strive for uniformity! Give the children the freedom to paint. Don't forget that the most important thing is that they are painting.

b   The second exercise from this fairy tale concerns the disappointment and sadness that the princess feels when she loses her ball. It fell into a well. What now? The princess is crying! How can she retrieve her ball? Have you ever lost something that was special to you, something that you had lots of fun with? A few children go out into the hall and try to come back as sad as possible. Oh my, how sad! Which color should we choose if we want to paint this? Red, yellow or blue? Freedom of choice is very important; there are no wrong answers. By repeating and experiencing this again and again, all color moods will be given a chance and the children will learn more and more about the colors.

c   A third exercise is about the princess's anger. Finding a frog in your bedroom is not fun. What now? The princess stomps and screams. Has anyone ever been that angry? Yes? Why? What happened? Can we paint the princess's anger? With what color?

After the children have chosen the first color for each exercise, they can choose a second one that fits well with the first and makes it even happier, sadder or angrier.

5 *Exchanging colors*

By changing the place of the color on the paper, or by changing the form, we will change the mood.

During the previous lesson the children painted a color mood with two colors, for example blue and red. In our painting today, let's switch colors. Look closely at your last painting: Where you see blue now, you will paint red, and where you see red, you will now paint blue. Is that going to work? It's pretty hard at first. This is an exercise for later in the year and should be repeated and expanded in the coming years.

6 *A Yuletide exercise*

"Today we will begin by painting brilliant yellow in the middle of our paper. Now we'll paint points on all sides of the yellow. What is it? The sun? No, a star, a shining star! Try to paint it so that the yellow becomes thinner and thinner on the way out. How many points does your star have? Five? Six? Or a lot more?

"When the star is done, you may choose red or blue to paint around it, but make sure you keep the sharp points."

Christmas star. (Students, age 6)

3   Painting in second grade
Opposites

Lisa pulls her chair to the desk where everything is set up for the painting lesson. She adjusts her brush, nice and straight and to the left of her water jar. The sponge is at the top right of her painting board, and the paints are perfectly placed in their rack: first the two yellows, then the two reds and finally the blues. She loosens the lids a little bit. That will make it easier later. Carefully she dips her sponge into the water. Where should she start? At the top this time. She neatly dabs the paper with the wet sponge. Sometimes she looks at it from an angle to see whether the whole sheet is wet. With great care, she picks up the paper by the corners and flips it over. She wets the other side the same way. This is great, all these painting supplies. What color should she start with? Most of the children answered "blue" to the teacher's question, but she's not so sure. Should I start with red and then add blue? Lisa looks around. Most of the children have already started. She had better start quickly, before the teacher says something. With enormous concentration, Lisa dips her brush into the carmine red paint. She strokes the side of the jar again and again before she puts the first stroke on the paper. There, she has taken the first step...

1. Complementary colors

In second grade we continue to explore color moods. The moods are more extensively expressed in the subject matter for this grade, which is full of great polarities: The fables and saints' legends are all about virtues and vices.

Character traits are described concisely and powerfully in the fables. The animals have brief adventures, in which two opposite types often meet: wolf and sheep, bear and fox, fox and raven, and so on, accentuating their differences. Each animal thinks, speaks and acts according to its own nature.

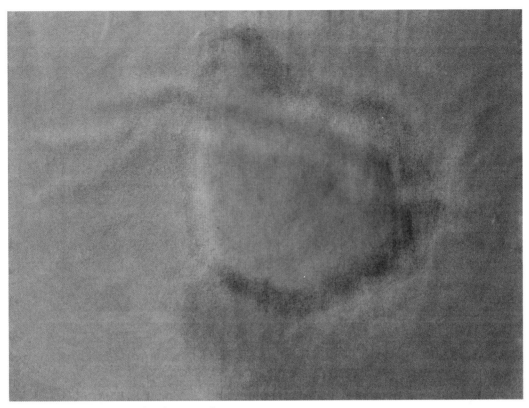

Complementary colors. (Student, age 7)

Thus, animals that are sly and naïve, silly and clever, industrious and lazy all meet each other.

In color theory we speak of complementary colors. Goethe calls these strongly contrasting colors "harmonious": red-green, blue-orange, yellow-purple. Each of the three primary colors is represented in one of the combinations: blue opposite yellow-red, and so forth.

We also often find these contrasts in the legends of the saints. A human being, confronted in all sorts of unique situations by his lower or "animal" nature, tries to overcome them by following an inner path. Where hunger gnaws, a person decides to fast. Francis of Assisi calls his physical body "brother donkey." He tries to distance himself from it in order to understand it. He imposes his will upon it, supported and inspired by his faith. These images in the fables and legends fit the development of this age group. Painting lessons can support and reinforce this by consciously putting primary colors next to secondary colors so as to attain balance and harmony.

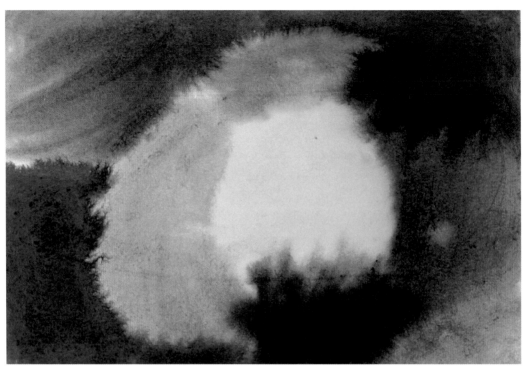

Complementary colors. (Student, age 7)

"How big and strong do we need to paint peaceful green when it meets powerful red, so that neither one will be the boss?" Time and time again it becomes obvious that we need to limit the quantity of an active color so the other one has a fair chance to be equal.

The children have already encountered how secondary colors are created. We now have a choice: creating purple from blue with red painted over it, or vice versa. There is also no need for one color to be always in the center with the other one around it. Any composition is possible; the children can decide for themselves. Borders between colors can also be painted in different ways (curved and meandering or straight and angular). These exercises will enrich the painting of the subject matter.

If a child happens to have her birthday on painting day, the following exercise can be given: Yellow is in the middle, beaming, because today is its birthday and it's having a party. Red and blue are coming, and their gift to yellow is purple. Yellow beams even more now because the dark purple lets yellow's strength shine more strongly. This is how the complementary colors influence each other: They strengthen each other. Red becomes even redder next to green, orange more fiery next to blue.

2. The legends

Legends give many opportunities for color conversations with the children. They have already heard how Saint Francis, with a single gesture, tamed the ferocious wolf, who had been making the city of Gubbio unsafe for quite some time, and how he brought him back to the city meek as a lamb. To keep the children from painting a representation of the story instead of a color conversation, it is recommended that the painting exercises be done a number of weeks after the story is told. Bit by bit, both teacher and students must recreate the story so they can once again visualize the motif. If the teacher only says something like, "Today we are going to paint this and that; I'm sure you remember because I told you the story not too long ago," the children will be left to their own devices and lose themselves in the external aspects of the story.

In the story of Saint Francis, his first meeting with the wolf is an important motif and can be used as an example. The teacher can search for such characteristic situations in the large number of stories available. They are ideal for painting assignments and are a fruitful topic of conversation with the children. "What did Francis feel when he suddenly met the wolf in the forest? And what about the wolf? Did he give up immediately?" Let everything the children say be considered as much as possible. "If we want to paint this meeting, what colors should we pick? Which one would you choose for Francis? And what about you? Why? Good, you take that color and you try your color. And now the wolf. Who has chosen a color for the wolf?"

Thus the class lets the colors appear as if by magic. Each child chooses a color combination; surprisingly enough, the majority chooses the same combination. However, those who have chosen a different combination are like icing on the cake; when the paintings are put up the next day, these examples encourage more discussion and exchange of ideas. If the children are used to painting from color area and mood, no naturalistic wolves or Francis figures will appear, but different forms will appear out of the color areas and the qualities of the colors. The color movement comes forward. The color chosen for Francis moves toward the wolf color: Does it retreat or advance strongly? The paintings give the answers. They are like windows to the child's soul in which this wondrous meeting has taken place.

3. Adding colors

In the course of second grade, we replace the three primary colors with two yellows, two blues and two reds, thus expanding the color possibilities. Lemon yellow and golden yellow, vermilion and carmine red, ultramarine and Prussian blue are needed to obtain a richer variety of mixed colors. Fresh green is a mixture of lemon yellow and Prussian blue. Ultramarine (which contains a lot of red) together with carmine red creates a beautiful purple. Vermilion with golden yellow produces a warm and festive orange.

Thus the children discover rich color nuances through experience, and the opportunities increase. The children should feel that the world of color is endless and not limited by what is made available, in this case by the teacher.

A short example by Steiner suggests many aspects of painting exercises for second grade:

> You can speak with the children in the world of color. Over there
> is the coquettish lilac, and a cheeky little red is right beside it. The
> whole stands on a humble blue.[5]

Where is lilac in the color circle if it is to be "coquettish" lilac? Is coquettish lilac large or small, and where is red? If something is cheeky, how big is it? Such questions regarding the positions, sizes and places of colors in relation to others on the color circle are all questions we can ask the children. Each painting will be different. Between the introduction by the teacher and the process of painting, there is a great deal of room for improvisation—but this space is created through many talks about color, not by letting the children sort it all out for themselves. That would cause the work to lose its great pedagogical value.

Thus, the feeling for color is further developed in second grade. The qualities of the colors are brought forward even more. Through developing a feeling for contrasts in word and image and by doing, the eye and heart are educated. The young child will experience each step as a new discovery and is given space by the teacher to use these newly acquired skills.

By second grade children feel at home in the world of colors and have mastered basic painting skills. However, it remains important to continue to pay attention to correct painting posture and handling of the materials. Painting while standing instead of sitting gives the children the ability to look at their work from a distance and allows for more freedom of movement. But it can also create distraction and commotion. We must decide continually which is more important: peace and quiet while sitting or more commotion and movement while standing. Children also have their own preferences. The important thing is that they should not become cramped, and they should maintain a relaxed posture.

4. Examples from second grade

1   A story in colors
In this example, the story is told step by step while painting.

a   At the bottom of the paper lies dark green. It is sleeping. [...] we paint dark green at the bottom of the paper. Yellow sees it or hears it snore [...] time to get up! Tingly yellow grows toward green, but doesn't touch it. I'll help you, red says. Red steps onto the paper where there is still some white. It comes to help yellow. Oh, orange! Part of the yellow has been turned into orange by red. Why don't you tickle the green? red says. We rinse the brush and dip it into light yellow. Carefully at first and then with a few strokes, we change part or all of the dark green. Green wakes up.

b   The color story by Steiner cited earlier can be given as an exercise. We see a playful, coquettish lilac and, close beside him, a cheeky, impudent red. Together they stand on a humble blue. The class can get to work immediately; a class conversation is possible, but not necessary.

2   Color moods in the legend of Saint Martin
Going from moods to color movement and gesture.

a   Martin, a knight, is in the service of the Emperor Julian. As the army enters the city of Amiens, Martin rides at the back of a procession of knights with his loyal servant beside him. At the gates to the city, he is approached by a beggar who begs him for help. Two people meet each other: beggar and knight. What colors could meet each other here? Which would you choose? And what did Martin do when the beggar asked him for help?

After the children have told the rest of the story together, the following question can be asked: So the one helped the other. How can you show that in your painting, in one movement from one color to the next? Wow! What would that look like? Let's try it.

To clarify, this exercise is not about portraying naturalistic human forms, but about a meeting of colors in which one color "helps, supports and makes the other one stronger...." Thus a courageous red could stand diagonally across from a gloomy blue, or next to a pleading yellow-green.

b   Another part of the Saint Martin story gives an ideal image for a painting exercise. In a dream, Martin sees a shining figure, wrapped in the piece of cloak that he gave the beggar at the gate. A brilliant color (yellow) could be painted with red around it, and yellow could then move outward into the red, transforming it into orange. After this dream, Martin decides to be baptized. He is allowed to leave the army after he makes sure that an important enemy of Emperor Julian surrenders without a fight. This story is a great source of inspiration for various exercises in which the children work on color movement and/or color gestures.

3. Color transformations

There are many examples of transformation in the saints' legends. Elizabeth of Hungary's sadness (blue) changes into a sacrificial purple. The impulsive Christopher (vermilion) changes into an inspired person (golden yellow). The knight Martin (red) changes into a thoughtful, spiritual man (violet).

In the story of Saint Francis of Assisi we can also find the example of Saint Clare, who wants to join the Franciscan order. "On Palm Sunday in the year 1212, Clare sat with her family in San Rufino for the last time. She was very quiet and introverted (violet in yellow). No one could guess what she was thinking. Shortly afterwards, she left her family and joined the Franciscan order. Later Francis founded a second holy order for women, of which Clare was the first member." The yellow around the violet is changed into an active orange with golden yellow tones, by adding red. When Clare makes her decision, silent yellow changes into decisive orange. The colors can be chosen by way of a class discussion.

4 Color exercises

Trading places.

a   The children attentively observe a painting created in an earlier exercise with the three primary colors. Where are all the colors on the page? Shall we see what happens if on a new paper we put yellow where blue is now, red where yellow is now... and what about red? Here comes blue! We look at the different outcome. Together, we give names to the various compositions. After an exercise with the three colors next to each other, it is

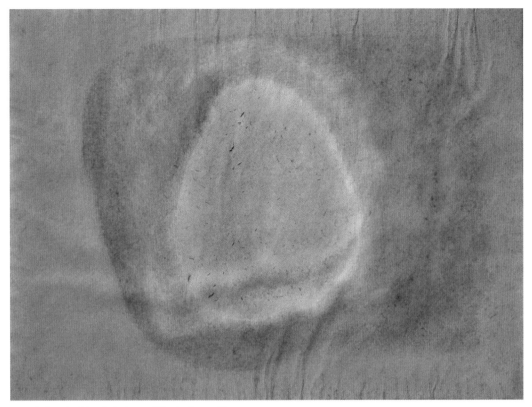

Colors that traded places. (Student, age 7)

also fascinating to paint an exchange of three colors that surround each other. For example: Red is in the middle, blue around it, and yellow around the blue. The end result comes out as yellow in the middle, red around it, and blue around the red, giving a completely different mood, a different experience. Give the children space to experiment with this sort of color exchange.

5 Exercises with complementary colors

a   A riddle: We'll paint two colors using three colors (red, yellow and blue). How is that possible? Today we'll start with red. What will the second color be? What if we started with yellow? Or blue?

b   The riddle continues. Now begin with purple. Which color haven't you used yet? What if you started with green or orange?

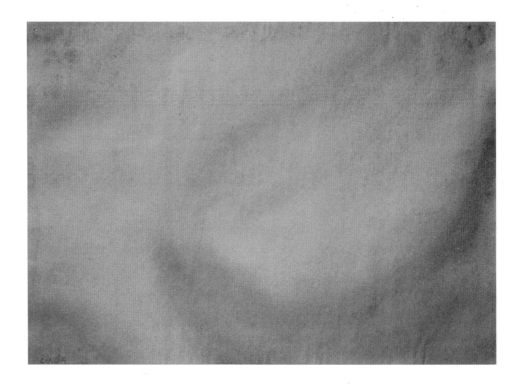

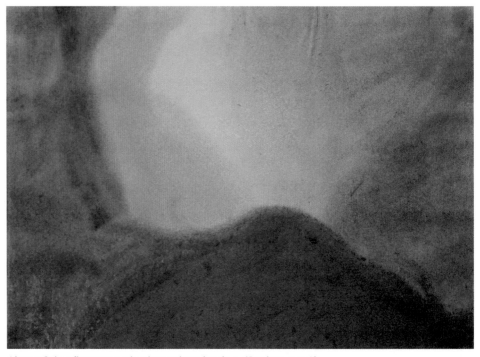

Above: Colors flow into each other without borders. (Student, age 8)
Below: Three colors with borders, three without. (Student, age 8)

4 Painting in third grade
Drama in color experience

Martin thinks Tuesday is the stupidest day of the week. And now it's Tuesday again, yuck, painting. I'd rather draw, so I can decide how the drawing will look, Martin thinks. With the wide brush and those watery colors it never turns out the way he wants it to. It's almost as if it always turns into the same mess; it never looks good. But his drawings! Houses, cars, airplanes and boats are what he likes to draw. But he likes trains best: Amtrak, the Erie Lackawanna line, freight trains. If he finishes his painting quickly he should have some time left over to work on his last drawing.

First the whole paper is painted yellow—that looks happy. And then today... paint a house with red. Wow, that's something different, more up his alley. His teacher told wonderful stories about building houses this morning. You need workers who know what they're doing: bricklayers, carpenters... Martin concentrates on his painting and for the first time, he is the last one finished.

In third grade, the students complete the phase in their painting careers in which colors are expressions of emotion. The foundations for their paintings are soul moods. The subject matter, the Old Testament, offers a dramatic climax of soul moods. Joy and tragedy alternate in these stories: the creation of the world, the Flood and Noah's Ark, Joseph betrayed by his brothers, his high position in the Egyptian Empire, the long, adventurous journey of the Jewish people under the inspirational leadership of Moses, the young David beating Goliath. There are plenty of passages full of imagery to inspire painting lessons, resulting in colorful paintings without falling into representation ("head" work). The drama of the world of color takes place in the feeling world of the child. We can avoid hearing "But it doesn't look realistic!" by continuing to emphasize color, character and gesture.

The thread that began in first grade and weaves through the curriculum continues: drama in color composition via contrasting color qualities; color transitions involving either delicate nuances or stark borders. The children control the elements, whether limiting the size of color areas or allowing colors to flow together or not. They have the necessary skills with water, paint, paper and brush at their fingertips.

1. Color circles, color changes and the rainbow

Color circles, either with colors flowing seamlessly together or in separate zones next to each other, are favorite painting subjects. They become even more exciting if only part of the circle contains separate colors, while the colors in another part flow together where they meet. The two zones could differ in each new painting, involving different areas of the circle and creating a different effect every time. The children discover how important both the restricted and looser areas are: the fixed vs. the fluid, an "awake" element as opposed to an "asleep" one. Each color acquires its own form and gesture, and together they continue to comprise the whole. This whole fits in perfectly with the development of this age group, in which the world is still experienced as a unity, although not for much longer.

The eight- or nine-year-old will still easily join in the events of the class. He is not yet critical. He sees the teacher as an authoritative figure who leads the group through the flow of activities in the school day. Painting lessons have their own undisputed place in the flow.

2. The Creation in color

Stories about the creation of the world are a rewarding subject for painting lessons. Each day in the first week of Creation contains new elements to paint. The children can still understand these through the moods, gestures and movements of the various colors: Yellow streams out, always coming from a central point; blue turns inward, feeling its way toward the center, and can become sunk in itself; red moves on its own, both outward and inward. The secondary colors contain nuances of these three movements.

Depictions of the days of Creation do not have to be realistic representations; this does not yet appeal to the child's soul. Not until fourth grade will the painted image need to correspond to what the children see around them. In third grade we can look within the colors themselves for the best way to represent the Creation. What colors tend toward a fixed form? Which ones love to be thin and tenuous, to help us portray air and water? How can we paint each color either airily or solidly? Blue's tendency to form can nevertheless be painted airily, and light, bright yellow can be painted solidly, restricted and heavy in form. The children can now search among the colors and create their own world in the process.

3. Painting over a base color

Another suggestion for the teacher is to lay down base colors. For one of the days of Creation, first paint a light carmine-red wash over the entire paper. Its warm, expectant glow will be a good foundation for the colors to come, binding them together. Surprisingly, the foundation will not be visible in the final painting, though its effects will remain. When we read Steiner[6] on the first phases of the earth's development, we discover that the initial phase he describes is a condition of warmth weaving within itself: an inner warmth, also called love, as a basis for all further development.[7]

Painting over a foundation creates many new possibilities. A yellow or blue undertone will make a huge difference in a painting; the children will discover the effects of the various undertone colors for themselves. And there is another advantage to having the class put down a base color during the first part of a painting lesson: It creates a calm, contented environment. Painting their foundations, the children will bring their papers and themselves into the right mood. Beginning the painting this way also helps keep the focus on the color, on painting "out of the colors" rather than preparing to paint images. For the teacher, this moment can also be an opportunity to observe how the students are handling their brushes and to offer corrections where needed; some children tend to press down too hard, going through the paper instead of over it.

Starting this way, we could paint the first day of Creation using two primary colors over the soft carmine red base. With each new day, a new color will appears. Finally all six colors of the color circle are present, painted either in strong forms or creating a subtly atmospheric mood. Thus the children are creating their own world out of colors. At the same time, we could tackle the creation of plants, animals and Adam and Eve in drawing lessons, along with details like the serpent, the apple and the Tree of Knowledge.

4. From movement and gesture to color

Depending on the class, the students could start painting actual human figures during the second half of third grade. When we start from color quality and movement, the emergence of the human figure is only a small step. However, it can also be a trap for both class and teacher if figures become too representational. Outlines and stick figures quickly appear, nullifying the many skills and artistic processes we have carefully built up so far. It should be obvious that painting stick figures is not our intention. We can take our inspiration from the great images of the Old Testament when we embark on this artistic process, with color at its center: Color movement evolves into the expression of a character's soul mood.

We must exercise caution when turning a soul movement described with words into a soul movement expressed in color. The figure that appears need not always even be human; no details of faces, arms or legs are required as yet. Wrath, joy, doubt and sadness frequently appear in the Old Testament stories. Sleeping, dreaming and waking could also be motifs to work on. Yellow, blue and red could yield a Christmas mood, a theme that can be used in all grades.

5. Mood, shape and surroundings

The story of Joseph and his brothers may be a good introduction to the human figure. "How does Joseph feel? What color best expresses his mood?" Once we establish this fundamental color mood, we can paint the entire sheet a corresponding color. On top of this base, using the same color, we paint the figure as one color area, incorporating an inward gesture, slightly inclined toward a sad mood. Thus, a "monotone" painting emerges. It might be blue on blue. The advantage of choosing the same color for the figure and its surroundings is the fact that the figure will not jump out but remain an integral part of the whole. The figure's contours barely contrast

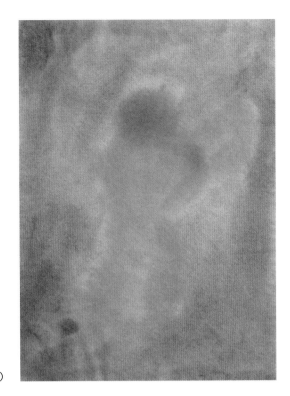

Joseph in the well. (Student, age 8)

with its surroundings; we thus avoid failed attempts or "mistakes" as much as possible.

After painting the figure, the children can decide on a color that will intensify the figure's color, to be added to the surroundings or background. If they choose blue for Joseph in the well, they might be inclined to add red for a purple background or yellow for a green background. The color below the figure should be strengthened, so that the figure isn't floating in midair but resting on a solid base. It is important for the figure and its surroundings to be in (color) balance, preferably of equal intensity. This creates color perspective instead of featuring a dark subject on a light background, which creates a silhouetted figure instead of a play of color. This can be a challenge for the teacher as well as the students. If you are constantly fine-tuning the color intensities, you are moving in the right direction. The results will also be immediately visible when comparing the children's work. Actually, the children already practiced this theme at length in their exercises on complementary colors in second grade.

Thus, we can distinguish three steps: determining the color mood for the foundation, painting color movement, and adjusting the surrounding color. Joseph's somber mood in the well is very different from the happy, radiant mood in the painting of Joseph as viceroy. The colors speak for themselves.

Another example is Moses coming down the mountain with the Ten Commandments and seeing the people worshiping the golden calf: "Moses is not merely angry; no, we speak of the wrath of Moses. Children, what color is the wrath of Moses? What movement does this color make? What does that color want?" The conversation leads the way, and the children proceed to choose appropriate colors.

The task becomes more challenging if the colors for the figure and for the basic mood are located next to each other in the color circle, for example, a purple figure in red or blue surroundings, or a golden yellow figure in green or orange surroundings. Depending on the class, we could also attempt pairings that Goethe would call "characteristic": yellow with blue, red with yellow. The children will find green with purple especially challenging, but why not try it? Can we think of appropriate figures for all these color combinations—either from the Old Testament or, perhaps, figures from a seasonal festival?

Painting several figures together and painting with complementary colors are assignments that will be covered in fourth and fifth grades. The teacher will determine the pace by way of accurate observation and proper insight into the class's limitations. All assignments based on the human figure, from Aaron (third grade) to Zeus (fifth grade), extend over several years of instruction and can be covered in dedicated lessons. We must always make sure that the figures do not stand out like cut-out stencils on a background, but remain color movements in their surroundings. The color should not jump out at us. Anything that looks like a silhouette distances itself from the child's feeling life and becomes fixed. The whole, the harmony within a painting, should constantly be kept in mind.

By alternating assignments, by having the students repeat the exercises in different ways and by reviewing them together afterwards, the students' powers of observation are constantly trained and their soul processes are met and addressed. (See Part 2 for more teaching hints.)

To summarize, we could say that third-grade painting lessons form a kind of climax in the children's color experience. Painting nuances within one color is one of the main skills practiced in this grade. Mixing colors on paper and setting colors off against each other give the child plenty of room to experiment. Finding a balance between too wet or too dry is a skill most children will have mastered by this point. They have also mastered painting as a craft, which connects well with their main lesson blocks on many other crafts this year. This synergy will add to their sense of security and trust and prepare them for their next phase of development, which will begin in the coming years. During this next phase the children will look more and more to the world around them, giving a new dimension to imagination in color and form.

6. Examples from third grade

1 Color circles, color transformations and the rainbow
These exercises are related to our earlier discussions of colors with or without borders.

a   We let the children paint a color circle, filling the paper with a circle composed of yellow, orange, red, purple, blue and green. Each child may decide what color to start with. When the final products are discussed later, many differences will be evident. Some children will let all the colors run into each other, creating a loose, boundless atmosphere; others will give the colors more form.

A next step could be for all the children who let the colors run into each other to paint them again, now in a more confined form, and for all those who confined the colors to let them flow together more, creating delicate nuances of color.

b   In the next exercise we could combine the two: Now we paint part of the color circle in an earthly way (the colors have definite borders) and the other part in a heavenly way (the colors flow freely).

Variations on this theme might include: Let the warm colors be confined and let the cool colors run free; confine the bluer shades as much as possible, surrounded by a fan consisting of all the other colors.

Students can paint color circles all the way through the upper grades. This is always a challenging exercise because it is not finished until all the colors are on the paper.

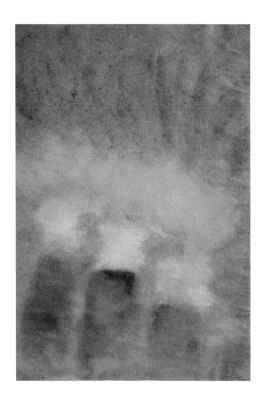

The Three Kings. (Student, age 9)

2 Old Testament stories

We can use these stories as inspirations for painting from mood to color movement and form.

As discussed earlier in this chapter, we have now built up enough basic skills to paint the first human figures. Ever since kindergarten, the children have been drawing human figures, progressing from rudimentary stick figures to "the farmer sowing and reaping" for the Farming main lesson in third grade. Whatever Old Testament characters you choose as painting subjects, the most important step is for you and the students to identify the right basic mood. First decide for yourself which color you would choose to depict the wrath of Moses, Joseph as pharaoh, Noah making a burnt offering to God, or Cain getting angry. Mary, Joseph and the Three Kings could also be beloved subjects during the Christmas season.

After painting the whole paper in one basic color mood, it's time for the second step. Now paint a figure using the same color, or a different shade of the color (ultramarine instead of Prussian blue, golden instead of lemon yellow, etc.) depicting a mood or a characteristic gesture, preferably as large as possible so as to create a good color combination. The result should

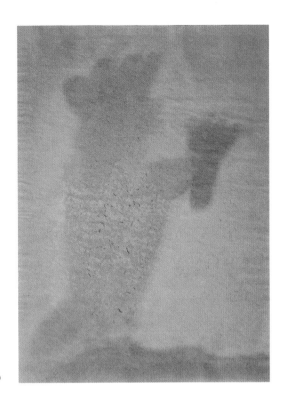

Joseph in Egypt. (Student, age 8)

not be a small figure on a large sheet of paper, but a good-sized color area surrounded by the base color. When making human figures, it may help to paint from the head down (following the development of the young child).

The third step is to change the color combination—let's say we have a blue figure surrounded by blue—by painting over the surrounding color with red or yellow. We now have a blue figure in a green or purple environment; let the children decide what they think would fit best with the figure.

Next we could change the figure itself by adding another color. To avoid getting too detailed (which is actually good for older children), we should keep the figure's base color as much as possible. We could also change the form slightly at this point, if it is too small or too large. But make sure not to fuss with it for too long.

As a final step, it is always good to let the children decide whether something is still missing that might enhance the colors' interactions. Maybe the color beneath and around the figure should be darker, to look more grounded; maybe the top of the painting needs some lighter colors, or we could even add a recognizable detail to the painting.

Building up a painting in five steps is typical for lessons from third grade onward. We work on the mood, subject, surroundings and everything else in consecutive steps for all paintings, including those with animals, plants, etc. (For more information, see the three upper grades.)

3 Seasonal festivals and moods

a Autumn. We start with small areas of ultramarine blue, carmine and vermilion: These are leaves that have fallen to the ground. Our brush is the wind. It carefully blows the leaves, using lemon and golden yellow. This creates a playful scene with warm fall colors. Afterwards, the approaching winter can be created with light brush strokes, but make sure the blue doesn't overshadow the other colors. A song about autumn could accompany the play of wind and leaves.

b Winter night. We paint the dome of the sky blue, starting from the corners until a rounded arch is created. The blue can be lighter at the bottom, for below the arch it is still day. We now create stars on the light blue and white; the yellow dots are barely visible. Darkness is falling. With a clean, wet brush we move the blue already on the paper around the stars, lightening them. If more blue and a tiny bit of carmine red are added to the blue on the paper, they will begin to shine.

c Spring mood. (Note to the teacher: The color movement in this painting is a spiral, leading from the top middle of the paper to the lower right, the lower left, and then to the center.) The order of the colors is as follows: We begin at the top with warm carmine red that becomes more intense as we approach the lower right. We add ultramarine blue at the lower right, creating violet. The red slowly becomes a powerful violet. We continue with a soft Prussian blue at the lower left. Now lemon yellow comes in from the upper left and touches the Prussian blue, and spring green bursts forth!

4 Intensifying colors

d What if we need to continue working on a painting at a later date because the colors are too pale? How can we avoid that dry "painted over" look? We turn the paper over and carefully wet the other side of the sheet with a moist sponge. Let it soak in for a minute, then turn it back over. Never touch the "right side" of the painting with the sponge; small irregularities can be carefully touched up with a brush.

e   Now we can resume work on the painting, changing it where necessary or intensifying the colors. Be careful that the colors stay transparent and that the forms do not become too fixed.

5 Depicting professions

a   Baking bread. We paint the entire sheet lemon yellow. The oven is painted as a blue arch on the top half of the paper. Under the arch we start with carmine red, then vermilion, and finally golden yellow. A light yellow area is left at the middle bottom: This is where the bread is. The children can now use their imagination to intensify the orange tones in the oven and decide what shape the bread should be.

b   Baking bricks: The baking process shows up as a color transformation. We begin with a blue rectangle in the middle of the paper. From the outside in, we now paint yellow that eventually goes over the blue, creating green and yellow. Keeping the outside yellow intact, we now paint golden yellow from the outside over the green, creating a warm green. We leave a stroke of golden yellow next to the light yellow and paint vermilion from outside into the warm green: This creates brown as the mud is slowly baked. Finally we paint over the brick with carmine red, making it glow, until it is baked hard and almost black.

5 Painting in fourth grade
From color mood to soul mood

*September: Michaelmas! Today we are going to paint Saint George
and the dragon. Well, that sounds perfect to Robbie! Saint George,
the knight, is going to be holding a huge sword in his hand, and watch
out for the dragon, he's going to be terrifying! Gaping jaws, huge
teeth, lots of flames. The jar of red paint is almost finished—Robbie
is starting to get hot himself. "Can we open the window? I'm dying!"
and he tears off his sweater. Oh, the sleeve rubbed the painting... too
bad, it was going so well. Thank goodness there's still a little red in the
jar so the dragon can be repaired: The sleeve mark is no longer visible.
What about the paint on his sweater? Oh, mother will know what to
do about that...*

Between the ages of nine and ten, children acquire a new relationship to the
world around them. They start to become more aware of their home and
school environments. The look in their eyes changes: The open, expectant
look becomes more questioning, even judgmental and critical. This criticism
is aimed not only at the world around them, but also at themselves and their
work. They are embarrassed by their paintings and drawings: "It's all wrong, it
doesn't look like it's supposed to." Other people aren't spared either: Parents,
teachers, fellow students suddenly have to suffer comments about their
clothes, hair, funny nose or big ears. Everything has changed. The children
are full of insecurities; their love and sympathy for adults has disappeared.
The scales have fallen from their eyes, and not everyone around them finds
it pleasant. The child may start to feel lonely; death sometimes seems near.
Insecurities may be masked by confrontational behavior, foul language, the
need to act tough. "How this child has changed in the last few months!" the
teacher sighs to a colleague. During a parent-teacher conference, parents
bring up the child's sudden anxiety: "She doesn't dare to be alone at home
even for a minute, and we need to leave the light on all night." You may
remember this phase from your own childhood.

Twilight of the gods. (Student, age 9)

This new relationship to the world also has a flip side. For one thing, the children may make surprising discoveries in nature at this time. Things they took for granted before are now revealed to be something completely new. The curriculum responds to this newfound interest in the environment with main lessons on Human and Animal (zoology) and Local Geography. Through these subjects the children discover that images and forms they only experienced inwardly until now can also be found in nature. In the style of Goethe, the teacher tries to let the children experience natural phenomena for themselves and recognize the forces at work there. Everything having to do with soul moods must now undergo a metamorphosis, a change from soul mood to nature mood.

The child's attention is now drawn outward to the world of animals, the closest kingdom to our own: animals in the wild, whether terrestrial or aquatic; birds in the sky; various habitats. Animals are formed and colored to fit in with their environments; their feeding habits reflect their habitats. Our intense relationship with them becomes obvious in the Human and Animal main lesson. A lifeless naturalistic view is avoided, so that the nine- and ten-year-olds learn to discern the creative forces at work in the realm of nature.

1. Earth colors

When painting nature moods, landscapes and animals, the children feel the need to use colors that are darker and more complex than the bright primary and secondary colors they have used until now. They may already have (inadvertently) encountered "muddy" shades of brown and grey in their paintings; these colors are now particularly inviting, though some children may find it hard to leave the rainbow colors behind. These new colors are almost like a shadow cast on the paper.

Being able to appreciate this new color quality depends on the child's individual taste. Where one child sees only "mud," another will discover many interesting color nuances. The color exercises given in the Basic exercise 6 for the teacher (see page 81) are still too hard for this age group, but some versions of them are possible, like using complementary colors to create an earth tone: painting a blue wash over an orange created by red and yellow, for example. In main lesson-related painting assignments we can encourage use of earth tones so that, even though we are not painting naturalistically, the animals we depict can really be seen as on and of the earth. Connecting with the earthly element is important for this age group.

2. Heat and cold

In the Norse creation story, we can find ample motifs to complete this transition from soul mood to nature mood in painting. One way into a conversation about nature moods could be the difference between warmer and cooler colors, in combination with the four elements of earth, water, air and warmth or fire. In fact, the way we introduce landscape painting is based on these factors.

The Norse creation stories tell of two worlds. Niflheim, the land of mist, is the home of fog, cold and darkness. It is a vast wasteland, with ever-blowing icy winds. In Muspelheim heat reigns, scorching and fiery, burning everything. Between these two areas is a deep chasm, the Ginnungagap.

On one side of the paper, have the children paint cold, icy colors; on the other side the warm, intense colors of heat.

We can expand this imagery further in a second exercise, with instructions to paint these two worlds using only two shades of blue: cool Prussian and warm ultramarine.

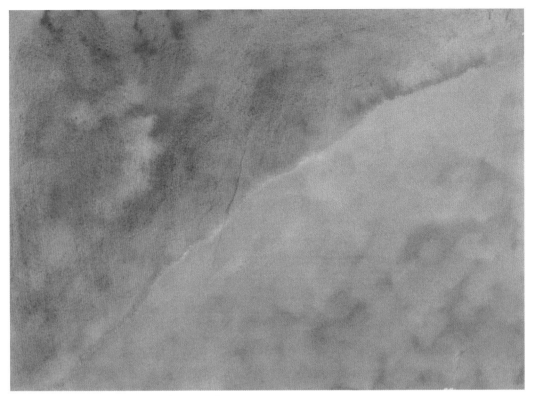

Creation of a landscape. (Student, age 9)

As a third exercise, the two worlds could be created using the two reds. Vermilion lends itself easily to portraying heat; the children may have to search for an icy, cold climate in the carmine red, perhaps mixing in other colors while keeping it predominantly red.

In exercises of this kind, the child develops a feeling for subtle nuances. Many surprising landscapes will be created, usually with heavier, earthy, cooler elements below and warmth above. But if we turn the paintings upside down, they will often be even more striking. Conversations about color and landscape can now begin: landscapes in warm and cold colors, in warmer and colder regions of the earth.

3. Landscapes

Many landscape possibilities appear when we paint the elements of water, air and earth. Details are not yet important; what is important is the mood of nature. Aspects such as time of day, season, geographical location and weather will be expanded upon in fifth and sixth grades. For now, one principal mood must always prevail. No matter how harsh the contrasts in a painting, the colors should form a unity, an organic whole. Trees and forests can still be omitted in fourth grade to let the children create landscapes from color first, rather than from representation. Much depends on the teacher's choice of words. A landscape can be beautifully described in a conversation with the children, especially if they have visited such a place; their experiences are important.

   After such a conversation the moment arrives when descriptive words must be translated into color qualities. "So is it light or dark, warm or cold, pleasant or mysterious in that place? Might there be one color that expresses its fundamental mood? Perhaps a purplish blue, or a more greenish blue?" Just as the children head out to explore their own environment during Local History and Geography lessons, they travel in painting class by means of landscape colors. What they observe is internalized and then consciously brought out again in the painting lessons, an important pedagogical aid for training thought processes.

4. Maps

Maps can be painted and drawn in connection with the Local Geography main lesson in fourth grade. It is interesting for the children to be able to view a number of historical examples of maps, so they become aware of their development. For example, the earliest maps depict side views, not bird's-eye views from above: The mapmaker's standpoint was still on the earth. Not until later are landscapes painted or drawn as seen from above. Maps as we know them today—full of color areas, lines and symbols—are a little abstract for the students; it will take most of them a while to really understand a modern map.

   The next exercise involves building a bridge from the world the child knows to the information we would like the child gradually to understand.

This is accomplished by means of simple color sequences that will allow the student to understand the meanings of colors on a map.

We first paint three colors with the children: yellow, green and blue, one after the other. Now we ask them to imagine what it would be like if they found themselves in the yellow part of the paper and to write down what kind of landscape they would see. Next we "walk" from the yellow part to the green part. The students describe this trip in their own words. Finally we arrive at the blue part. How does it look there?

Various experiences and ideas will result. One student started out in a desert and reached the sea by way of an oasis; another started in the hollow of a sand dune and walked through the woods to a lake. It is important for them to use their imaginations as much as possible and to describe the surroundings, together with any adventures, in as great detail as possible. The students thus bring their inner worlds into connection with external information.

Our three-color sequence could now be replaced by a different set of three colors, for example a sequence from the color circle: from purple via red to orange, or from green via yellow to orange. The students will expand their descriptions to include mountains, valleys, swamps; differences in temperature, altitude and land use may appear. In this way the students learn to orient themselves in their imaginary environments. Elements such as roads and towns could also be added.

This painting exercise could parallel the creation of the students' first maps, which result from careful observations (the classroom, the school building, the immediate neighborhood). To conclude the colorful painting project, the students could try to include the entire color circle on a journey, either in their own surroundings or in distant lands.

There are many ways to give children the experience of discovering their own personal viewpoints and gaining an understanding of the process. Thus, we could easily begin by painting maps, which will include increasing numbers of features until they become too detailed to paint with wide brushes, and colored pencils take over.

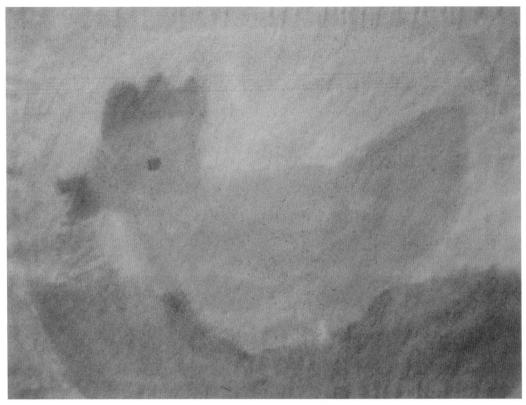

Chicken. (Student, age 10)

5. Animals

In setting up painting exercises to accompany the first lessons on animals, we should make sure it is an animal's essential qualities—not its immediate outward appearance—that we express in the painting, in forms that arise out of color. The essence, the characteristic gesture of an animal species is what is most important. What is it about a bird that allows it to fly: Which elements are involved? What is the essence of "cowness"?

We must search for examples that will show clearly how the animal lives in its habitat, as well as its position and tasks in nature. In the painting lesson, the children should be able to experience how the animal's habitat is shaped by the different elements: cold, warm, air, light, water and earth. We first look for a base mood and its corresponding colors.

Let's say we start with the cuttlefish. We describe the underwater world: "Have you ever kept your eyes open underwater? What did you see?" The students will share various experiences, from which a palette of underwater

134

colors, ranging from light to dark, can be established. The children could paint an entire sheet with these thin, weak colors, everything flowing together in motion, with no fixed shapes. In the midst of this the cuttlefish moves. Greenish and pinkish colors shoot along its tentacles; colorful clouds float across its body. One remarkable aspect of this creature is that all colors are reflected in its large eyeballs. The children will paint it the way we describe it. Onto the foundation of soft color, they now paint the cuttlefish, starting with the head. Different colors move in all directions; the cuttlefish floats and swims in a bath of color. A few cuttlefish might be fending off an enemy and will therefore need to be partly obscured by a dark, inky cloud.

Another semi-transparent water creature is the jellyfish. It floats along with the movement of the water and shows wonderfully soft colors, like a solidified, flower-like mass of water. The fire jellyfish will need some stronger red accents; other types of fish could also be painted on a delicate multicolored background. Afterwards the surrounding water might be painted in darker shades so that the light, mirroring quality of the fish scales shows up better. The children identify deeply with the water element during these assignments.

6. The cow

If we set out to paint a cow, completely different qualities are involved. The most essential parts of this animal are its remarkable digestive organs. In fact, we could say that the cow is an enormous stomach lying in the grassy meadow and chewing its cud. Its body is at the mercy of gravity. Large-scale, time-consuming processes take place in the cow's digestive system; it has to eat its weight in food several times over in order to stay alive. The cow's warmth organism is very strongly developed; whoever has been in a cowshed in winter knows how warm and humid the atmosphere is inside.

Human beings are also warmer in the abdominal regions (about a tenth of a degree) than in the head. The warmth needed for digestion is the most important element of the cow. This warmth can initially be painted with a light vermilion wash across the entire sheet; the cow itself can then be painted starting with the curve of the rump.

Steiner describes how humans, unlike animals, developed from the head.[8]

> With humans the head is first to evolve. The remainder becomes
> an appendage, which hooks itself, as it were, onto the head.
> Humans, in their cosmic evolution, grow from the head down. ...
> The human starts with the development of the head, then adds
> the chest, the chest metamorphosis, then in turn the digestive
> organs. The lion starts with the chest, then adds the head and
> then, simultaneously with the human during the moon time, he
> receives the digestive organs. The animals of which the cow is a
> representative, first build the digestive system and then growing
> from this the chest and head organs are seen. So you see: The
> human grows from the head down, the lion from the chest upward
> and downward, and the cow, so to say, compared with the human,
> entirely upward, toward heart and head.

The cow is best painted lying down so we can avoid dealing with the four
legs. We paint the animal as large as possible to create a clear, powerful
color tone; afterwards we can paint the surroundings a delicious juicy
green using yellow and blue. The green will darken slightly due to the red
foundation color. Sky and horizon are not important: They would pull the
children toward a naturalistic representation, giving the painting a depth that
would not benefit the color tone. The color areas, not the representation,
are what evoke spatial effects in the painting. We should, of course, paint
lighter tones at the top and somewhat darker ones below, especially under
the cow, because a free-floating cow is definitely out of place. Finally the
children could paint over the cow's warm colors with blue, so that peace and
harmony can reign; after all, a cow is not a bull. It is important to give the cow
eyes, for, just like us, the cow looks into the world. This step should be last,
since it is not easy when painting with the wet-on-wet technique.

Painting over the cow (or any other animal) with blue requires further
explanation. If we only paint animals with pure primary colors, they remain
cosmic, otherworldly creatures, not connected with the earth. Adding
the blue, painted over the entire creature like a veil, reflects the earthly
connection. The "luster" character of the original color is changed and, in a
way, covered by this darker veil. Steiner describes this process in relation to
the division of colors into luster and image colors. The primary colors are the
luster colors: They express their essence directly in the color, just as sunlight

136

gives us direct light and warmth. Blue painted over any luster color gives it an "image" character (blue over blue requires a different artistic-technical solution). Like the image colors, the new color has an indirect effect; its essence remains somewhat hidden to the eye and works behind the color, as it were, similar to the way we experience the difference between sunlight and moonlight.

The new quality which then arises when we paint animals is what Steiner calls image luster (see page 271). Blue represents the "luster of the soul." Painting a thin blue layer breathes life into the animal, as it were. The blue has the effect of a shadow on the luster color, giving it "image character." This theoretical background sounds complex, but it can be put into practice immediately with and by the children; its effect is obvious and astounding. The children do not need to know the reasons behind it, of course. For them, painting blue over the creature and seeing how the new color connects the animal with its surroundings is sufficient.

7. The eagle

We also find the luster quality when painting birds, for example, the eagle. Eagles can move freely in the air, using the warmth from their bodies in and between their feathers. The warmth element is carried by the cooler surroundings; birds ride on rising columns of warmth called "thermals." Without a single flap of the wings, eagles circle upward and seagulls soar along the dunes.

> The bird is, one could say, a warmth-air creature, for the true
> bird is the warm air extending within the bird; the other parts are
> the luggage it drags through this world. ... The bird feels the air it
> draws in as its essence. Schematically speaking, the bird actually
> feels as its essence that which penetrates it as air and spreads out
> over its entire body. This air spreading within it and warming it is
> its essence.[9]

We begin by painting a warm color within a cooler color; then the children can start on the bird itself. Starting with the small head and curved beak, the eagle spreads its enormous wings diagonally across the sheet, using yellow, golden yellow and orange. Next we adjust the surroundings, strengthening the airy element here and there. How can we make the eagle appear to be soaring rather than falling like a stone? How can the colors support this? Here's the secret: If the colors beneath the bird are stronger, they will appear to be propelled upward. Using stronger colors for the bird itself could also intensify this effect. Let the children experiment for themselves. Reviewing the assignment later, we can note which birds seem to be flying and which ones find it hard to stay up in the air. Which eagles are rising and which are coming in for a landing?

Enough food for discussion. If we finally paint over the plumage carefully with blue strokes, beautiful brownish hues appear. The bird, creature of the sun, comes toward us golden and shining. The essence of "birdness" is expressed in these paintings, creating a direct link with the subject matter discussed in the Human and Animal main lessons. Using colors artistically enriches our knowledge of and insight into the animal world.

This way of painting animals can be applied to all sorts of other animals as well. We follow this series of logical steps: Paint a fundamental mood color expressing the essence of the creature; paint the animal itself; adjust the surroundings; and paint over the animal with a soft blue so it becomes part of the whole, since no animal is dissociated from its environment. If we paint a squirrel, its quick movements can help us choose the right colors; fox and mouse will be similar in this respect, unlike the lion, elephant or camel. These animals will be covered in the upper grades, and are best not painted until then. Animals with particular features are rewarding subjects for drawing lessons: Horns, tufts, tails, manes and hoofs are best left for drawing, following proper observation. The teacher should always consider this when deciding whether an animal will become a drawing or painting assignment.

The artist, teacher and color analyst Julius Hebing wrote in his diary:

> The objective of the painter is to internalize the outwardly observable to such a degree that he becomes innerly rich. Only then can a landscape, a flower or an animal be painted as an image in such a way that it approaches the spiritual reality more and more. From the inside it is born anew and passed on in a changed form.[10]

Though the children will not walk this path consciously, artistic education may allow them to spontaneously create animal types that ring true.

8. Themes from mythology

Let us now return to stories. Figures from Norse mythology can be painted following the same steps as those discussed for third grade. The gods, with their diverse personalities, lend themselves perfectly to color interpretations: Odin and his wife Frigg (or Fricka), Thor with his hammer Mjölnir, or the tricky and cunning Loki. One of the most exciting moments is when the blind Hodur, supported by Loki, shoots an arrow at his brother Baldur. The children will find colors for these figures without much difficulty. The gods' surroundings can be depicted in many colors; Bifrost, the rainbow bridge linking the realms of gods and humans, and Heimdal, its guardian, are favorite subjects for the children to paint.

Initially, the Norse themes are best painted in rainbow colors, made sufficiently intense where the mood requires it. The World Tree Yggdrasil and the Bifrost bridge should remain dreamlike images; if painted in earth tones, they will become too earthly. An important moment for the fourth graders comes when they paint conflicts among the gods, using disharmonious, dark colors that result in blackness.

9. Examples from fourth grade

1   Color exercises from tales from the Edda
a   Yggdrasil, the huge life-giving World Tree, can be painted in such a way that its trunk connects two colors, for example yellow and blue. One color is painted at the top of the paper and the other at the bottom, and they touch or merge in the middle, creating green. Starting from the roots, the trunk can grow blue up to the sky and spread into green in the crown. Yellow straight out of the jar can then be applied to the left and right of the crown and drip down onto the earth. We could also paint this with the paper horizontal, instead of the more obvious vertical. This exercise can be repeated with other colors: red and blue, yellow and red... we could also put blue above and yellow below. Through the meeting of the colors, we repeatedly create Yggdrasil by letting its trunk and crown "grow" from the bottom up. In painting the twilight of the gods, Yggdrasil (painted in this way) could be covered with complementary colors, darkening them all. But be sure to save a small part at the base of the trunk: the beginning of a new world!

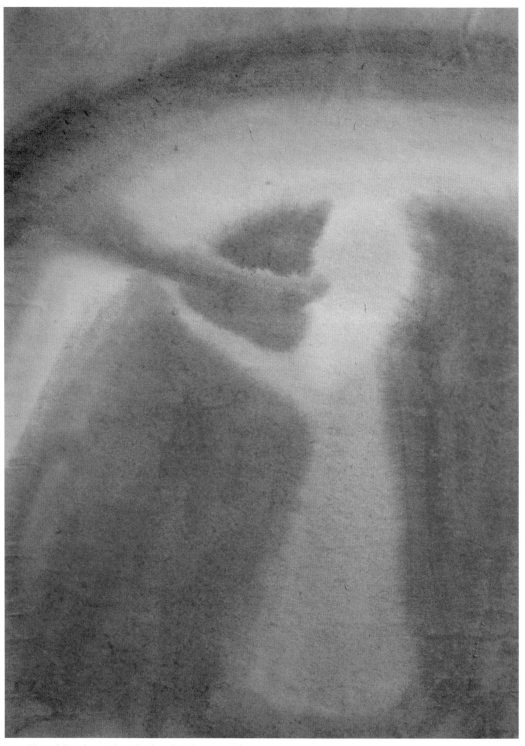

Heimdal at the rainbow bridge. (Student, age 9)

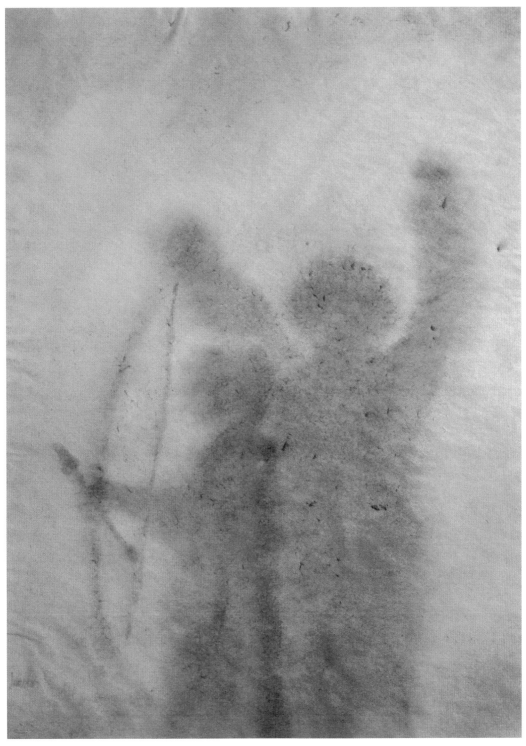

Right: Loki and Baldur. (Student, age 9)

b   Many of these stories can be painted with pure colors: Heimdal at the rainbow bridge, Thor with his hammer. In this assignment, however, the pure colors are covered up: "Thor throws lightning bolts across the sky." White zigzags (left free of paint) are surrounded by rich yellows and reds; these are then painted over with blue from the edges of the sheet, creating rich secondary colors. Be careful not to overdo this; stop in time, and paint over the lightning bolts with a clean brush and a thin blue wash.

c   Another assignment for creating darker colors is the scene in which Hodur, helped by Loki, is aiming the deathly arrow at sweet Baldur. The paper is first painted light yellow; then we use golden yellow, leaving the figure of Baldur blank. At the sides we add a color transition from green to blue. In one blue or green area, we add the figures of Hodur and Loki, using green for Hodur, blue for Loki. The surroundings can now be darkened by adding carmine red, creating violet and brownish tones.

2 Exercises for discovering tertiary or earth colors

a   Local Geography and Human and Animal are part of the curriculum for nine- and ten-year-olds. The children look out at the world around them and wonder, "Who am I? Where am I? What do I see? What is my horizon?" At this age the color circle is enriched by new arrivals: the tertiary colors or earth tones.

b   "Heavenly colors become earthly colors," the Basic exercise 6 for the teacher, provides good information for the upper grades; we will simplify the material a bit for fourth grade. We start by painting the primary colors in three areas of equal size. We now mix two of them together—the children can decide which. Once the secondary color has arisen (purple, orange or green), the remaining pure primary color is painted over it. A new color appears: an earthy color, deeper and darker than those we are used to.

Some children take time to get used to this new palette. The pure rainbow colors have now made room for muddier, harder-to-name colors like eggplant or indigo, which may not seem very attractive to some children; others will love them. In either case, the students often have an intense reaction.

c   We can now use this new experience to paint landscapes, animals and seasonal moods. A few examples: A cow in a brilliant green field will not look too believable; the brightness of the green needs to be toned down. If we add some red, we'll create a browner, more plantlike green, and the cow will now look connected to the field. If we paint a mouse in its hole surrounded by a primary or secondary color, it will look magical rather than realistic. Mixing in a third color brings the painting down to earth. Similarly, an eagle needs some blue over its golden yellow wings so it will not be mistaken for an angel.

3 Painting animals

This is a challenging assignment. After a number of animals have been discussed in main lessons and students have completed small individual projects, animals can be painted as well. To practice an animal's form and proportions, it might be a good idea to make a drawing of it first.

Two ways of painting animals are appropriate for this grade. The first begins with a particular color combination, for example, orange surrounded by blue. The figure of a quick, agile animal, such as a squirrel or a fox, will be suggested by the orange and can arise out of it. The second way starts from the colors that best describe the essence of a chosen animal, as was described earlier in this chapter with the examples of the cow and eagle.

a   First let's take animals that arise out of certain colors. The children paint an orange area of undetermined shape, surrounded by blue. The orange reacts strongly to the blue: It doesn't want to be controlled, it wants to move and play with the blue. What animal is like this, swift and alert? Perhaps a squirrel or a fox. We start over with a new sheet of paper, again painting an orange area surrounded by blue. This time a fox or a squirrel can appear in the orange. Animals are best painted starting from the trunk and adding the head and limbs and, in the case of both squirrel and fox, a beautiful bushy tail. Let the orange mix with the blue somewhat, to give a nice brownish color. The surrounding blue can turn into shades of green by adding some lemon and golden yellow.

Now, what animal could we create using the same colors, but with blue in the middle this time? Maybe a sea lion! The orange could then be transformed into a sunny beach, using golden yellow. The children can work this way with other color combinations as well. First we look carefully at how the colors interact: What do they want? What are their tendencies? What can arise from them? Have the children paint the animal as large as possible, as they painted human figures in third and fourth grades.

b   When we paint animals starting from colors we have chosen for them, we could follow the five-step plan outlined in previous discussions of the cow, the eagle and the human figure.

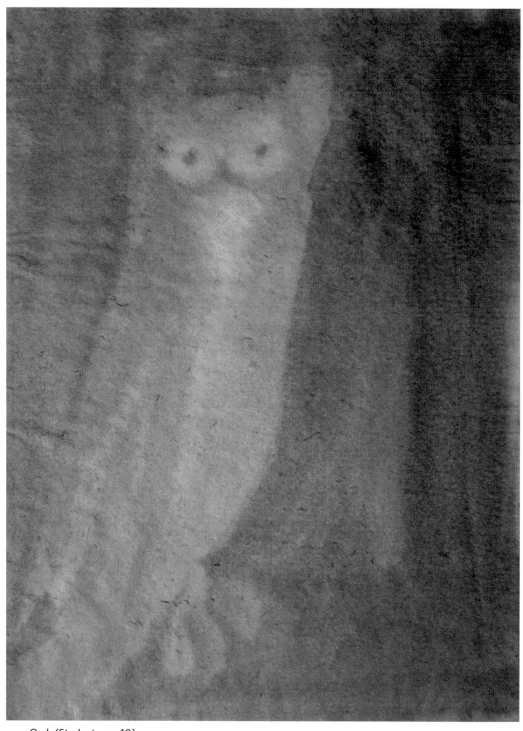

Owl. (Student, age 10)

First we apply a base color. In the case of a cow, this could be a soft carmine red; for a lion, golden yellow; for an elephant, a warm blue; etc.

In the second step the animal appears, starting from its trunk or belly. What color best expresses this animal's character? We are not looking for a realistic representation, just an expression of the essence of the animal's being.

In the third step we work on the color surrounding the animal. Green is important to the cow, as well as to the elephant. The lion prefers the yellow-brown tones of the savannah. A feeling of warmth is important, too: The sleeping lion, with its balanced heartbeat and breathing, feels comfortable in warm tones. While we work on the surrounding colors, we can work on the animal's form too. Make sure the color of the environment has a connection with the color of the animal. This exercise recapitulates the earlier color exercises of the lower grades.

When painting animals that live in or on water—fish, ducks, swans— we can either leave blank areas for them in the colors of the surroundings or remove some paint with a slightly moist brush to create spaces for them.

Step four focuses on the animal again: A faint blue wash can be (very carefully!) painted over the animal, allowing it to lose its otherworldly brilliance and come down to earth.

In the final step, the children examine their paintings and add more colors where they think they're needed. Later, when we observe the finished paintings together, we can usually discover many more types of animals than we initially intended, making things more interesting. For example, why did this cow, with its long neck, suddenly turn into a horse? Or why does this cow look like a sheep, with its head low on its body? At the end of the exercise, all the animals should be given eyes, for they are creatures with souls!

Thus, the children slowly discover the world of animals.

4 Color circle exercises: dragons and castles

In these exercises, we create dragons and castles by following a sequence in the color circle. Such assignments are appropriate for the highest grades and have many variations. We can start with any color; the results will be different each time. Of course, in the fourth grade it is easiest for everybody to use the same sequence and starting color, so things doesn't get too complicated.

a   The castle on the mountain. Let's say we agree on the color sequence yellow, orange, red. Paint these colors, with smooth transitions (not easy), from the top to the bottom of the paper: yellow at the top, orange

Castle from a color sequence. (Student, age 10)

next, red at the bottom. Which primary color is still missing? Blue. (In these exercises, it doesn't matter which blue the children use). A mountain is now painted in blue from the bottom up, with a castle, perhaps in ruins, on top. Unexpected colors will appear in the blue because of the underlying red, orange and yellow. As a final step, the children can add anything they think is still missing. For the next castle exercise, they could begin with a different sequence—say, blue, violet and red—and paint the mountain and castle in yellow. What different effects do we see now? If we do this exercise through the whole color circle both clockwise and counterclockwise, we'll get twelve variations on the theme!

b   The dragon. We paint a dragon with two adjacent colors from the color circle: blue and green. We begin with the blue tail, the legs, the belly, and then the green head with its mouth wide open. The path from blue to green is an S form. Which complementary colors belong with blue and green? Orange and red. We now paint around the dragon with these two colors. Red surrounds the green head; as we travel down to the dragon's blue

The dragon appears! Teacher training course in Ireland.

tail, the red becomes more and more orange. When this exercise is repeated using different colors (and if the children are up to it), we can give the dragon three adjacent colors, for example yellow-orange-red from tail to head. Painting as large as possible on the paper, we start the surrounding colors at the bottom again, using the color next to red on the color circle: violet around the tail, changing slowly to blue, ending with green around the head. This is a surprising exercise with lots of possible results: Each child will create his or her own dragon! It isn't easy, since it uses all six colors; therefore for fourth graders we recommend starting with a two-color or even single-color dragon, using the complementary color(s).

5 Painting the Mississippi Delta

Aspects of this exercise can be adapted for a map of your state, for the Local Geography block.

a   We first paint lemon yellow from the upper left to the lower right of the paper. We paint golden yellow across the top: These are areas of higher altitude. The Mississippi River (Prussian blue) meanders in curves down to the yellow area at lower right. A green area, the Mississippi delta, appears near the shores of the Gulf of Mexico. From the Gulf waters at the lower right we paint ultramarine blue toward the green, creating the delta. The intricately etched coastline is created where blue and green meet.

b   The same painting can be enlarged in scale to show the whole state of Mississippi, with higher-altitude areas in golden yellow and vermilion.

c   These paintings have a north/south orientation, which could, of course, be changed if desired.

6 Maps

An introduction: colors and their meaning on maps

a   The students make their first maps during the Local Geography main lesson. We usually begin with the classroom, the school, the neighborhood and the town or city. To allow the children to become familiar with the different colors used on maps, the following assignment can be given.

b   Choose three consecutive colors from the color circle, for example, yellow, green and blue. Paint these colors next to one another on the paper, in clearly delineated blocks. You have created a tricolor flag.

c   When the painting has dried, the children can use a red pencil to draw a dot in the yellow area and one in the blue area. Now draw a road, either straight or winding, leading from the dot in the yellow area (a village, city or castle) to the dot in the blue area (a location in the mountains, the ocean or a lake).

d   Now have the children write or tell a short story about the trip from one place to the other. What might the yellow area be? A beach? A desert? A field of sunflowers? We then go through a green area: forest? jungle? meadow? And finally we arrive at the blue: water? Or have we come to some high mountains?

e   The children use their imaginations to give meaning to the colors on this first "map."

f   After the children have practiced this with a number of other colors (for instance red-purple-blue or orange-red-purple), they could look at an atlas to see the different meanings that are assigned to colors in maps. A color may be used to denote land use in one map, altitude in another, and so forth.

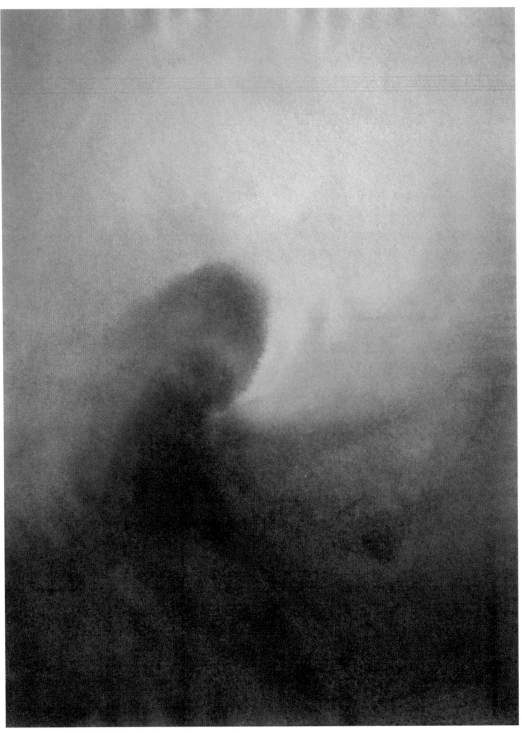

Color exercise. (Student, age 10)

6 Painting in fifth grade
Experiencing processes

Rosemary bounces into the classroom. Yay, painting! As soon as she gets to her desk, she gets ready to wet her paper. The wet sponge falls on the paper, which expands unevenly. Wait a minute Rosemary, the teacher says, let's all start together. Rosemary still tries to even out the paper; she can't wait. Once all the children have their papers neatly in front of them, she is still battling with the paper and water. Oh well, Rosemary thinks, I can start with it like this, it doesn't really matter. As she paints, the colors flow into each other slightly, forming little colored pools. It looks nice! Wow, cool, her neighbor says. The class is painting red roses on a green background. Rosemary's roses stay pink; the green runs off the paper. The teacher looks at Rosemary's work: Your roses look like butterflies today. Let's check tomorrow to see if they've flown away!

In fifth grade, the children's horizons broaden. In Botany main lessons they discuss plants, flowers and trees. The plant world inhabits a thin, vulnerable layer between heaven and earth. The form, color and growth of plants depend on local conditions. Roots burrow into the earth; stem, leaf and flower grow upward toward the sun. Sunlight and warmth are essential to plant life. The plant moves between the earth's darkness and heaven's light, an upward ambition in spite of gravity. Flowers appear in all shades of color and emit wonderful fragrances, and their seeds float on the wind.

This world holds the interest of the ten- or eleven-year-old. We can observe developments in different plant types that can be related to phases of development in the growing child.

Mushrooms grow in the bosom of the earth, with only a small part sticking out aboveground. Ferns unfurl their leaves slowly but surely. In a series of such examples, the students can see and experience plants becoming ever more complex, including rose stems becoming hard and woody. In the shapes of flowers the children discover five- and six-petaled stars; in the patterns of leaves on stems, or at the heart of a sunflower, they discover spiral shapes. Everything in the plant world is created, grows and flowers between the polarities of light and darkness.

The spring sun coaxes the first fresh green from the branches. In the summer, the greenery becomes heavy and saturated. In autumn the summer's warmth expresses itself one more time in the leaves' bright colors before they return to earth, their warmth extinguished, while fruits and seeds guarantee the continuity of life through the winter months.

These annually recurring processes in nature are the source of inspiration for our artistic work. In fifth grade we are not concerned with the schematic or analytical representation of plants. The children should be led to experience that the plant is one with its environment and participates in the four elements. The course of the plant year is a closing circle, but also an upward spiral of development. Living and dying are closely linked; from what is apparently dead, new life germinates.

1. Color processes in botany

The children can experience the processes of plant life while painting: darkness below, radiant light above; on one hand yellow, which makes light visible to our eyes, and on the other blue, the first color created when darkness is illuminated. We must still begin, however, with a soft carmine-red wash, just as we did with the creation images in third grade, calmly spreading warmth—which underlies all creation—across the paper. Yellow can then shine through from top to bottom, meeting blue coming from the bottom up; in the middle, green automatically appears. The red makes this a darker green than one mixed simply from blue and yellow. Steiner says that the plant character of green is only shown to its full advantage if it is painted darker than it looks in reality. There is a close relationship between the plant and the color green; the word "green" is related to the old Germanic word *gehre*, meaning to germinate or grow. Thus green and growing are connected.

The green we observe in the plant world is not the most essential part of the plant; the living, growing element is. This living element has a different color, red, which Steiner calls "the luster of life." The green is an image of this living element, not the life itself. "Green is the lifeless image of life." The red points of new shoots on plants and trees are noticeable in the spring; this living "luster" element then fades as summer approaches and gradually dies (color-wise) into a heavier green. A beech forest in early spring also shows this pink glow in its foliage; after a few weeks a green shadow falls over the forest, and red does not return until autumn, to give a last sign of life. Red is the luster of life, green the lifeless image of life.[11]

2. Plant green

We incorporate this concept when we paint a red undercoat beneath the yellow and blue. Prussian blue will yield a sharper, colder green than ultramarine, which contains more red and will create a mossy green. If we add more red, we can create earth colors with blue and yellow. More blue in the painting suggests a humid climate, red reinforces the element of warmth and woodiness, and yellow the light, blossoming element. The children can experiment with all these elements during the painting lesson to discover the various ways of creating green.

Basic exercise 8 for the teacher (see page 85, "Plant green: from luster color to image color") can also be done by the students to experience this color. Without having to draw them, a leaf and stem can simply be created from the color. Forms automatically appear where lighter greens sit next to darker greens. When we strengthen the warmth element in the airy/sunlit part of the painting, the students can make flowers appear as if by magic: first in red, orange and yellow and finally in blue and purple. A flower is a climax, a point of concentrated warmth, a certain realized potential in the plant before it becomes further concentrated into the seed. Different types of plants can be painted in fifth, sixth and/or seventh grades. The dandelion remains a marvelous example to paint in fifth grade because of its distinctive taproot, leaf rosette, red stem, shining yellow flower and white fluffy seed-head on a fragile yellow-green-pink background.

Narcissus. (Student, age 10)

3. Trees

For discussing trees with children during a Botany lesson, Steiner said the following:

> Look, imagine that plant next to this tree. What does this tree look like then? Yes, it has roots at the bottom, certainly, but then there is not a stem but a trunk. Then it spreads out its branches and it almost seems as if on the branches actual plants grow. For on those branches are leaves and flowers, small plants. We can see a meadow in a completely different light; across the meadow yellow buttercups grow. The meadow is covered in plants, all having their roots in the soil. But with a tree, it is as if one has picked up the meadow, lifted it up and bent it round, so that all those flowers started growing up there. The trunk itself is a piece of earth. The tree is the same as the meadow in which the plants grow.[12]

The step from painting a plant to painting a tree is a small but important one. With a tree, the trunk pushes up the earth element, and the foliage is created in the air/light element. In painting class, without specifying the type of tree—we are most concerned with the process of becoming—we can focus on the tree's various stages through the seasons. We should, however, discuss the correct proportion of trunk to crown, otherwise many "kindergarten trees" might show up, with thick trunks and small crowns.

One way to give the tree a more shining, living character is to paint the surrounding areas darker: This will lighten the leaves. Blossoming trees in spring can be depicted in many delicate colors. The children will discover that, by changing colors, they can produce different trees in different seasons. To conclude, here is another description by Steiner:

> There is the sun. The sunlight falls on the tree. Now one should not start from the tree and draw, but one should start from the light areas and dark areas, so that the tree is created from this contrast of color, coming from the light. Not to start with the abstraction: The tree is green. Do not let the leaves be painted green; the leaves should not be painted at all. Light areas should be painted.[13]

4. Mythology

In fifth grade the students hear stories from Greek mythology; they are surrounded by the adventures of gods and goddesses. As the year progresses, it becomes clear that humanity is gradually taking control more and more, and the gods are withdrawing to holy Mount Olympus. This transition is often accompanied by alarming and catastrophic events: After all, Zeus wants to retain power and control the lives of beings both divine and human. The prophecies that play a large part in these stories, for example, the story of Oedipus, refer to ancient clairvoyant abilities which are gradually waning: The world of the gods must yield to the world of human beings. Freedom of choice is dawning.

Sports were of central importance in Greek civilization: the Greeks' aim was "a healthy mind in a healthy body." This harmonious, athletic image is typical of fifth graders, who have reached a temporary balance between growth spurts in height and width. They are readily identifiable next to upper grades students who may look clumsy and gawky due to their rapid growth.

Many figures from Greek mythology provide excellent subject matter for painting assignments. Cunning, revenge, strength, despair, jealousy: All sorts of soul conditions weave through these stories. A class discussion can provide ample color ideas to start from, as we follow our five steps: first the mood, then the figure, the surroundings and further individual details. Children want to express drama, so the teacher should encourage sharp color contrasts, suggestive nuances of color and imaginative forms.

5. Ancient cultures

Ancient civilizations, from India to Egypt to Greece, are discussed in main lessons. Details of pattern, decoration and architecture are best shown in drawings; painting color areas doesn't always suit these subjects. However, many themes from this main lesson block are quite suitable for class painting. Sculptures, temples, ornaments and the like, painted large with lots of color in different media, can cover the walls during the main lesson block, inspiring the class and giving an impression of the enormous structures that were built during these civilizations.

6. Maps

Maps of Egypt and Greece provide suitable painting assignments. For example, the Nile, which connects all of Egyptian civilization, flowing through the desert, is a nice blue/yellow exercise in which fertile green land can spring up along the river. Mountainous areas can be painted orange and red, to make the contrast between the Nile valley and the inhospitable desert visible through color.

The map of Greece, with its thousands of miles of irregular coastline, rocks, beaches and peninsulas, is very different. The redness of the rocks contrasts with the blue Mediterranean in a powerful color combination, emphasized by myriad groups of islands and high inland mountains. Thus the children can experience the totally different characteristics of the topographies as well as the civilizations of Egypt and Greece. If a country or continent is rich in color qualities, working on it in a painting gives us many more possibilities than drawing: We can look at the qualities and colors of the polar forces from which the landscapes arise.

Thus we can also paint maps in which the climate becomes visible in color. On the European continent, for example, different climate zones meet: from the west, blue; from the north, green, purple and blue; from the south, the warmer hues of red, yellow and orange; and from the east, red from below and blue from above, creating purple. These could meet on a yellow foundation. It becomes a lively whole, in which the high mountains and lower coastal areas are portrayed together with climate conditions.

7. Landscapes

Slowly but surely, an understanding for warmer and cooler colors takes hold—the basis of landscape painting. Morning, evening and night moods are discussed with the children. After sunset, is the earth cooler or warmer than the air? The air always cools down quickly in the evening, while the earth retains warmth longer. The earth even releases vapors which we see as mist trails in the landscape and over water. At daybreak the reverse happens: The sun heats the air quickly, while the earth is still cold from the night. The children distinguish the alternation between warm and cold and choose colors with this in mind. Prussian or ultramarine blue? Lemon or golden yellow? Carmine or vermilion? In the night mood, indigo is effective:

Night mood. (Student, age 11)

Prussian blue with a little vermilion gives a beautiful, cool, dark tone against pale white/yellow moonlight. Is water reflecting the moon, or is there a clearing in the woods, full of shadows?

The time, place and region of each landscape can be discussed with the children before painting, perhaps in connection with geography instruction. A base or foundation color can yield special effects—for example, a pale vermilion will immediately speak to the children of warm, tropical lands. In our vivid descriptions of these countries we can also include animals.

8. Animals

The format for animal painting this year is the same as it was in fourth grade. The African elephant can be built up from a blue base, in a jungle or rainforest environment; the camel, from golden yellow. With a blue wash, the figures will acquire warm brown tones. Owls painted in brown and grey emerge magically from an indigo night mood. Let the children paint the animals large, using characteristic colors. "What are the conditions like where this animal lives? Where have you seen one?" Try to include the students' own experiences in assignments; their relationship to the artistic process will be strengthened and they will feel more involved, even if only one child has actually seen a certain creature and shares his experiences.

9. Color perspective

Working with color areas is still important. The effect of three-dimensional depth in a painting is created by the interactions between different color areas: Some colors pull back, others come forward. Especially when painting mountains, children may be tempted to make one side darker, which has a remarkable effect and emphasizes the work of light and shadow. This will be covered later in black and white drawing. The children should try to achieve the effect of depth only by using different colors, creating so-called color perspective. We find marvelous examples of this in the work of many Impressionists (e.g., Cézanne); it gives fullness to the color and adds dramatic shades to the landscape. This contrasts with the starkness of contrived optical effects such as artificial shadows, which create a depth we aren't looking for in a painting.

If some of the children are strongly inclined to pursue such a graphic or light/dark approach, the teacher can dig up various color exercises from previous years to let the students immerse themselves in color. Meanwhile, their need for graphic representation can be met by engaging them in sketching exercises. Painting and drawing are opposites: areas vs. lines. In landscape painting these two elements come close and even intermingle; there will always be examples of paintings in which both elements are visible. These examples can be pointed out during class discussions of student work, allowing the teacher to formulate questions that can be answered only by the children's careful observations.

10. Seasonal festivals

From the third grade on, we paint color combinations linked directly to the seasons: light red with green and yellow (spring mood) or golden yellow, red/ orange and blue (autumn and winter moods), as yet without any particular images. Images for fifth grade might include the Madonna and Child, the

Three Kings, Saint Michael and the Dragon, children with Martinmas lanterns, or a midsummer (Saint John's) bonfire. If the children discuss the color mood, soon enough the figures will leap out in a lively interplay of colors. Use the suggestions given in the discussions on figures in the third and fourth grades (see pages 120 and 139).

11. Examples from fifth grade

1 Main lessons on culture and storytelling

a   During the lessons, teachers must continually decide what aspects of the subject matter are suitable for drawing and which work for painting. Depicting architecture requires exact lines, so drawing with colored pencils or crayons is preferable. However, the mood of the majestic Pyramids can be expressed very well in a painting; the interplay of colors is more important for this than exact forms, though the children will try their utmost for architectural accuracy. The shapes of the Pyramids could be left blank after painting the background color, which could then darken around them.

b   The Parthenon, high on the Acropolis, could be left blank in a delicate yellow sky color and its supporting rocks painted blue and red, from the bottom up. Finally, the temple's columns could be indicated by lightly painted vertical lines, and golden yellow could accentuate the decorative tympanum above them.

c   Figures from the Greek legends can be painted large, always starting with their color quality. What color would suit Zeus? Hercules? Prometheus chained to his rock? We could even paint hieroglyphics on rolls of wallpaper, testing the boundary between painting and drawing.

d   Ceramics are important in Greek culture. When discussing the black and red figures on Greek vases, we could ask the students to pretend they are Greek vase painters. We paint the entire paper in golden yellow and vermilion, the colors of baked clay. Using Prussian blue, we now leave an empty space in the shape of an amphora, preferably as large as possible. Only when the painting is dry can we continue: We now use indigo and fine-tipped brushes to paint figures and ornamental patterns on the vase. The children can also choose to paint these in black or red, though the latter is much harder: The figures to be painted in red must first be blank areas

160

in the background color. Small details can be added later. Arising from the mixture of golden yellow, vermilion and Prussian blue, the indigo designs are a beautiful color.

2 Maps

Color qualities combine with climatic features when painting maps.

a   Maps of North and South America can include colors representing the different climates and altitudes, for example, from cool blue (Canada) to warm vermilion (Mexico), from the pale green Great Plains to the dry Rocky Mountains (pale vermilion), from the golden heat of the Deep South to the bluish-purple of New England. Painting these features lets the children process geography lessons in a totally different way; they learn through a different modality while painting.

b   Greece, with its volcanic base, can be painted in warm red tones. It stretches into the Mediterranean Sea like a hand. We use blue to flow around the intricate coastline and the many islands; the mountains can be accentuated with carmine red.

c   Various climates can be discussed when looking at different continents. For example, Australia contains vast deserts, fertile areas in the east, and mountainous zones; we could begin with golden yellow-vermilion, surrounded by blue. A subtle transition from warm ultramarine at the top to cool Prussian blue at the bottom gives a good idea of different sea temperatures; ocean currents can also be included.

d   In contrast, the small country of the Netherlands has a damp sea climate. Its land was created by mud transported by rivers, which settled behind coastal sand dunes. Thus a map of this country could feature a meeting of yellow and blue, resulting in green bordered by blue. Other colors could be added to indicate the dunes; all areas above sea level could be shown in red.

3 A dandelion

This is a perfect assignment for plant-based paints, which already have a reddish tint. We could begin with a meeting between indigo blue below and warm yellow above, transitioning to green in the center. The violet-colored soil is created by painting red over indigo, making sure to leave a blank area for the taproot. We now paint the dandelion's rosette of leaves and its stem with indigo into the green, topping it off with a golden yellow flower. Adding some red will give the flower a warmer shade.

4 Seasonal festivals: a Saint John's bonfire

a   Sequences in the color circle can be the basis for many assignments; the "dragon and castle" exercise was described for fourth grade. This assignment is: Paint a fire. Use bright colors!

b   We begin by painting a brilliant yellow area in the middle of the bottom half of the paper, leaving white space on the right and left sides (likewise for steps c, d and e).

c   Into the yellow we paint orange toward the center of the paper, using golden yellow and vermilion.

d   By adding carmine red next to the orange, we create a wonderful color transition from yellow to red. The fire has been lit!

e   We paint the red streaming upwards and mix it with ultramarine blue. An intense purple appears.

f   In the remaining white space at the upper edges of the paper, we now paint Prussian blue, coming downwards from right and left and mixing with yellow to create a green area at the bottom of the paper. The green touches the yellow—this is where the fire begins.

g   At the base of the fire we paint small pieces of wood, twigs and branches, using orange and red over the green and blue, creating brown.

h   As a final step we can look to see what else the painting needs. Does it need more color, more form? It is important for the bonfire to be confined on all sides by blue, so it can glow outward from the center.

5 A toadstool

a   Paint the whole paper a light lemon yellow.

b   Paint a light shade of carmine red over the yellow.

c   Add a wash of Prussian blue, making sure to leave blank spaces for one or two toadstools, with their caps and stalks.

d   Add the toadstool cap in intense carmine red, leaving little spaces for its white dots.

e   Now take both yellows (lemon and golden yellow) and paint over the blue, creating different shades of green around the toadstool. For example, lemon yellow at the top and golden yellow at the bottom will produce warm shades of plant green and brown.

Toadstool. (Student, age 10)

f   The stalk, a pinkish yellow, might need to be painted over with a slightly moist, clean brush to define its final shape, since the outside color often moves into the space reserved for the stalk.

g   Finally, colors can be added at will to create a nice autumn mood.

h   Variation: Use the paper vertically and paint one giant toadstool!

7 Painting in sixth grade
On the road to exact observation

Julie, a sixth grader, says: I think all the colors flow together so nicely in wet-on-wet. Other types of paint don't do that at all. That's why you can paint rainbows so well with wet-on-wet. I didn't like it so much at first because I like lots of details, and you can't paint them all with wet-on-wet. Usually paintings represent something, but I don't think that's really necessary. With wet-on-wet it can be really beautiful without being a picture of anything, just wonderful colors.

In kindergarten we put all kinds of colors together, and sometimes we got brown or almost black. But my paintings in kindergarten were often really nice. Since then I've learned to paint much better, more beautifully. The teacher usually told a story, and then you had to paint something from the story. Or you could paint something from the main lesson. For example, if we were in a Botany block, we painted a flower. I always picture exactly what I want to paint and then when I'm painting it turns out completely different, but just as pretty!

The new subject of Physics is typical of the sixth grade approach to the curriculum. From the realms of light, sound, warmth, magnetism and electricity, simple subjects are chosen that appeal to the children's intellectual capabilities. The point is not to impart abstract information, but to let them discover laws and formulas based on dozens of experiments. From a pedagogical point of view, the following method is used.

The class sees, or does, a number of experiments. No one speaks while the experiment is going on: They observe carefully. Watching and observing intently with the eyes, ears, indeed all the senses, is vital. After the experiment is over and the materials are put away, the teacher reviews with the students what they just did. Judgments and opinions are withheld: The students simply describe what they saw, not what they think they saw. The next day the procedures and observations are repeated, this time from memory. Now we can draw some conclusions. Observations and conclusions are then written in the main lesson book, and the experiment is illustrated as accurately as possible.

Thus, the students get a little practice every day in observing, remembering, hypothesizing and recording. They enjoy the dawning of causal connections and logic. This is, of course, only the very beginning of a long-term process: Noticing and experiencing abstractions is not the same as being able to deal with them. The children start relating their observations to other phenomena, or find new ways of applying them. They are waking up, becoming more confident of what they can see, think and conclude, learning to judge according to what they have observed for themselves. Twelve-year-olds could also be tempted to seek refuge in a make-believe world, isolating or alienating themselves; so building a bridge into the world, using new foundations they have constructed for themselves, is very important for this age group.

Optics experiments fit in well with what we know from painting. The students are quite familiar with the colors of the rainbow and are now surprised to witness experiments that demonstrate the objective reality of things such as color sequences. As the bright light of a projector is gradually obscured by several layers of wax paper, yellows, oranges and even a dull red appear. ("That wax paper was white, wasn't it?" someone wonders.) Light obscured by darkness gives rise to the warm colors of the spectrum.

Next the children look at a piece of black cardboard through a fish tank full of water, lit by a bulb shining into it from the side. If we add some milk to the water and stir it, a bluish glow appears in front of the black cardboard: Light shining in front of darkness gives rise to blue. Similarly, complementary colors are evoked by staring at a colored area, and prisms reveal wonderful colors at the borders between light and darkness.

These excerpts from sixth grade Optics lessons show how the children are beginning to look differently at color, making new connections and seeing painting in a new way. They are becoming more aware and critical and have a better understanding of color relationships. From this moment on, all painting assignments, no matter how simple, seem interesting again, as if they were doing them for the first time. These new adventures conjure up a new "first grade feeling." The painting curriculum for sixth, seventh and eighth grades responds to this need.

Left: Continuous color circle, with white outside and black inside. (Julius Hebing)
Right: Continuous color circle, with black outside and white inside. (Julius Hebing)

1. Crystals and the veiling technique

The sixth graders now meet a new subject and a new technique that give them what they want. They descend into the earth to discover the minerals, a world in which light radiates anew through rock, despite total darkness. They gaze at minerals in amazement: exquisite quartz crystals in all shapes and colors. "Can we paint this?" We do some wet-on-wet exercises and manage to express the mood, but those crystal forms are especially unsatisfactory because of the oozing wetness. "Children, today we are going to stretch thicker paper than usual on our painting boards. We'll wet it on both sides, making sure it is nice and tight on the board. Now we'll take four strips of gummed paper tape, wet them on one side, and tape the paper down by sticking about one-third of the strip to the paper and the rest to the board. Press the tape down from the center to the edges, on all four sides of the paper. Now we have to wait until tomorrow."

The next day the paper will be nice and tight, unless it has dried too quickly or isn't taped properly, in which case it might be partly loose. As it dries, the paper contracts and pulls on the tape—it becomes stretched. If there are traces of grease on the board, the tape may not stick well. To avoid disappointments it's always a good idea to stretch a few extra sheets, because everyone wants to get started right away.

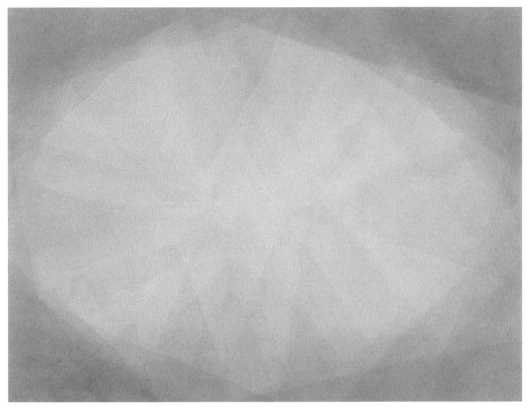

Crystals painted with the veiling technique. (Student, age 11)

To make the veiling process clearly visible, we choose a very watered-down Prussian blue and paint it on a piece of test paper. A blue haze is visible. "Now we must learn to paint as dry as possible."

"How can we do that with wet paint?" a student rightly asks.

"Dip your wide brush (preferably #20 or wider) into the paint and wipe it off well. We'll start by painting an area in one of the corners. Start on the tape, so you can see how much paint you have on your brush—and here is the most important rule for veil painting: You may paint on the same spot only once or you'll be removing paint that's already on the paper... which would turn it back into a wet-on-wet painting! Now lay down an area of color with a nice straight border, not using long, heavy strokes but with small brush strokes in all directions. Keep it lively, but make sure the outside of the color area is razor-straight. No, no angles yet. And here's another ground rule: Dip your brush only once for each area. Imagine you are halfway through painting an area and you get a new brushful of paint: splash, a big puddle in the middle of the sheet. So use up all the paint in your brush before dipping again. Now go ahead and paint color areas in the other three corners, without having them overlap."

The children need this repeated many times. "This is hard, with all those rules." "Yes, but it does look good," one can hear the class say.

"You may start painting a new area only when the paper is dry as a bone. Be strict with yourselves, and check the dryness by looking at the painting at an angle: If it's shiny, it's still wet. And here's another tip: It will get incredibly boring if you paint the same thing over and over again. Make each of those color areas a little different!"

When the children have mastered these first steps, they can continue. Coming in from the corners now, they paint obtuse angles, then acute angles. Some are having trouble controlling the amount of water. Only a little white is left in the middle of the sheet; we can cover it up now. The paintings are glowing with transparent areas of color: A crystalline world has been created. The class can work on their paintings a little every day, for example during the first thirty minutes of main lesson. If they are still using too much water and the drying is taking too long, the teacher can tell a story or other work can be done.

After four or five veils are down, it becomes apparent that the new ones are fainter than the first veils, so the time has come to make the color less thin and watery. Once the whole paper is covered in color, we apply darker areas from the outside in, creating a radiant inner world; the more darkness we add, the stronger the light shines. The children learn to leave blank spaces where new crystal forms will appear. Glancing into the room, it looks like the tables are covered with enormous diamonds. The effect is enhanced when the dry paintings are cut off the boards (with a sharp knife inserted between paper and board) and mounted under a white matboard frame. The dirty tape is gone, the color shows up wonderfully, and the crystals light up.

The children need to learn the veiling technique step by step; it will test their patience. In many ways, this process corresponds to their Physics lessons: Conclusions are not drawn until the next day; the work requires space and time; and the students are constantly confronted with their work from the previous day. All the veils remain visible, and the students carry on where they left off. They observe, step back to look from a distance, make decisions, and continue working at their own pace: There are fast, dry workers and slow, wet ones. Never before have the effects of our actions been so visible; however, mistakes reassuringly disappear as the veils are progressively built up over them. For the next veiling exercises, more colors can be used; the children discover that this increases the degree of difficulty. Oddly enough, yellow turns out to be an awkward veiling color: It is so radiant that it easily becomes overpowering. Subtlety is essential in the veiling technique.

Have the students clean their boards as soon as the paintings are off. The tape will come off easily if it is wetted with plenty of water: About ten minutes of soaking and it can be scraped off with a palette knife.

In sixth grade many other subjects can be painted using this technique: waves in water, Gothic stained glass windows, cubes, buildings, rock formations and color compositions out of the imagination. The children come up with plenty of ideas. They notice that colors look much stronger with this technique, especially when dry. Now it becomes possible to work on color quality. Not all children will take this step at the elementary school level, but with careful encouragement, they can go a long way. At the secondary level, from tenth grade onward, they can pick up this technique once again. In addition to veiling, the children can still do plenty of work on wet paper.

2. Mineralogy

The creation of various rock formations is discussed during the Geology block, including igneous and sedimentary rocks. The polarity between limestone and granite mountains can be created easily with color. One example of sedimentary rock is caves full of stalagmites and stalactites; many colors are visible in the dripping white limestone. The following verse may serve as inspiration for the children to paint this mysterious underground world:

> In the subterranean corridors
> Leading to cavernous vaults
> Sounds without interruption
> A murmuring river.
> My newly lit torch
> Casts many a capricious shadow,
> Reflects in the water
> Mysteriously.
> Only now do I see the world
> I'm entering,

So many colors
To meet me, radiating
As if rainbows
Are always shining here.
I feel overwhelmed:
Whoever suspected
That so deep in the earth
Secrets are hidden
That only reveal themselves
When light shines around them?

Igneous rocks originate in volcanic action. Granite is a good example—an extremely hard stone from which countertops and floors are made. We could express its hard character with an intense red. Mountains could be reddish-purple, contrasting dramatically with a blue sky. Or we could paint a rocky, craggy coast: Red meets the green-blue water, solidity meets movement.

Volcanoes are also a much-loved subject, spewing fire, smoke and magma into the world. We could first cover our paper in fiery colors, then paint the volcano in indigo, which looks almost black in contrast to the warm red and orange. Rocks hurtle into the air, flows of lava erupt down the mountainside: It is a world of extremes, very attractive to this age group.

3. Trees

From sixth grade on, we can paint the different varieties of trees.

A drawing assignment—for example, observing the characteristic gesture of oak branches—could precede the painting. What basic color mood do we choose for the oak, with its powerful, obstinate quality? Warm tones with yellow and blue overlays could form the crown; the trunk and branches could be vermilion. The surroundings should be darker rather than lighter, to accentuate the oak's strength.

The beech is a stately tree whose branches extend almost horizontally out into the world. Hardly anything will grow under it, so we can put blue and purple tones around the base of the trunk.

The pale, silvery birch is thin, agile, bright and sunny. Its whitish trunk sets the color mood and announces the tree's delicate character.

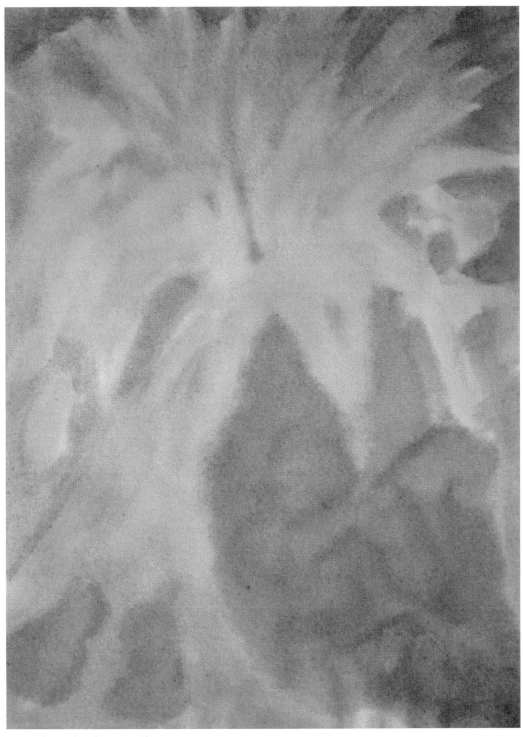

Volcano. (Student, age 12)

The weeping willow at the water's edge looks into the mirror; its long, graceful branches stir the surface of the water.

Trees can represent multiple moods of nature: Each student will have his or her own favorite, or feel somehow related to one type of tree.

4. The blank-space technique

A space that is to be left blank in a painting must be visualized and thought out in advance; foresight is required. Leaving spaces open for future color forms means exploring what is as yet invisible, which involves a degree of difficulty that can only be asked of students beginning in sixth grade. It is an indirect way of visualizing something. This skill is closely connected to the transition into adolescence. It now becomes possible for the students to leave blank spaces to be filled in later.

What subjects lend themselves to this technique? If we're painting animals, how about a swan? First we cover the sheet with a soft wash. Then we continue painting with a darker color, but we leave the silhouette of the swan blank, so it stays the wash color. There are many other possibilities:

"How about a flamingo? They're such a great pink."

"We could just do a polar bear," another one grumbles.

"Why all the soft colors? I want something stronger!"

"Why don't you all paint lots of small, brightly colored patches next to each other today," says the teacher.

"What's it going to be?"

"Wait and see." A multicolored collection blooms in the classroom.

"Now we'll take a strong Prussian blue and leave a blank space for… a parrot."

Mayhem now reigns as big, gaily colored feathered friends appear in all the paintings, as if we were suddenly in a vine-laden rainforest.

"This week, think about what we could do next time. Then we'll paint the best idea together."

Indigo. (Student, age 12)

5. Indigo

In sixth grade the need for precision arises, hand in hand with the need for perspective. Both these areas can be addressed in drawing. In painting, the blank-space technique can satisfy the desire to create starkly delineated shapes; and a desire for stronger color, more intense dark-light contrasts, or more three-dimensional effects can be met by working with indigo. First we could tell the students the interesting history of the dye that produces this color.[14] As they do some painting assignments involving the almost exclusive use of indigo, they will experience its unique darkening effect. Added to the six rainbow colors, it now becomes number seven: A completely new range of possibilities arises.

Unlike the new veiling technique, which seems to hold on to light, indigo introduces a world of forms, shadows, darkness. The teacher should introduce indigo to the students step by step, so their powers of imagination can keep working as they process this new color.

173

6. Examples from sixth grade

1 Moving into tertiary colors, step by step

a These exercises were given in the basic exercises for teachers and in lesson examples for fourth grade. The former emphasized color transformations; the latter, the creation of tertiary colors or earth tones. In sixth grade this can be good practice for creating dramatic landscape moods: storms with lightning and racing thunderclouds or thick, murky fog.

b First the students paint the primary colors, strong and intense, each taking up about the same amount of space. In the next step, the primary colors are turned into secondary colors by painting yellow over red to make orange, red over blue to make purple, blue over yellow to make green. If there isn't enough paint on the paper, use a little more from the jar.

c There are always some children who feel an intense need to keep a little bit of the primary colors in the painting: a little yellow, red or blue amid the orange, green and violet. This now becomes the assignment: Traces of the three primary colors must still be visible, somewhere on the page.

d In the next phase, the students paint over the colors again, with complementary colors this time, to obtain the earth colors: many shades of grey, brown and black. If we now leave bits of the secondaries showing, glimpses of primary and secondary colors will shine enticingly through the new tertiary colors.

e If the students now look carefully at their paintings, the makings of a landscape will become visible. Look, that could be the horizon! And are those mountains or pounding waves? By adding a few more colors, we have painted a landscape into existence.

By experimenting with the amount and size of primary or secondary colors left in, we can thus create dramatic tension between light and darkness, like a threatening sky just before a downpour. These exercises can be repeated many times and will always provide new challenges. They require courage! A touch of pink in all that indigo creates a remarkable mood, but can we stop before we go too far? It's easy to overdo it.

2 Sky phenomena

The phases of the moon are studied in the Astronomy block.

a Until this year, the children didn't give much thought to the phases of the moon: It was pretty much either a crescent moon or a full moon. Now things are different. When is the next full moon? What about that crescent

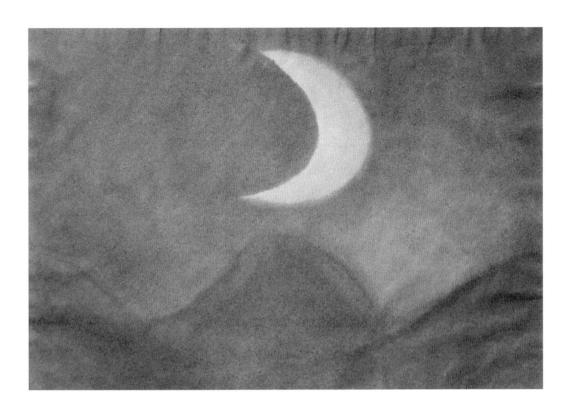

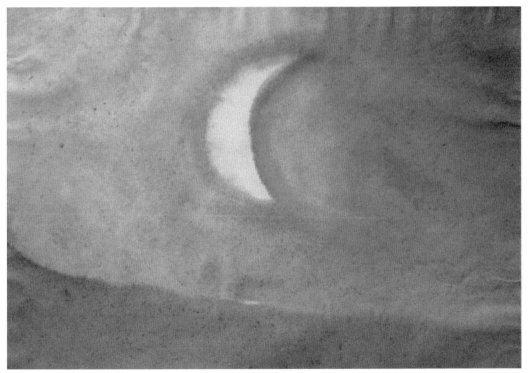

Above: First quarter moon at sunset. (Student, age 12)
Below: Last quarter moon at sunrise. (Student, age 12)

shape: There are two different ones, right? Which one do you see in the morning and which in the evening? The way to remember it is DOC, right? Answering these questions will require attentive observation.

b We're going to paint an evening mood. The sun has just set. The sky looks the way it did last night, with a beautiful red afterglow and purple and blue streaks. The moon was already up, and we are going to paint that, too.

c As a base color we paint the entire sheet a pale, soft lemon yellow, the color of the moon.

d Now we begin with a succession of warm colors from right to left: orange, red, violet and Prussian blue. We leave a blank space in the blue shaped like the crescent moon. At sunset the crescent moon always looks like the D in DOC, with the setting sun illuminating its right side. It's the first quarter. The moon shines brightly in the blue next to the strong, warm red-orange tones.

e Now for the landscape. Is the ground warm or cold? It was warmed during the day by all that sunshine, so we'll paint the landscape by adding blue, yellow and red over the colors already on the paper. We have created an exciting painting: Dusk has fallen on earth.

f After painting the sunset, the children will undoubtedly ask to paint a sunrise. Once again, we start with light yellow over the whole paper.

g We now paint the sequence orange, red, violet and blue (the warmer ultramarine this time), starting at the left. When painting the blue, we again leave blank the shape of the crescent moon—but which is it, D or C? (The O represents the full moon.) It must be C, since the rising sun is illuminating the moon from the left. It is the last quarter.

h The earth has cooled off during the night, so we can create the landscape with cool Prussian blue. These two exercises are really for advanced students or especially skilled ones, for they involve many colors and, in addition, a shape to leave blank. Here is one more challenge, for students who will soon enter high school:

i The sheet of paper is placed vertically. First we lay down the base of soft yellow; then we use Prussian blue, leaving the blank space for the moon as large as possible. We paint a landscape across the bottom: mountains, valleys or a flat prairie. Now, we change all the blue to indigo by using vermilion. Everything becomes much darker and more mysterious.

j A variation on this theme is painting water (a lake or a river flowing out to sea) under a full moon: The moon is reflected in the water! The children will enjoy all these possibilities.

3 Flower series

a In fifth grade we discussed flowers and painted a whole plant, emphasizing the growth process, from root to flower. Once the children have done those exercises and all their variations, they can begin the following series of flower paintings.

b Composition and color combinations are important in this series. We begin with warmth: The whole sheet of paper is covered with soft carmine red, painted somewhat unevenly so as to create warmer and cooler areas.

c After warmth comes light: We paint lemon yellow over the red, changing it to golden yellow-orange.

d The first subject in this series is the rose. The children choose three to five places on the paper to place spots of carmine red, each about the size of a fist, and lighter around the edges so they don't look like cutouts but fit together into the whole. A conversation on composition is now called for. For example, we should never put a spot at the edge of the paper. The children can practice on the blackboard.

e Now we surround the spots first with lemon yellow, then Prussian blue. We now have red spots in green. During this step the red spots can be enlarged or made smaller. The students should realize that they can always change what they have painted; self-correction is important.

f Now we focus on the roses themselves. We shape the red spots into rounded flower forms using more carmine red, always painting the red outside the roses a little into the green, to create a connection between subject and surroundings.

g The students may now add blue and yellow around the flowers to imply leaves and stems—but don't go overboard! A profusion of lines will appear; however, if we look closely at real flowers, very few stems are actually visible. Try to keep the focus on the interplay of color areas. Finally, the students may add whatever they like to finish the painting. During the next assignment, the green can be made lighter (with yellow) toward the top of the paper and darker (with red and/or blue) at the bottom.

h Many different flowers can be painted using the above steps. If we paint spots of ultramarine blue instead of red, and then add green around them, we can create blue harebells. Four or five hanging bells, nice and big, create wonderful color harmony with the green surroundings. Follow step g to finish the painting.

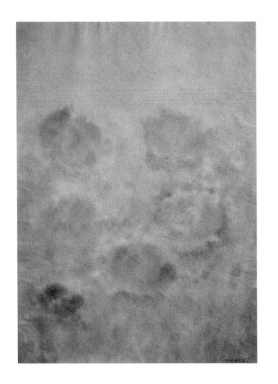

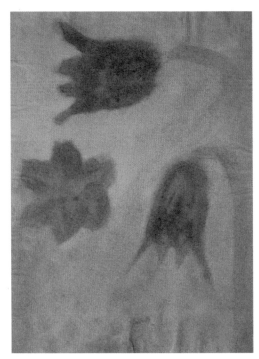

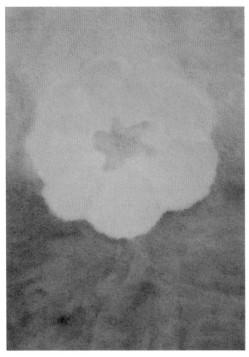

Upper left: Red roses in green. (Student, age 12)
Above: Blue harebells. (Student, age 11)
Left: Yellow flower. (Student, age 12)

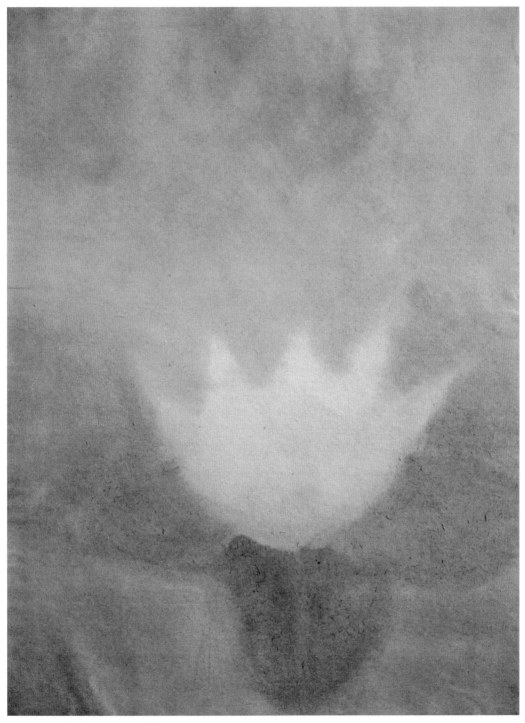

Water lily. (Student, age 12)

i   After the harebells, we could tackle yellow daffodils or sunflowers. One large sunflower is especially impressive in a summer-green background.

j   Orange and purple flowers can be painted in the above way. White flowers require a special procedure: We begin with three faint pastel washes of the primary colors (as we will with the winter tree, below). If we choose to paint water lilies, we will then use Prussian blue and leave the crown-like lily forms blank. Yellow added to the blue will give us large, floating green leaves under and next to the flowers. The lilies can be further elaborated: A yellow heart might become visible here and there. The blue water can be made even darker with red. The darker and more intense the blue, the more brilliant the "white" lilies become. In this flower series, all the colors of the rainbow can appear in the green sections; except for the white flowers, each painting has a base of carmine red (warmth) followed by yellow (light).

4 Trees

In these exercises, we will paint deciduous trees in the four seasons. Each painting is set up differently.

a   *The spring tree.* The spring tree is in full bloom. Cover the entire sheet with small, pale patches of color next to each other: pink (light carmine red), yellow and blue. It should look as if blossom petals blown by the wind have fluttered down onto the white paper. Don't use vermilion for this exercise, as it creates an autumn mood. Using warm (ultramarine) blue, we now paint the element of air, leaving a blank space for the tree's crown and trunk and for the ground beneath it. We paint from the outside of the page to the center, visualizing what will fill the form that we're leaving blank, and keeping an eye on the proportion of the tree trunk to the crown (often the trunk will come out too big and thick compared to the crown). Now the light yellow-blue-pink areas of the crown are connected using a pale red, creating a whole. The trunk can now be darkened—a suitable brown can be created with orange and blue—or we could leave it a lighter color. The ground beneath the tree can then be adjusted to blend nicely with the whole, using a light spring green of Prussian blue and lemon yellow. The same green should also appear next to the trunk so that the tree will not look like a cutout on a hilltop. The students can now add whatever they wish, keeping in mind the spring theme. The more intense the blue around the crown, the more the blossoms will shine.

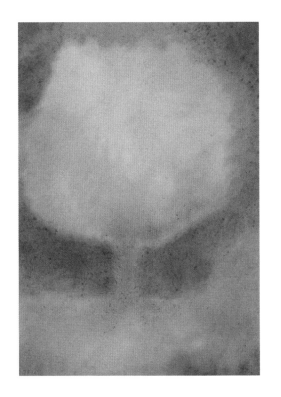

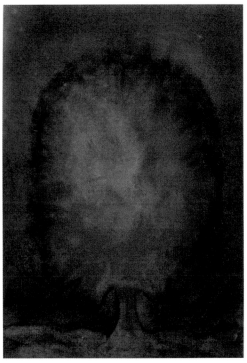

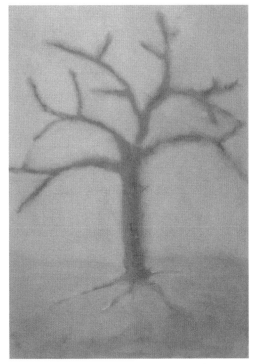

Above left: Spring tree. (By an adult)
Bottom left: Autumn tree. (Student, age 12)

Above right: Summer tree. (Student, age 12)
Bottom right: Winter tree. (Student, age 12)

b *The summer tree.* We can paint this tree taking our cue from the processes of nature. We begin with warmth, a soft carmine-red wash across the entire sheet. Then comes light: an intense lemon yellow shining through the red. With Prussian blue we create the earth element, starting at the bottom; it grows upwards to trunk and crown. Green appears. The area around the crown can now be strengthened with yellow; this prevents the green of the crown from contrasting too much with the area around it, creating a silhouetted effect. The tree arises out of (two-dimensional) color perspective, not from a (three-dimensional) illusion of depth created by contrasting light and darkness. The children can now further develop the trunk and the ground; perhaps it will be a mighty trunk with many strong roots in the summer green.

c *The autumn tree.* For this tree, we start with a mirrored color circle: Beginning at the top with yellow, we paint green in both directions into the corners, blue down both sides, and purple in the bottom corners, moving along the bottom into red at the center. Next we paint orange straight up into the middle of the page, filling the remaining space. We have created a symmetrically mirrored color circle. Now, using Prussian blue (orange's complementary), we paint around a blank tree-shaped space. The existing colors under the blue give it a lively character. The crown shines out at us, brilliantly autumnal amid the dark surroundings. The trunk and ground can now be given a more colorful autumn mood with yellow and green. If we paint a bit of the surrounding blue into the crown, a beautiful brownish orange will be created. All the colors must be intense, but they mustn't be too wet or they'll all run together, which is not the desired effect!

d *The winter tree.* Can we actually paint white onto white paper? If we paint small areas of very pale red, yellow and blue next to and over each other, they will cancel out each other's one-sidedness and create a grey-white mood. On this foundation we paint a bare tree in strong Prussian blue, aiming for realistic positions of the trunk and branches. Important: Paint the trunk and branches by moving the brush across them in short, horizontal strokes, building them up little by little, as it were; this gives a completely different result than from moving the brush vertically along the trunk and branches, following their direction. Four or five specific branch shapes work better than lots of indeterminate shapes. We then paint over the blue with vermilion, making the tree indigo; this, too, should be applied in short, horizontal strokes onto the trunk and branches. Use the vermilion sparingly, or the tree will become orange instead of indigo.

To connect the tree with its environment, we rinse the brush well and apply it horizontally to the trunk, stroking toward the sides; using the tree's blue color, we can alter its surroundings as we see fit. Later, a yellow tint in the air can intensify the winter mood, or we could paint a red-orange suggestion of a sunrise or sunset. There are many possibilities.

If we now put the four paintings next to each other, we can recall that the spring tree came out of space left open for a variety of pale base colors; the summer tree slowly emerged from warmth and light processes, with blue added; the autumn tree was created from a mirrored color circle; and the winter tree was achieved by drawing/painting on the "white."

Of course, there are many ways to paint trees through the seasons. The spring and autumn trees could be created out of natural processes; a tender green-yellow spring tree could arise from the color circle; and so on.

The sixth-grade students could create birthday calendars from these exercises using the seasons, each with its own color mood.

5 The industrial landscape

For assignments dealing with this subject, we direct you to Basic exercise 9 for the teacher, which is a good introduction.

6 Optics main lesson topics; color theory

Complementary color exercises with possible variations.

a   Hold up a red cloth in front of the class and ask the students to stare at it for 30 seconds. Then remove the cloth and ask them to stare at a white sheet of paper. A greenish shape will appear: red's complementary color. This experiment can be done with all six colors of the color circle. The afterimage will not only appear on the white paper; it's everywhere you look—on the palm of your hand, further away on the wall, on the desk in front of you, and even when you close your eyes! We can immediately connect this experiment to a painting exercise.

b   The students paint red in the middle of the paper; they look at it long and hard. Now they look at the white paper next to the red, and a greenish color appears. We're going to paint that color. We can't make it as light as you just saw it; that's not possible, because what you saw was inner light. But let's try to come close to that color, using yellow and blue.

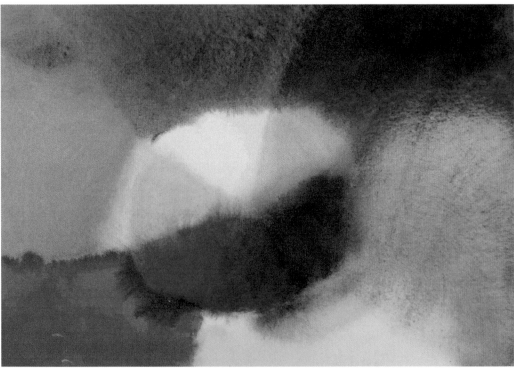

Above left: Double color circle. (Student, age 11)
Below left: Double color circle. (Student, age 11)

c   As soon as the children have become adept at painting the complementary colors arising from this experiment—next to each other, one above the other, in each other's arms, etc.—we can make the assignments more difficult. The students paint yellow on the bottom half of the paper. From golden yellow at the right, it transitions into greenish yellow at the left, creating three shades of yellow next to one another. If the children have mastered the skill, the three colors could flow into each other where they meet.

d   Above this yellow bottom half, the children now paint the color that is complementary to each shade of yellow. They already know purple will be above the middle shade. But what color should go to the right of purple, above the golden yellow, and to its left above the greenish yellow? Six colors will result—two rows of three, complementing each other beautifully.

e   This exercise also has a more challenging variation. In the middle of the paper, leaving room on all sides, we paint violet, red and orange next to each other, in any shape we want: Angular and geometric might be interesting. The assignment is to paint complementary colors next to and around these three colors. What colors belong with violet, red, orange? Yellow, green and blue. Looking at the six colors, we discover the color circle. By starting with different colors in the middle, six variations on this exercise will result. If each student chooses a different starting color, all the possible variations will appear in the classroom; things couldn't get more colorful!

f   Now for the double color circle. Paint a color circle in the middle of the paper. The circle should have a definite border on the outside, but at the colors' internal borders with each other, they can meet in a friendly way and flow together. Outside the circle, we now paint all the complementary colors, creating a spacious double color circle that fills the entire page. This is a festive and colorful way to end sixth grade.

8 Black & white drawing in sixth grade

Black and white drawing is a new challenge for this age group. It requires the students to practice their observational skills, and therefore fits in well with the Physics main lessons. To make the best use of their observations, we use charcoal, which allows us to create many shades of grey between light and darkness, white and black. This technique is also related to our painting lessons because we are working with areas rather than lines. Using a piece of charcoal flattened on one side, we can create with one movement all kinds of forms in various shades, from very light to very dark. Sketching from life inside or outside the classroom, we can use the slanted tip of a charcoal stick or the side of a pencil point.

1. Materials

Paper. Paper used for wet-on-wet painting is perfect for charcoal. Textured paper is not as good—it should be as smooth as possible. It's best to work on a smooth surface so no wood grain or other pattern becomes visible on the paper. Rough surfaces can be made softer by taping a number of sheets of newsprint to the table, using masking tape so they can be reused. You could also use several sheets of painting paper on top of each other, but they might get covered in black smudges from the charcoal.

Charcoal is available in many sizes. Buy charcoal sticks with a diameter of at least 10mm. Break off pieces about 1 to 1½ inches in length, and make one long flat surface by rubbing it on a piece of paper.

We advise against using erasers. If we make mistakes, we need to learn to deal with them; it will be good practice for future exercises.

Hold the piece of charcoal in one hand, keeping the other hand clean to hold down the paper. It is a good idea to keep about a half inch around the edges of the paper clean, so you can easily pick the page up without leaving black smudges. Quiet can be maintained in the classroom if you don't let the children wash their hands until the end of the lesson, after they hand in their charcoal.

Two exercises will usually fit into each lesson period, so the children can practice a particular theme or technique.

If possible, it is good to hang the students' work up after each lesson and discuss it immediately, so you will not need to spray fixative on the drawings. Only spray the final product of a series of exercises, which will go into the students' portfolio. Fixative is quite expensive.

2. Making your own charcoal

We could make our own charcoal in the first lessons! Doing this will give the students a good connection with the material. Using chunks of hardwood, light a fire outdoors in the barbecue pit; cover the fire after the wood has burnt well, so it can turn into charcoal. It's fun to create all kinds of grey and black tones with charcoaled pieces of wood. You'll notice that after this experience, the children will have more respect for store-bought charcoal sticks.

3. How is charcoal produced?

Charcoal is produced by removing moisture and volatile chemical compounds from wood by heating it. The trick is to produce exactly the right amount of heat (by burning other materials) so that the wood turns into charcoal instead of burning down to ashes. Making charcoal requires a lot of experience; it's not for nothing that it has been a profession for centuries.

First of all, a post is pounded into the ground at the center of a circle 20 to 25 feet across. Slabs of wood are then piled around the post, larger pieces at the bottom, smaller pieces at the top, to create a dome shape. The dome must now be covered with an airtight layer of sod and earth. To prevent this from disrupting the charcoal burning process, the pile is first carefully covered with small, thin pieces of wood, on top of which the sod, moss and soil are packed. To make sure the fire has air and the smoke can escape, the charcoal burner pokes holes of about an arm's width into the earth layer.

The woodpile is now lit at the top, where the post sticks out. It will burn for a week. To keep the fire burning optimally, the charcoal burner controls

Left: From light to dark with soft gradations. (Student, age 13)
Right: From dark to light with hard borders. (Student, age 13)

the air supply by continually opening up new holes and closing others. As the wood heats into charcoal, it gradually shrinks, so the charcoal burner climbs up with a ladder and stamps on the pile so that the charcoal inside collapses. After about a week, all the wood has turned into charcoal. The holes are now stopped up so the fire will go out; all that remains is to dig out the charcoal and sort through it.

4. Charcoal technique

Our first assignment will be to slowly turn a white sheet of paper grey by "clouding it over," not uniformly but in a way that contains interest. The students experiment with methods of slowly darkening the paper. At first they will find working with charcoal quite challenging. Some will simply fill the sheet with big pencil strokes, which won't create a lively grey; the lines just sit there. To prevent lines we need to keep the charcoal touching the paper as we move it around. By learning to move carefully and subtly, we eventually create areas that no longer look scribbled; they develop a life of their own and become peaceful. The children especially need to develop the skill of creating as many shades as possible between grey and black.

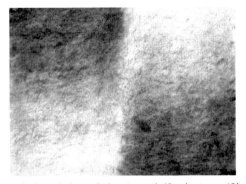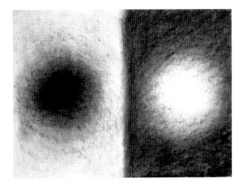

Left: From light to dark, mirrored. (Student, age 13)
Right: Darkness in light, light in darkness. (Student, age 13)

5. First exercises

The first series of exercises focuses on practicing with light and dark. First we create a uniform gradation from white to black and from right to left, slowly getting darker, with no borders between the shades. Next, borders are added. Now each step of grey between white and black has a definite boundary. How many steps can the children produce? Some can manage only three different shades of grey; others can get up to five. If the paper is placed horizontally, landscapes can be created with this exercise, with areas representing mountains, water, clouds, and so on.

Another exercise is to create light within darkness on the right side of the page, and darkness within light on the left, with or without boundaries. We can also create a movement from light to dark on one part of the page, surrounded by the exact opposite progression, from dark to light. If we were using color, this would be described as adding the complementary colors.

Sunrises, moonlit landscapes, forests, prairies, industrial scenes, locomotives (see Basic exercise 9 for the teacher, page 87)—everything can be rendered in charcoal. Always start with an area as opposed to a line, and use as many shades of grey as possible.

With this technique, when we leave an area blank we tend to draw around the space, outlining it. The children need to develop the self-discipline not to do this. It is important to discuss this when critiquing the class's work, in which examples of it will often be visible.

Once the students have mastered the technique of creating different shades of grey with and without edges, they can start drawing arrangements of one or more objects.

The play of light and dark. (Student, age 13)

6. Objects in light and shadow

The next step is to connect powers of observation with the newly acquired skill of drawing with charcoal. We can start as follows.

A tube made of a rolled-up sheet of thick white paper, about 4 inches in diameter, is placed on a large piece of white paper. Make sure the background is white as well.

Shine a strong spotlight onto the arrangement so it illuminates one side of the tube. The light should not be too high up or too far from the arrangement. The tube's shadow should be visible on the white paper.

Now ask a number of questions to wake the children up. What do you see? Today's exercise is not about saying what things are, only about what you see, the play of light and dark. Where is the light? Where is the darkness? Where are the transitions? Where are the sharp contours between the two extremes? These questions call attention to the different qualities of light and dark; they sharpen and deepen the students' observational skills. The students will learn to express what they see in well-chosen words that will be clear to the others.

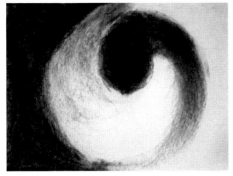
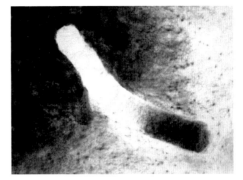

Left: Light and dark spiral. (Student, age 14)
Right: From light in darkness to darkness in light. (Student, age 13)

Before we begin, we turn off the light and remove the paper tube. Now let's start:

First we apply a light shade of grey over the entire sheet.

Now we leave a blank space for the tube while applying a slightly darker shade of grey to the rest of the page. The tube's top and bottom are rounded; its entire shape is left blank.

Now color the shadow on the tube a slightly darker shade than the surroundings. This is exciting because we need to remember how the tube looked inside; the shadow actually falls in a different place on the inside. It's challenging to make this area grey without drawing a line first.

Finally, we add the shadow cast by the tube onto the white paper, using the darkest shade of grey.

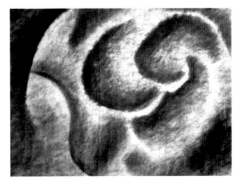

Left: Grey areas. (Student, age 13)
Right: The play of light and dark, restricted and unrestricted. (Student, age 13)

191

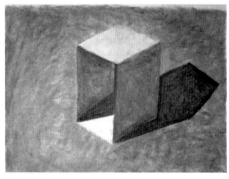 

Upper left: Ball with shadow. (Student, age 14)
Upper right: Bowl with shadow. (Student, age 13)
Lower left: Box with shadow. (Student, age 14)
Lower right: Box with shadow also cast on the wall. (Student, age 14)

When we look at our finished work, we see that it is composed of four different shades ranging from grey to black. Now we recreate the arrangement on the table and turn the light back on; the students assess their drawings. Did they remember the arrangement correctly? If not, what needs fixing?

Following the above steps, we can go on to draw balls, bowls, boxes and cubes; the difficulty level depends entirely on the class. The main thing is for the students not to see the arrangement once they start working. They must work from memory. At the end of the lesson they can look at the arrangement again with their work in hand and discuss the assignment with each other. Each student can see his or her own rate of improvement and can decide what needs working on during the next lesson.

Part 4

Grades 7–8 curriculum

Dragons in complementary colors from a teacher training course, Ireland.

1 Seventh grade
Discovering new worlds

The assignments for this grade are a continuation and an elaboration of the work completed in sixth grade. Children in this grade who have little experience with wet-on-wet painting will benefit from exercises from fifth and sixth grades. Many differences in ability will become evident in a given class, and even in a given student. Landscapes, trees, plants and flowers can be worked on at various levels appropriate to the individual.

After their first veil painting experiences, children ask for new subjects to work on. Their skill in painting the veils, finding the necessary patience and making the right choices, is improving.

When painting maps, as we described in fifth grade, the children travel the world. In seventh grade they learn about the Age of Discovery, when Europeans traveled to all corners of the world in search of new horizons. For some, vivid expectations became reality; for many others, disappointment or disaster. This uncertainty fits the seventh graders' new stage of development, an age of turbulence and insecurity. What has happened to the serenity of past years? Everything now seems to take a toll on the students' energy. Girls, especially, experience growth spurts; the boys lag behind them and may make up for it with nonstop wisecracks and (they hope) greater assertiveness. They all look up in awe to the high school students. They internalize and protect their emotions, yet will often express them bluntly or with feelings of shame. When painting, the seventh graders may seek harsh, overpowering colors, or yearn for grey, indigo and black, with only a hint of color.

Night mood with full moon. (Student, age 13)

1. Sky phenomena

When the students painted night moods in the lower grades, they had few questions about the phases of the moon. It all just came naturally: The moon was either full or a crescent shape. But things are different now. When was the moon full? Which way should the crescent face?

"We are going to paint an evening mood. The sun has just set, like last night when the sky had such a beautiful red afterglow with purple and blue streaks, and the moon was already up. We are going to paint it, too. Let's paint a soft yellow base color. The moon can be that color. Now add vibrant evening colors, leaving a space for the moon. What shape was the moon last night? What phase is it in—the first or last quarter?"

The students try to remember. They want to understand this and be able to explain their answers. "We see the round side that's lit up by the sun. The sun was to the right of the moon. So that means it's the first quarter."

The twilight colors come out strong and beautiful. This is also a nice assignment for parents in a parent evening. About a third of the little moons will face the wrong way; we wouldn't have paid attention to this in the past, but now the students have observed the phases of the moon and know them and will be happy to offer corrections.

Next time we talk about the full moon. "Wow, it's huge when it's just coming over the horizon. In the winter it's really high in the sky all night, and at sunrise you can see it just setting in the west."

Luckily, we can see the last quarter out the window during main lesson. We see the moon creep closer to the rising sun every day until it finally vanishes. The children choose morning mood colors: usually vermilion, golden yellow and red, with the landscape shrouded in cool colors.

Next we paint the starry sky with a yellow base color. To make sure the stars are in the right places, we paint them first; then the night sky around them in Prussian blue and indigo, with vermilion making them almost black.

The children now want to see their own Zodiac constellations in the sky. The main lesson books are produced, and Aries, Taurus and all the other star signs are reviewed once again. "Do you all remember that your star signs are high in the night sky six months after your birthday?" With much enthusiasm, the students paint their star signs the next day. Some manage to capture the constellation recognizably; others simply paint a nice group of stars. By exploring the world and being able to explain it, the students build up a measure of security in these turbulent years of adolescence.

2. Voyages of discovery

History and Geography, especially the latter, provide us with ample subject matter for painting. Travelers have lots of stories to tell. Explorers bring back new, unfamiliar products from faraway countries and describe fantastic, unknown regions for the first time.

When we let the children immerse themselves deeply in this subject, they will be happy to paint many of these new lands. We can offer guidance by asking, "Is the climate dry or wet, warm or cold?" Using combinations of elements (dry-cold, dry-warm, humid-warm and humid-cold), we can now create polar regions, rainforests and deserts starting from the color mood. If we begin with an appropriate base color that reflects the mood, it will be easier to build up the landscape. These assignments can also include seasons and times of day: sunrise in the desert, night in the rainforest, northern lights in Alaska. Using the skills we have learned, we paint the world from the viewpoint of the four elements.

We also continue painting maps in which the continents derive their colors from the climate. This could lead to a large-scale group painting. The students should feel that they have enough working space in the various artistic disciplines. Through experience they should be able to consciously manage color and form.

Seventh-grade veiling assignments relate directly to the students' experiences in sixth grade with this technique. Those exercises can be repeated and expanded in terms of color. Plenty of experiences and discoveries can still be gained by doing simple assignments.

Teachers can draw color inspiration from the Human Physiology and Chemistry main lessons. The science of nutrition provides a new entrance to the world of plants. Sour and sweet, salty and bitter tastes could possibly be found in the color circle. By finding in these new subjects, the qualities of color, form, area or line, by expressing them artistically, we place them in a larger context and enrich them.

In Chemistry fire plays an important role. A candle flame contains nearly the entire color spectrum. The sometimes spectacular experiments in Chemistry main lessons often involve dramatic color changes. Seventh graders like to explore and redefine boundaries; let them do so, within clearly defined assignments. Individual differences in ability will become more and more apparent. At this age, educating the powers of observation

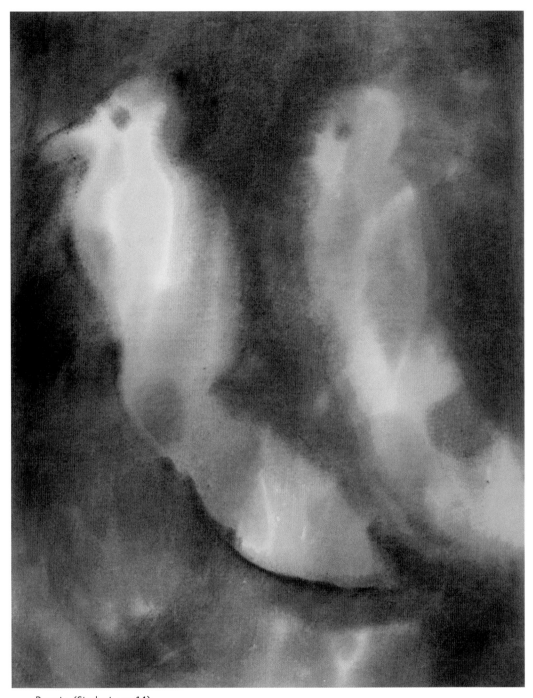

Parrots. (Student, age 14)

includes inquiring and researching what might lie beyond color, on the side of darkness as well as light.

Many subjects involving light and darkness can be drawn and painted during Chemistry main lessons, for example, a color circle surrounded by black, from which bright complementary afterimages arise as if by magic when we close our eyes.

2 Eighth grade
New developments

In eighth grade one phase of the painting curriculum comes to completion, because, for pedagogical reasons, little or no work will be done with color in ninth grade. This fact is related to the major changes taking place in the students. A multicolored emotional life arises in thirteen- and fourteen-year-olds. If students can accept the teacher's authority at this point and follow her lead, they will be on their way to a freer relationship with her. This phase is often characterized by Steiner's words, "Each one of us must choose the hero in whose footsteps we toil up Mount Olympus."

From the way they dress to the way they decorate their rooms, the children become more somber. Their internal richness of color, their strong feelings of sympathy and antipathy, can no longer bear the riotous colors of childhood. Everything needs to change: Posters from childhood are traded for images of pop-culture idols, and bedroom wall colors change on a regular basis. Important changes are also taking place in their bodies: Heart and lung capacities increase, by up to fifty percent in the case of the lungs. Soul moods and movements directly influence breathing and circulation, and emotions are experienced more intensely in adolescence.

Individual soul life thus starts to connect more deeply with the physical body, causing a more intense experience of self: increased self-awareness, self-consciousness, feelings of loneliness, and the common complaint, "Nobody understands me!"

To accommodate the changes taking place in the eighth graders, we can give them color exercises they've done in years past, but include more stringent requirements of technique and control. Working on a large scale, too, can present a new and welcome challenge. Exercises in which dark tertiary colors are built up from concentrated primary and secondary colors can be especially rewarding for this age group.

1. Trial and error

It becomes evident repeatedly at this age that not all the students have internalized the skills they were taught in sixth and seventh grades. Many of them still struggle not to paint too wet or too dry. The way they deal with painting often reflects their inner state. Sometimes they need to find out for themselves what works, all over again. Remarkable contrasts show up in the same assignment: loud, acrimonious colors next to soft, subtle shades. Sometimes there is a strong urge to draw outlines or to exaggerate details. Once again the teacher should demonstrate that it really is possible to achieve the desired results if we just paint two-dimensional color areas.

Even though some of the students have been working with these same painting techniques and materials for eight years, we can't help noticing that they still tackle their painting assignments with concentration and pleasure. Water jars tend to tip over easily once again, perhaps in part because of the students' newfound physical strength.

It is important for the teacher to guide the lessons with enthusiasm. Some students will resist assignments they recognize from the past, protesting, "I really think we know how to do this by now." But often, once they lay down their first brush strokes, they're involved again; their joy in painting is rekindled.

The students now pay much more attention to classmates' work than they used to. When the finished paintings are displayed, one can hear murmurs of admiration: "How did you get it to look like that?"

If in previous years we already covered veil painting and indigo, we can now emphasize subjects that are both intellectually challenging and interesting from the point of view of painting.

2. Global studies

Once again, we will find such subjects in Geography. We can explore various nations and cultures by painting landscapes and climates, with a new emphasis now on the people: what they wear, how they work, how their dwellings are constructed, what their cities are like, and so on. All these subjects require a sense of appropriate color surroundings and detail. The students like to focus on the task of artistically illustrating their studies, which is why it is important to relate painting assignments regularly to main lesson subject matter.

A display of work by 14-year-old students.

3. The Industrial Revolution

In eighth grade the Industrial Revolution can supply ample material for wonderful paintings: steam trains, iron bridges, steel mills, blast furnaces, glowing molten metal, mines, factory landscapes, workers, etc.

We must, of course, provide the students beforehand with imaginative and technically accurate descriptions of these features. Thereafter, the students can pretty much be left to create their own visions, as long as their work contains attention to detail where needed, as well as a rich and dramatic use of color and light/dark contrasts.

In Basic exercise 9 for the teacher, we gave an example of such a painting, with a simple light/dark exercise as a foundation. It is important to stay with these kinds of exercises when, together with the students, we look for the best way to set up a scene we can already see in our mind's eye. The teacher should continue to offer help in identifying appropriate base colors and basic shapes; otherwise, such paintings too quickly turn into illustrations, tempting the students to work with lines rather than color areas.

> What we have to make our habit again is to use color perspective, not line-perspective: the sense of area, a sense of what is far off and what is close by, not via line perspective, which always wants to magically create sculptural forms on the area, but on the area via the color itself, which yields or comes closer intensively, not extensively.[1]

In one assignment we could require students to produce the greatest possible color contrast in one painting, from pale yellow to deep violet-brown and blue-black. Steam, smoke and soot lend themselves well to this theme. We can draw inspiration from the work of J.M.W. Turner: Out of light and darkness, amid swirls of color, a steamship appears on the water at sunset. The same assignment can then be given in charcoal. Working out a theme in various ways and techniques will be covered in the next grades (see also page 88).

If a class is familiar with the veiling technique, the above subjects can also be painted that way; if not, it might be better to start with simpler assignments. Eighth-grade drawing and painting lessons usually take up two class periods, so we need to remember to keep things lively by alternating activities: wet-on-wet painting, veiling, pencil drawing, charcoal drawing. Thus, we can accommodate the students' need for variety.

3 Black & white drawing in the upper grades
Light and darkness

Black and white drawing starts in sixth grade with charcoal; if a particular seventh or eighth grade needs more practice, they should repeat the exercises given for sixth grade. Other options for black and white drawing include Siberian chalk (a type of compressed charcoal) and India ink.

We can now choose different subjects out of the curriculum, as long as we remember to work with areas, form, composition and the interaction of light and dark to create atmosphere and depth. In addition, it is important to stress the need always to finish what we're working on, no matter how eager the students may be to move on to the next project.

By the end of seventh and the beginning of eighth grade, we can introduce more complex elements into the sixth-grade charcoal assignments, including possible variations within a lesson. An object's shadow could fall first onto a side or back wall; next, onto a staircase.

The students could also draw multiple objects that cast shadows on each other, for example a cone with its shadow on a cube. A square box opening on several sides makes a good subject, with the inside of the box included in the intricate arrangement of shadows.

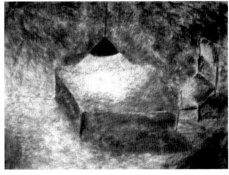

Left: Interior. (Student, age 14)
Right: Pyramid with shadow. (Student, age 14)

205

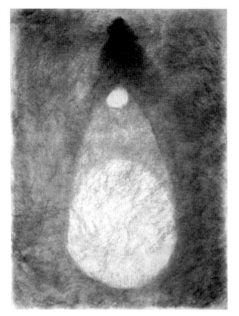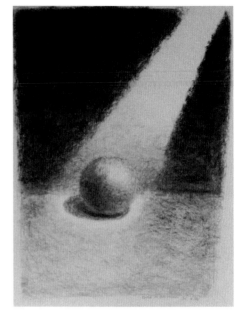

Left: Person walking with flashlight. (Student, age 14)
Right: Ball in a beam of light. (Student, age 14)

Before the drawings are finished, it is a good idea for everyone to step back, observe from a distance, evaluate progress and see what needs more work. The drawings arise through the interaction of cause and effect, observation, experimentation and control; each spot of light or shadow has its own reason for existing. Through doing, the students' capacity for observation connects to their thinking, and they begin to be able to form judgments. They wrestle with their ideas during these assignments, testing their boundaries, giving themselves increasingly difficult tasks.

Gradually, over the course of the upper grades and the first two years of high school, we move from drawing out of the creative imagination to drawing what we see in front of us: the still life. If the use of black becomes too confining, the student needs to seek an alternative; if things are blurry and unclear, the work will ask for form and structure. The spatial effect of the drawings is great; perspective is created. As the students draw what they see, they seek balance, harmony between light and darkness. Fourteen-year-olds feel the approaching darkness of loneliness, but also the light of a slowly dawning process of consciousness, in which they are learning to ask questions. By letting them experience artistic processes, we can help and support them in this uncertain period of adolescence.

4 Perspective and intersections in 7th and 8th grades

In seventh grade the students want to learn to draw accurate buildings, landscapes and architectural features. Their main lesson-book drawings no longer satisfy them: "This really doesn't look like it's supposed to." "It's all at the wrong angle somehow, it just doesn't look right."

There is always a student who knows how certain lines and planes should be drawn to make a scene look "real." Someone taught him some tricks, which earn him the admiration of his classmates.

How does perspective drawing fit into the sequence of skills the students have acquired? The concept of depicting one object in front of (or behind) another was first encountered in fourth grade form drawing. With Celtic knots, we consciously gave a flat design a three-dimensional feel by drawing the strands of the knot as if woven over and under each other.

In fifth grade we drew geometric forms freehand, without compass or straightedge. In fifth- and sixth-grade paintings we developed color perspective using different color areas to create the effect of depth in landscapes.

In sixth- and seventh-grade Geometry, we learned to construct geometric shapes with the help of a compass and ruler. In Physics we experimented with color, light and darkness. We learned to observe the way light falls and shadows are created, and we drew it in charcoal. In Astronomy we studied the heavens, orienting ourselves in space from our human perspective. All these experiences precede, underlie and support the introduction of perspective drawing in seventh grade!

One day the seventh grade students and teacher take a short walk in the neighborhood. On a street with houses and trees on either side, the teacher asks them to stop. "Please take a look at the end of the street. What can you tell me about the trees or the cars parked along the sides?"

The answers come immediately: The further away things are, the smaller they are. "Okay, let's keep that in mind, even though it's perfectly obvious to us."

Now the teacher takes them to a spot with a wide view of the surrounding landscape. By way of questions and answers, she confirms that the students are in agreement: Everything looks smaller in the distance.

A few days later, the lesson continues. The students are sent outdoors with drawing boards, drawing paper and pencils. They find the same locations and try to sketch what they see. Later in the classroom, they each choose one drawing to develop further, using colors or charcoal.

After some more sketching practice, the students can try their hand at interiors, for example, the long corridor outside the classroom or the classroom itself. This is more challenging: Things inside are so close to us. The schoolyard, the garden plot, the brook nearby with its little footbridge—everything will work for this assignment, which is to discover perspective through sketching.

At this point, we can impart instructions and assignments. Not until the children have experienced and drawn for themselves objects decreasing in size with distance, or lines and surfaces approaching each other as they move away, are they ready for the subject's abstract, technical aspects, aided by a ruler.

It is striking that many children cannot yet conceive of the idea of a "vanishing point." This is related to their development. Before the age of thirteen or fourteen, one can't really experience the degree to which one's personal vantage point affects what one sees. If this development is delayed in some students, we bring it to consciousness.

We can now apply our newfound knowledge to main lesson drawings, for example, the foam on the wake left by Columbus's departing ships. Thus the vanishing point becomes a manageable concept, although there will still be students who cannot "see" it; they are given the time and space to do so.

Not until eighth grade, when the second seven-year period comes to a close, do we fully cover perspective drawing. We draw two cubes side by side. If one is smaller than the other, it will lead to a series of cubes, each decreasing in size. If we draw a cube with one of its edges facing us and other cubes lined up behind it, we will suddenly see that we are dealing with not one, but two vanishing points—sometimes located on the page, more often outside it. Now the class really comes alive, for they discover yet another peculiarity: An invisible line connects the two vanishing points, which makes structures appear either above or below us when we draw them above or below the line. As the cubes pile up in the drawings, a third vanishing point appears; impressive (perhaps oddly distorted) buildings loom.

We can now transform our cube into a rectangular space open on one side. Doors, windows and (hopefully) stairs are properly constructed in it, and a roof above. This requires a special step: To find the peak of the roof, we draw diagonal lines connecting the corners of the front and back walls; from the points where they cross (the center of each wall), we draw vertical lines to give us the roof peaks, which we connect to form the roofline. We can now construct all kinds of structures using our imaginations and the strict rules of perspective; even some with curved lines, like Roman arches.

1. Albrecht Dürer

One way to begin eighth grade drawing lessons could be by discussing and recreating the perspective device attributed to Albrecht Dürer. A woodcut from Dürer's 1525 *Instructions for Measuring with Compass and Ruler* shows a device by which the image of a three-dimensional object can be transferred onto a two-dimensional surface.

The draftsman sits before his drawing, which is mounted on a vertically hinged frame. The frame stands on a table, on which lies the drawing's subject, a lute. A helper swings the frame open, turning the drawing away; the artist looks along a thread coming from the wall behind him, whose loose end the helper is holding on a point on top of the lute. The thread enters the frame at a point that the draftsman marks exactly with horizontal and vertical threads. The thread to the lute is now released and the drawing swings back into position; the draftsman adds the new point to the drawing. The drawing is turned away once more, and the thread is held onto the lute at another point; its position is again marked, the drawing swings back into place, and the new point is added. This process is repeated many times.

Slowly but surely the lute's shape is created from these points, in correct perspective. According to Dürer, this is a practical device for painters, goldsmiths, sculptors, stonemasons and carpenters. He wrote that no one was compelled to use it, but that those who studied it could carry on his research and discover much more than he could demonstrate.

One could pursue this approach to perspective drawing by attaching a grid of horizontal and vertical threads to a small window at school. For many children this will be a new, unexpected experience. We could also examine drawings and paintings by various artists, asking, "How did they manage to suggest depth?" In Giotto we find human figures overlapping each other;

Dürer's perspective device.

Fra Angelico painted an accurately constructed building around Mary in The Annunciation. More recently, Escher tricks us all with his marvelous illusions; what eighth grader doesn't want to discover the secrets of the perpetual waterfall, or the objects that could never actually exist but look perfectly feasible on the page?

At home the children could make a pinhole diorama. By drawing, painting, cutting and pasting, the assignment is to suggest as much depth as possible in a small shoebox. Lighting, window shapes and color are important in this experiment. We may encounter highways disappearing into tunnels, with cars becoming appropriately smaller, or beautiful interiors with furniture giving the impression of rooms of vast depth, or imaginary landscapes with mountains, valleys and lakes. Some students will use little mirrors, wool or beeswax to help fool the eye.

2. Manipulating a cube

Finally we have the assignment of manipulating a cube. With the help of two vanishing points, we draw a cube as large as possible, with one edge facing front and the top visible. Now we "remove" a smaller cube shape from one of its corners, leaving the corner empty; but the small cube now reappears on the opposite corner, as if we had simply pushed the small cube through the large one, all the way to the other side. In principle, one can do this exercise from any angle. The students then discover they can also "push out" the middle of one of the cube's surfaces and have it come out again on the other side. By assigning each plane a particular color or shade of grey, the changes in the cube can be made clearer. All these exercises, plus many more, will give the children a firm foundation and enable them to create skillfully constructed drawings in their main lesson books.

From seventh grade on, the development of perspective drawing runs parallel to the drawing of cross-sections. These exercises are related to black and white drawing in previous years.

In his second lecture on the curriculum, Steiner described[2] how technical accuracy must be connected to beauty. He proposed the following as an example for seventh grade:

> Here is a cylinder dissected by a wooden beam. The beam needs to be thrust through the cylinder. You must show what type of section is created in the cylinder on the spot where the beam goes in and comes out. This must be communicated to the children. The children must learn what happens when bodies or planes dissect each other, so that they know the difference between a stovepipe going straight through the ceiling or at an angle, creating an ellipse.

Manipulating a cube. (Students, age 14)

Intersections in charcoal. (Student, age 14)

It is up to the teacher to think of other assignments in seventh and eighth grades, using these examples. Round posts can be intersected by square beams, and vice versa; round posts intersecting each other are more challenging. We are surrounded by things that intersect at various angles: How are handles and spouts attached to pots and jars, chimneys and dormers to houses, balconies and greenhouses to buildings? Once the children have acquired an eye for this, they will come up with many different examples. When students of this age make the connection between technical accuracy and beauty, the results are often spectacular, especially if the drawings are in black, white and grey.

Part 5

The high school curriculum

Linocut. (Student, age 15)

1   Introduction

Around the fourteenth year, the physical and emotional changes of puberty, which Steiner calls "earth ripeness," take hold of the adolescent. These changes are often already apparent in sixth and seventh graders' artistic (and other) school work. The period of rich imagination—age seven to fourteen—comes to an end. Little by little, individual judgment develops; new feelings undermine old certainties. A new phase of development begins.

The changes that accompany this new phase are expressed differently in girls and boys. There is a considerable difference in the way they experience things. Feelings of loneliness and insecurity alternate with recklessness and unbridled exuberance.

A totally different attitude is now called for in the teacher: The trusted, often revered class teacher is no longer the right kind of authority figure. First and foremost, the high school teacher must be a human being and an expert. At best, he will become a friend. The students express interest in his artistic abilities, sometimes even in his struggles. He is an authority in his area of expertise. His seriousness, and especially his sense of humor, will create the right atmosphere: a classroom where each student will feel able to work, where all sincere artistic acts will be respected and seen as a contribution to culture.

1. The art of black & white

In his indications on the psychology of the developmental stages, Steiner recommends dropping work with color in adolescence (particularly in ninth grade) to focus on black and white art, itself an appropriate image for the adolescent experience. Art history provides us with plenty of examples of suitable and varied black and white techniques. The fourteen-year-old strongly experiences extremes between light and dark. The inspiration of childhood, which helped her connect to the world around her, has

Monochromatic work on display. (Students, age 15)

disappeared: In the world of matter, death looks her in the eye. Faced with this death chill, she experiences an unfamiliar, uncontrolled inner life.

Through black and white art we try to understand the way light and shadow work. Light animates things in the world and gives them "color," even when we are working with black and white. In light and color the laws of the cosmos are revealed, and this helps adolescents in their insecurity. Light also makes beauty visible—beauty that can be experienced, and which consequently must exist despite everything. As evidence of a higher world, art is one of the few things the adolescent can keep believing in.

Themes for assignments should be kept simple, but attention must be given to their development and completion. The first assignments should emphasize nuances of light in an interior space; the next should focus on renewed experience and exploration of the world of color. The student must have mastered certain techniques and be able to implement them.

The teacher will have a different way of working with each class, because each group has a different character. Even the time of year can provide new themes. The particular interests of this age group can help us choose themes for working in black and white. It is particularly effective for students' work to be compared with the work of others, or for an exercise to be repeated and compared to previous attempts. Even two assignments at the same time, or a subsequent exercise that is a metamorphosis of the previous one, can be productive. In his school sketches, Steiner gives an example: sunrise and sunset. Trees in the sun and trees in a storm. One theme can change into another: Summer turns into autumn in the next project, and so forth.

2. Evaluating and exhibiting

Class conversations before and after a project require subtlety, especially at the high school level. Constructive criticism will suffice; one should say just enough to spark enthusiasm. We must look at enough art for the art to speak for itself and create interest; this applies equally to the work of known artists and that of one's classmates. The information with which we introduce an assignment, as well as the wording of the assignment itself, is extremely important when "judging," "viewing" or "exhibiting" work. Before we evaluate results, the assignment's stated goals should be reiterated to everyone's satisfaction.

Student work should never be judged or exhibited without an accompanying explanation, though the tendency to do so in high school is great. The teacher should see to it that students sign and date (or number) their work, and, especially if it is exhibited, state what the assignment was.

3. Teaching instructions

In Waldorf art education, the most important part is the process, the practice. This distinguishes our attempts from "great art," although what we are doing is the same: creating an image from the connection between inner and outer concepts. Through practice, this process teaches the students what aspect of a subject they want to convey, for example, what it's like to be an Impressionist as opposed to an Expressionist.

Through practice the students also experience and learn the difference between an inspiration and an assignment, or the space between imagination and what the material demands: the moment when human freedom comes into play. Their awareness of the process of creation is further enhanced in twelfth grade, if they discuss Schiller's *Letters on the Aesthetic Education of Man.*

In all grades we pay particular attention to composition and color detail. Sketching is a skill that supports everything. In drawing from observation, the teacher should point out opportunities for expressing more than what is photographically, academically and technically correct. On the other hand, on occasion we must also ensure that spontaneous expressions of imagination are balanced by visible reality, or the reality of the assignment.

In eleventh and twelfth grades, after we review the history of drawing, culminating in our time with the technique of shading, we could do free drawings of rocks, plants, animals and people, perhaps in a sketchbook we have bound ourselves.

Steiner gives no indications on when to paint animals in high school; he does mention plants (see the eleventh grade curriculum). When we draw animals, sketching from nature is the best way to capture their living soul gestures.

Thus the high school students' skills in several techniques grow through well-planned assignments. We can't practice every single technique at school, but experience shows that technical skills built up over many years (e.g., watercolor painting) give students tools with which they can continue, even many years later, to give form, color and content to thoughtfully considered products of their imagination.

Even in the oldest students, total freedom to give oneself one's own assignments usually does not lead to satisfactory results. Pedagogically appropriate assignments, including some the students may find for themselves, are those that foster the development of slumbering potentialities in the students, thus creating a connection with other themes in the curriculum.

Creating something from nothing requires considerable application of the will. The assignment of making a picture book for a kindergartner to illustrate a particular story provides direction for the imagination and engenders enthusiasm, even though it limits one's possibilities with its specifications regarding target group, content, etc. By way of such projects, the students can experience the dilemma—and freedom—of the artist

Exercises in observation. (Students, age 15)

between assignment and inspiration, question and answer. It is the explicit task of the high school teacher, and specifically the art teacher, to provide the student with experiences that will help boost self-confidence and help him conquer the fear of dialoguing with himself about the world during the artistic process.

Steiner gave only as many indications for working at the high school level as the number of questions he was asked at the time. Even now we can find answers only if we know how to ask questions: out of our experience of working with students and with empathy. By properly taking Steiner's few indications into account, and by understanding how they still apply to today's high-school students, the teacher will discover contemporary, personal variations for the assignments in the curriculum. For this reason we have not given many teaching suggestions and refer to Steiner's indications only sporadically.

2 Ninth grade
Life between light and darkness

In ninth grade the art teacher is a subject teacher. She creates enthusiasm in fourteen- to fifteen-year-olds through her professional discipline. The unrelenting rules that must be followed when working with certain materials are the same for both teacher and student. Only teachers who have "walked the walk" know what they have overcome, and can therefore help students struggle through the process with authority and humor, for example, by proposing a new exercise such as the following.

Let us observe for a moment the effect of light shining through a small window into a shoebox. The light illuminates the bottom; it makes the walls various shades of grey. We draw this large with charcoal on a big piece of paper, starting with the grey areas on the walls, without drawing lines around them. We leave a white space for the window. The darkest area (where is that?) is strongly applied in black; between this black and the white window, as many grey tones as possible appear, with and without edges, ranging from darkest to lightest and vice versa. We begin to see more and more, even in such a small area; the large format lets us record our subtlest observations. The structure of the grey areas should not overrule the effects of the light. Shade with a steady, even hand; don't be content until all the areas have settled down harmoniously and all edges are sharp. At first this is a struggle for many students; but as soon as all the white has disappeared except for the window, the interior space starts to tell a cohesive story, making all the initially tedious work worthwhile.

1. Dürer as a source of inspiration for black & white drawings

Easy mastery of materials is one of the most important keys to working with adolescents. Artists like Dürer were Renaissance men[1] because of their desire to investigate and overcome the unknown and untested; Dürer's work holds a special attraction for high-school students. We can tell his biography

Charcoal drawing of Dürer's engraving
Melancholia. (Student, age 15)

and describe his times as an introduction; intrigued by his fascinating subject matter and technique, the students will now try to follow and comprehend the master. Studying his engraving, *Saint Jerome in His Study*, we can point out the significance of the light, simultaneously physical and spiritual, that surrounds the head of a saint. In his engraving, *Melancholia*, we find mystical images symbolizing the victory of light, inspiration, knowledge, wisdom over darkness. We do not need to analyze all the symbols up front; as the students observe closely and work on their drawings, their questions will arise spontaneously.

The first ninth-grade assignment could be to explore *Melancholia* with eyes and hand, not by sketching lines, but by indicating areas of shadow in charcoal. Gradually the mysterious images appear: the heavy angel figure, the smaller chubby angel, the polyhedron, the globe, the dog, the light in the distance. Enlarging the format is an excellent exercise, though it creates its own issues and takes more time; the enlarging process could be presented initially as a technical challenge for everybody. The students should work from an actual-size reproduction, possibly supplemented by a blackboard drawing by the teacher. "Where does the light come from?" we ask when the drawing is finished and our observations become experience. Our goal is an accurate rendering not only of the composition, but also of the light on and around the objects, which follows definite rules and has its own pictorial character.

We could also precede our study of Dürer's engravings by revisiting black and white drawing, starting with the simplest techniques.

Using graphite or charcoal (compressed or regular), we start with a black area at the top left of the page and go down the left side, getting lighter. The area reaches about the middle of the page, but with no drawn boundary; it continues to the bottom. We then fill the right side, transitioning from very light grey at the top to black at the bottom, with all shades in between. We pay close attention to the place where the two areas meet: No vertical black or white line should appear. We continually observe the work from a distance so we can adjust it. The same exercise can be done with horizontal or other boundaries.

We start a second drawing at the top again, with black across the entire width of the paper. In the middle of this area, which gradually gets lighter as it goes down, we leave a round space. This open circle is "colored in" starting from the top, with the lightest grey down to black. The roundness of the circle and the gradual transition of the grey can be worked on and corrected by the students when they view their work from a distance.

We can also draw a simple white object on which light and shadow show up well: a white ball or a roll of toilet paper. The surrounding area is shaded grey; the space for the object is left blank. We should be slightly above and fairly close to the object so its shadow will fall correctly in the background and foreground. The object, the background and the area under it should all be white; a sheet of drawing paper behind and underneath it works well. The white paper shows extremely delicate grey tones.

Another interesting exercise with white paper, ideal for observing delicate light-shadow nuances, is to draw a crumpled sheet of paper using a delicate drawing medium such as graphite. This requires great concentration, but as soon as half of it is done, the finished part kindles great enthusiasm, attesting to the student's improved powers of observation: White on white is accurately rendered with just a few strokes. This is an assignment for a single lesson: Working on it next time is impossible, because the slightest change in light will change everything, and it's also hard to create a second piece of crumpled paper exactly like the first!

We now take on a more challenging object from one of Dürer's engravings, for example the sphere, the bell, the key, the skull. Depending on the length of the lesson, this is an assignment for at least two classes, so we can distance ourselves from the work.

There are two ways of working on this. For the first drawing we have the actual object in front of us and we copy it. For the second, we take Dürer's engraving, observe closely how he drew the object, and reproduce it on a larger scale. Dürer uses lines; we can either copy these exactly or use a different approach toward the same effect, for example using the flat side of the charcoal stick.

By the way, it is best to use the "blank space" method described earlier. First we shade the background in grey, leaving a space open for the object; thus, we draw the surroundings, in other words, the light in which the object sits. Then we draw the shadow on the object (the object becomes spatial). Finally, the spatial object casts a shadow onto its surroundings (it removes the light). This shadow is usually the darkest part of the drawing; it needs to be dark enough to connect the object and the space.

The size of the paper we use should be compatible with the thickness of the charcoal or pencil lead. The paper shouldn't be too thin so we don't go through it. Working in a large format has an enlivening effect and prevents rigidity. The practice of keeping a white border around the edges of the paper has technical and pedagogical advantages: The sheet can be steadied (with a clean hand), and the size of the border area can be estimated and established by the drawing hand. Don't measure and draw a borderline; creating it by "thinking a line" is a valuable balancing act.

2. Exploring interiors

After working intensively on exteriors, we can now look at interior space; a good example is *Saint Jerome in His Study*, captured atmospherically by Dürer. To easily observe how light works within a space we can use a pinhole diorama; one pinhole and one window are enough. This will help bring outer observation and inner representation closer together.

We could also draw the classroom, darkened except for one window or doorway that admits light. Other examples of spaces that provide an opportunity to experience and reproduce extreme tension between light and dark on paper might include a door ajar, with light falling on a single table, or an empty (or nearly empty) room.

As a prelude to the larger work, we could draw a room like the one in which Saint Jerome is depicted, but empty; thereafter, we could make a rough copy of the Dürer engraving, enlarging the format. In this assignment we are concerned with the relationship between light and dark, not with how each individual object is drawn. Here again, line drawing must cede precedence to working with areas. On the blackboard or on a large piece of white paper, the teacher can sketch an idea of the proportions in the engraving; the students can follow along and begin working on the light-dark contrasts, each in his or her own way. Transferring the image by way of a grid will not help us understand the effect of depth created by the larger areas. Just as we drew the empty room in the previous exercise, we can now leave blank spaces for the objects and for Saint Jerome, including the light around his head. Alternatively, we could start with the images themselves, or work horizontally from top to bottom.

After working for a while, a few students offer their work for display and discussion; the teacher points out differences in their ways of working. We are better off not displaying too many examples, but with the help of a few we can call attention to several points, such as:
- evenly worked areas, helping the eye to go around objects as it is carried along into the space;
- sharp edges, making forms visible;
- proportions and invisible connecting lines throughout the drawing.

Based on Steiner's recommendations to "artistically develop the technical,"[2] ninth graders can draw all sorts of constructions, objects or spaces in black and white, while strongly emphasizing their aesthetic. We are less concerned here with producing a pleasant external effect than with bringing the lifeless, empty world to life again by means of light.[3]

In this year's curriculum, technical skills occupy important places in several subjects. Learning printing techniques, such as etching and linoleum-block printing, connects with the fourteen- to fifteen-year-old's need to become familiar with technical disciplines. The student learns to manage these techniques in stages; we do not stress experimentation or long-term design at this age. If the students are to learn these printing techniques, we should look initially for simple black and white themes in which the approach to light and dark is similar to that encountered in drawing. Afterward the students could write a report on the experience.

There should be sufficient work for each student, especially in the ninth grade. Working in smaller groups (e.g., half the class at a time) gives the teacher more opportunities to advise and encourage. The ninth graders' great urge to perform is held in check by gradual, step-by-step techniques.

Charcoal drawing of Dürer's engraving
Saint Jerome. (Student, age 15)

Simple, carefully chosen, well-monitored themes will help the students work more easily with the effects of light. A single example of work from previous years or higher grades, and the encounter with Dürer's masterpiece, usually suffice as sources of inspiration.

Steiner recommends the use of Dürer's engraving as suitable for fourteen- to sixteen-year-olds. If your students have already worked with Dürer's engravings in eighth grade, perhaps guided by an elementary-school colleague, find out what was done and how. You can then elaborate or vary what was already covered to fit the ninth graders.

3. Drawing and painting in connection with art history

The Waldorf curriculum is a whole, not only vertically through the years of learning, but also horizontally in connection with the various subjects. Art history occupies a central position in ninth grade in connection with drawing, painting and clay modeling. The strong physical and emotional changes taking place within the ninth graders have unsettled their relationship with the world; it is, therefore, very important for them to become acquainted with ideals such as those exemplified in Egyptian and Greek sculpture. Through the inexhaustible power of beauty, unity becomes apparent in a world that is falling apart for the adolescent.

Art History main lesson blocks (lasting at least four weeks) facilitate an intensive encounter with the essence of beauty. By recreating ancient works of art, the student grows closer to them. Museum trips, good slide presentations, prints and photographs and, above all, the teacher's careful blackboard drawings can help bring about this closeness. The most important ingredient, however, is how the teacher motivates the students to experience awe for what humanity has achieved via the hand of the artist in, for example, the specific works they are reproducing in class. Drawing, clay and painting assignments should all relate to a particular historical era.

In drawing or painting assignments, for example, in main lesson books, the teacher will attach great value to the way light and dark are expressed, especially when depicting sculptures. In painting this effect should be achieved by way of appropriate colors to express the mood of the time; for example, neon colors do not convey the atmosphere found in old icons.

The correct representation of proportions and perspective should also be stressed at this age, for example, by making sure columns are not drawn too thin or too short. Creating one's own well-thought-out drawings can capture the essence of an era much better than listening to endless lectures or viewing slides. Blackboard drawings and the prints we use as examples for the students must be of top quality. For example, prints should show the actual lines of the original, not the texture of dots we see in many prints nowadays. Many photocopiers yield poor-quality copies, and working with photocopies actually promotes a throwaway attitude. If good prints and other materials are stored in transparent sleeves or cardboard folders, they should retain their quality for years to come.

When making blackboard drawings the teacher should try to reproduce the atmosphere of an image, as well as the proper use of perspective. This can be achieved by working amply with color and using color perspective. We could also create large black and white examples. Rich blackboard drawings foster in the students enthusiasm for their own work; especially if they copy the drawings, they will remain bright inspirations in their memories.

3 Tenth grade
Movement and structure in black & white and color

The assignments described for the previous grade can also be used with sixteen-year-olds, in an expanded or different form. However, a certain stability or "ripening" characterizes the students' emotions at this age, enabling them to work not only on more themes related to observation, but also on black and white studies from the imagination.

Tenth graders can now learn from the tension and drama of Rembrandt's work, which he achieved by taking light away. Nearly abstract light-dark studies can be created, as well as studies of trees, landscapes, people, objects and architectural forms, in black and white as well as color. The students can also use their powers of observation for several drawings, or one or two large ones. For example, a backpack or shoe seen in a new light could be the subject of a drawing, or a school hallway, doorway or stairs, lighted a particular way.

Tenth graders have greater endurance than students in lower grades. They can work on large projects for a longer time and with more concentration. Thanks to their work in previous classes, they are also capable of technical refinement. If Dürer's work was not discussed in ninth grade, make sure to do so this year. The themes of the inspired scholar in *Saint Jerome in His Study* and the melancholy, brooding angel in *Melancholia* provide images of the human being on his way to self-awareness. Steiner stresses the importance of introducing the adolescent to these images; the eagerness with which the students work on these themes shows how accurate Steiner's indication is. As described for ninth grade, we are not concerned with perfect copies of Dürer's work, but with the study of light and darkness.

If the students are sufficiently familiar with these images, they can now be transformed into colors of the students' choice. This exercise can be introduced as early as eighth grade,[4] relating to discussions of the Renaissance man.

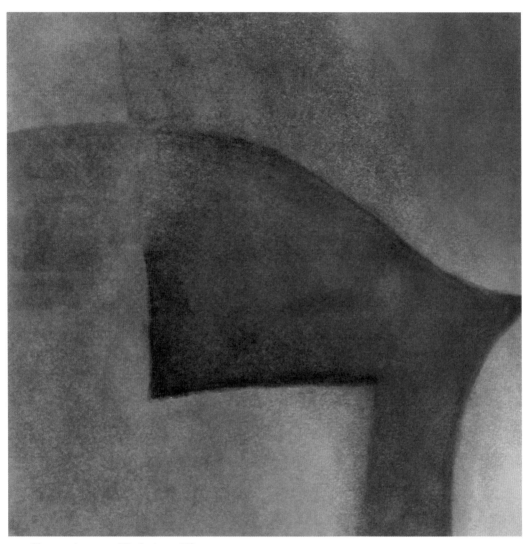

Blue meets orange.(Student, age 16)

In tenth grade an awareness of the Baroque (Rembrandt, for example) is awakening. Steiner's recommendation to transform Dürer's black and white work into color may seem like the obvious next step, but it is not an easy one. The practiced painter quickly realizes that rules about yellow (light) and blue (dark) meeting in green on one side, and red-purple on the other, should not be followed literally: This is most likely what Steiner means by "pedantry" when he says we can play with many possibilities *ohne* (without) *Pedanterie*. We need to go through, and fully experience, the process of observing and distancing, approaching and doing. No one can teach us this; we are creating something new.

In Dürer's work we find substance and atmosphere portrayed in black and white; the students became familiar with this in their ninth-grade work. Because black and white drawing largely replaced painting in the past two years, the students' imaginations may be quite spontaneous at the start of this main lesson block.

The first painting, an assignment to transform black and white into color, is best done at the beginning of the block using the wet-on-wet technique, for it is a leap of faith. *Saint Jerome in His Study*, for example, is to be painted using whatever colors one feels appropriate; the students may realize what this actually means only when the first results are viewed, for it will become obvious that some are still using colors as stand-ins for black and white: Blue denotes darkness, yellow denotes light. Now is the time to break this habit! A class discussion of the original engraving, including the atmosphere in the room and Jerome and his work, can help the students move toward more original color choices. Also, we should point out that, rather than constantly looking at the Dürer, the students should just try to remember it, consulting it in memory. This will help them move away from the illustrative details and start transforming the whole, including its main elements, into color. The painting will likely be re-wetted and worked on again at another time (see directions, next paragraph), so it is best to use the slightly heavier paper we used in the early grades.

1. Transforming black & white into color

"Transforming into color" should be interpreted as "...into whatever colors you wish." There is no preconceived scheme to follow. Establishing a system of colors for the grey areas would restrict us. We need to feel unfettered and free when choosing the colors.

When painting wet-on-wet, this assignment is usually not completed during one period, which is why it lends itself to re-wetting later so one can continue working; or we could use the veiling technique on stretched paper. (see the directions for sixth grade). To continue working on a dried painting do the following: Place the painting upside down on a dry table or board and wet the back with a sponge. The paper will soak up the water. Carefully lifting it by the corners, turn it back over and flatten it out, either while painting or with a clean sponge or cloth, until the surface is flat. The layers of paint we now add confirm and reinforce the forms and colors that are already

Black and white drawing transformed into color.
(Student, age 16)

there. They should be applied with more of a veiling technique, so first make sure there is not too much water in the brush, and then fearlessly lay down the color.

2. Color dynamics

In addition to transforming black and white into color, our renewed acquaintance with the drama of the color world will take place via wet-on-wet painting. Here are some examples:

- Red, blue and yellow, each coming from a different side, meet in the middle, flawless and pure. Now we paint blue over most of the red; then red over most of the yellow, and yellow over most of the blue. We now paint the outside of the purple with yellow, the green with red, and the orange with blue, creating shades of brown, but always keeping bits of the original colors.

- A vibrant red area is in the middle of green. Areas of black are created; here and there red pushes through the green. We seek harmony in color and form. All the "characteristic" color combinations can serve as starting points for this exercise.

232

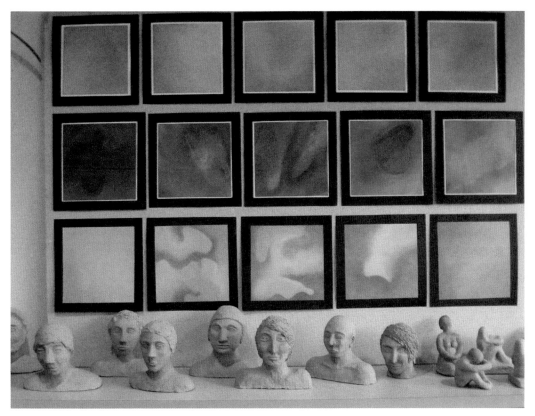

Color exercises by 16-year-old students.

- Purple and orange stand together amid the colors they contain the least of: yellow and blue. We slowly continue painting until a harmonious, balanced whole is achieved.
- Using indigo, vermilion and Prussian blue, we create black. Golden yellow is added and brown appears; mixed tones are created with golden and lemon yellow. This is an intensive exploration with earth colors, but some light should always remain.
- White at the top of the paper; a thin black wash flows into Prussian blue via indigo and ultramarine at the bottom. The white is kept; around it we add light yellow, radiating up to the Prussian blue and creating green.
- Create as many different color areas as possible, with strong edges. The colors can be mixed either on or off the paper; students can also trade colors. When all the colors are there, starkly separated side by side, take one color and paint over the whole thing, or just part of it, making all the colors darker, lighter or richer. (This last part might need to wait for the paper to be re-wetted in a subsequent lesson.)

233

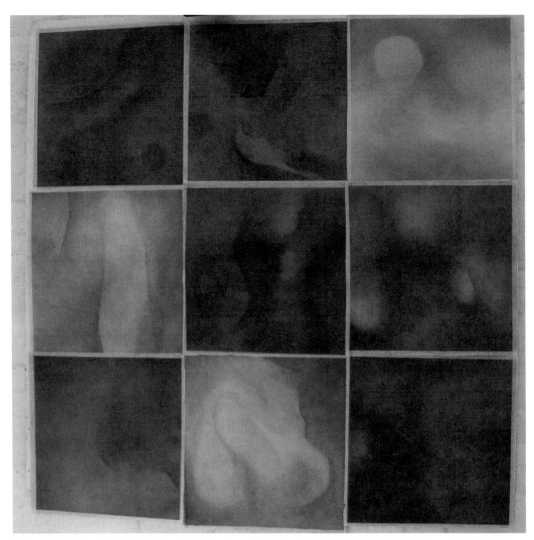

Above and right: Color exercises by 16-year-old students.

For veil painting, it is important for the students to get lots of practice, so begin with assignments as soon as possible. (See the next exercise as well.)

We begin with a dried, stretched watercolor paper. (Stretching the paper, preparing the paint and other initial steps were described in the sixth-grade section.) This basic exercise is about refining the technique and experiencing the tension between central and peripheral colors. We could start with any color and any veiling method (different brush strokes create different effects: large areas with straight edges, rounded areas, straight-edged and rounded areas, medium-sized or small areas... etc.).

When using diluted paints, as we do in veil painting, it is important to paint as dry as possible. The paper needs to be able to soak up all the water, so we mustn't use too much. When applying a new layer to an already painted foundation, a single brush stroke is preferable: If we go over the first brush stroke with a second one, the first layer will dissolve and come off, leaving a bare patch.

Having chosen the initial color for the outer area of our painting, for example a very diluted Prussian blue, we paint it in large curved areas. The stronger the color when we look at the painting from a distance, the clearer will be the pinkish-red afterimage on the white part of the paper.

We now choose a color for the inner area, perhaps orange. We concentrate on placing it strongly next to the blue, at least in some places. Where they overlap, accidentally or on purpose, a dark brown will appear. It is very difficult to "paint against" whatever form was painted first. If the painting is allowed to dry well between sessions, blending colors will not be a problem with this technique, unless the paints were not diluted sufficiently.

When we have balanced the inner and outer colors in terms of proportion, intensity and number of veils, we are ready for the next step. Leaving one or two sections blue and orange, we change the Prussian blue elsewhere by painting several veils of another color, for example yellow, over it. Now we have orange and blue in a predominantly green painting.

Next, some of the initial orange can be kept while the rest is partly covered with violet, created by mixing carmine red and ultramarine blue on a palette or mixing tray. A completely new—possibly unsatisfactory—color combination appears. The remaining orange and pure Prussian blue are still there, somewhere in the painting; the rest has been transformed by the subsequent layers. Deep black-brown tones are created until all the green and violet are gone. The violet-green contrast has become red-brown and blue-green, in which the original colors are still visible.

Experimenting in this way, we gain a lot of experience in creating color and color drama. Because of the step-by-step technique and our limited choices, we also encounter the rules and restrictions governing certain color combinations (see Part 6 of this book). A "monotone" combination is essentially different from a "characteristic" or "harmonious" one. It makes sense for us to become aware of this as we ponder: What color should I use to brighten or tone down this color?

Because veiling requires a lot of drying (and waiting) time, and because making comparisons highlights differences, we could work on three paintings simultaneously, starting all three with the same color combination, then continuing each one using two different new colors and ending with bits of the two original colors still visible. As we compare the paintings, we can try to describe the differences and come up with suitable titles.

3. Veiling, elaborated

We now stretch two sheets of painting paper (for a complete description, see sixth-grade instructions). On one sheet we veil-paint large areas; on the other, small repeating patches of various sizes. On the first sheet we place a blue area opposite a yellow area. Now we paint several more layers of each color in its own area, moving them a bit each time: yellow overlapping yellow, blue overlapping blue. On one side we let green arise by painting Prussian blue over yellow, or vice versa; on the other side we arrive at red, the other color between yellow and blue, by painting vermilion over the yellow and carmine red over ultramarine. The vermilion and carmine should overlap. Some white, but not too much, can remain in the center of the page. At the outer edges we now add complementary colors over the existing colors, creating shades of black: green over red, orange over blue, violet over yellow, red over green, etc. A crystalline image arises.

On the other sheet we paint a base layer of small areas from top to bottom, from yellow to orange to red through purple to indigo blue. In the vertical middle of the sheet these colors are "confirmed": We intensify the color sequences by applying several layers. To the left and right, each color fans out, creating many mixed colors all the way to black. Try to prevent a pointillist or blotchy effect due to too much water; aim for care and clarity so the colors start to shine into the grey around them. Examples from previous years, your own work, or that of known artists can demonstrate how veiling with watercolors achieves remarkable effects of light and color. This second painting can stay a mood painting or become a landscape.

Each student should now have a palette of dry watercolors or jars of slightly diluted paints. Small mixing bowls or white plastic trays can be used to dilute small amounts of paint for veiling. Each student also needs two or three water jars (for red, blue, yellow), broad and narrow brushes, and a cloth for removing excess paint or drying a wet brush. In addition to the how and why of water control when veiling, we should teach the students to correct any mistakes during each lesson. We could position the boards at a slight angle for veiling, so extra water can be easily seen and removed. The students need to find solutions that work best for them. Working at an easel makes it easier to view work at a distance, but requires greater technical skills.

Light and darkness: veiling in black. (Student, age 16)

Yellow, red and blue veiling. (Student, age 16)

Veil painting requires a degree of organization. Each layer needs to dry properly before further work can be done; once it is dry, a painting can be worked on several times each lesson. If drying is a problem, we could use a drying cupboard, in which boards are placed vertically as a heater blows warm air onto them from below.

We could also alternate veiling with wet-on-wet work. While waiting for veil paintings to dry, we could use the middle part of the lesson for wet-on-wet color exercises.

When one veil painting is finished, new paper should be stretched onto the board for the next project. There are many possibilities for further color explorations. The most important thing is for the students to use their imaginations, with the help of the preliminary exercises and explorations, when handling the brush and choosing colors.

Since veiling can produce real brilliance when applied over large areas, we can paint the radiant inner world of crystals when studying Mineralogy. Themes from cultural history such as Atlantis can also be portrayed by veiling.

Abstract color exercises afford many opportunities to experience the dramatic effects of color. The colors themselves, and our brushwork, then become the subject of the painting.

We could work on a color version of Dürer's *Melancholia*, whose masterful composition and wealth of images can be sources of stability and inspiration for young high-school students; they will achieve especially remarkable results by working on a large scale. Some might even attempt a color interpretation of Dürer's *Knight, Death and the Devil*.

Finally, doing two paintings of the same scene under different conditions is quite fruitful at this age, not just for the sake of "doing something," but to call attention to the transformations as one scene follows the other. We can learn a lot about evaluating our own work from this sort of project. The images themselves don't need to be complex: The colors will do the work.

Here are some examples:
- sunrise / sunset
- night / day
- sunlight / moonlight
- summer / winter
- storm / calm
- before the battle / after the battle

Sunrise and sunset. (Student, age 16)

Impressions of trees. (Students, age 17)

242

4 Eleventh grade
Seeking personal identity

In the sixteenth to seventeenth year, we see young people creating larger spaces around themselves. Childlike qualities are discarded; individuals distinguish themselves more clearly from each other; their emotional worlds and personalities are more openly expressed; love may be experienced for the first time. They are searching for their own identity.

The Parsifal main lesson in the Literature curriculum answers many questions, but it also helps one ask essential questions, especially about one's own inner world, of which the students are becoming increasingly aware. This world is now becoming important in the artistic process.

Biology, including Botany, occupies a central position in the Waldorf curriculum at this time. The plant's essence shows us an image of the soul. We can even recognize people in the characteristic gestures of plants. The contributions of religions in dealing with the world are also important building blocks for the young person at this age.

1. Growth processes in the plant world

Depicting the growth processes of the plant world in images is an entrance to the inner self. For this we have the following exercise. We will show the root, leaf, flower and fruit processes of a plant using one or more sheets of paper, either in wet-on-wet or in the veiling technique. There are many different ways of doing it.

    1 *The root process:* Crystalline, cool, star-like forms in a dark, warm environment.

    2 *The leaf process:* Blue and yellow come together in green, rhythmically repeating forms. Carmine red permeates the plant green!

    3 *The flower or budding process:* Light, airy carmine red and yellow above join with blue down below, creating green. We find a connection with

the insect world—bees or butterflies—by highlighting butterfly-like shapes in the flowers, mostly in light yellow and pink.

4   *The seeding process:* The seed inclines toward the earth. Each seed becomes an island of warm light: rounded shapes in a cool environment.

Interesting feedback results when a colleague who teaches eleventh grade Biology is asked to comment on the paintings. Question: How would we paint the process that lies between 4 and 1? In connection with this exercise we could study Steiner's watercolor, *Urpflanze (Archetypal Plant)*.[5]

When painting trees in eleventh grade, we should be mindful of Steiner's comment that trees should be painted "pictorially," not just green and leaves! We can use this encouragement in every lesson. We paint the tree as if surrounded by light, constructing its image with areas of color. Examples from both Impressionists and Expressionists, who worked so much with inner and outer impressions of natural phenomena, can help us define color and area as the painter's primary media. What was done playfully in fifth grade is now repeated, but with a new awareness.

We can go a step further by painting the same tree under different conditions of light, in different seasons and weather. When we compare paintings, we become aware of a deeper layer, expressed by color, that seeks a connection with our inner being.

After a first wet-on-wet painting of "the tree in light," we could divide a large stretched sheet into two or four parts, for two or four seasons. We can discuss color nuances with the students; for the rest we should follow the "pictorial" comment and not lose ourselves in details.

We now pay renewed attention to the presence of red in plant green. Without red it would have a cold, mineral quality. This concept can give rise to wet-on-wet paintings of flowering plants, for example daffodils, poppies, lupines, roses or various types of trees. The teacher describes the plant in such a way as to create an inner image. The description and expression of an image, for example the daffodil "heralding spring with its trumpet," can be discussed at length before painting. The plant or flower in question can also be brought in and observed.

Working on a light carmine red foundation is the best way to create plant green with the various yellows and blues. After some encouragement, the students will even dare to apply an extra layer of yellow-white over the plant in the final stage, as recommended by Steiner in his color lectures. They

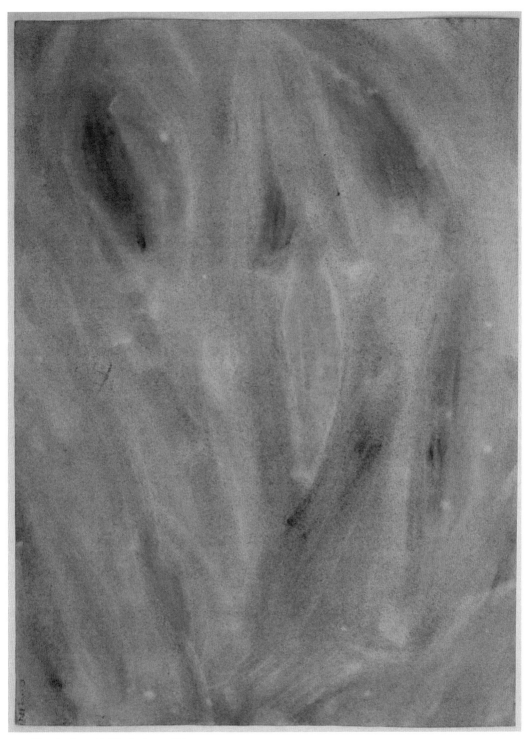

The plant world. (Student, age 17)

The plant world. (Student, age 17)

will see how the yellow, with its connecting quality, helps light permeate the plant.

In addition to these wet-on-wet paintings, we can work on spring or autumn flowers on stretched paper, perhaps in a large format. We could also paint the lily and the rose, a special challenge: The lily is more of a spring flower with fresh, juicy greens, while the rose blossoms on dark wood with its warm reddish shoots.

If every student chooses his or her own plant, a great deal of empathy is required on the teacher's part. But with proper preparation, with the students working actively over time on their renditions of the plant, this project can yield very personal and intensely experienced results. It is important for eleventh graders to feel a certain measure of freedom in working at their own pace. There is also ample room for their personal interests and contributions to appear in the work.

Repeatedly alternating between veiling and wet-on-wet will keep us from sinking into a complacent green. Most students no longer have trouble with these techniques; some may even show signs of mastery. Going deeper into the work of the Impressionists and Expressionists (flowers by Emil Nolde, for example) and into the artists' inner attitudes can strengthen the eleventh graders in their approach to their work.

2. Sunrise and sunset

The "sunrise and sunset" exercise is one we have assigned countless times, but it can always be newly experienced. The differences in color and contrast lie deeper than those simply attributable to weather or season. After a class discussion, the students can work on these paintings independently.

Some students, or even whole groups in a class, may be battling uncertainty as to their abilities. Encourage them by letting them transform black and white works by painters such as Rembrandt, Cézanne and Van Gogh into color studies. Once again, it is important for them to emphasize color, not the drawing aspect, in their paintings.

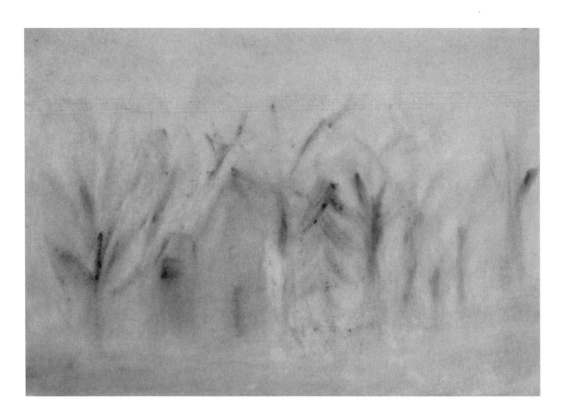

Night and evening moods. (Student, age 17)

248

3. Various techniques: shading
Plants, animals and human beings

In eleventh grade the moment arrives in which we usher the students into the realm of modern art, in both drawing and painting: the art of the turn of the 20th century, from Impressionism to Expressionism. In Music History, terms such as "Apollonian" and "Dionysian" are also discussed, giving the students an initial understanding of the two poles between which human beings experience themselves and which influence and "color" our ability to express ourselves. We encounter these extremes in drawing as well, spanning the entire range of possibilities from line drawing to light-dark shading, from observation to imagination.

Shading occupies a special place here. This technique enables us to directly render the spiritual effect of light in an image. Shading can be covered in eleventh grade, introduced by a study of drawing through the centuries.

Works by Dürer and Rembrandt as well as forerunners of this technique can be discussed. By copying and enlarging their work, we can study the techniques of the masters. Subsequently, we look at developments closer to our own time in works by Van Gogh and Picasso, for example. The way they emphasized different qualities becomes obvious. Later, when the students draw each other in different poses, they are not slavishly copying; they are learning to highlight specific elements. Alternating between thick and thin lines, the rhythm of shapes, the structure of areas, the relationship between light and dark, proportions and distortions—all of these can alter realism while strengthening expression.

After this introduction, we can start practicing a new artistic technique: shading. Shading requires a great deal of "I" activity, a degree of discipline that is difficult for the student to summon. This is why we also speak of shading, as explained by Steiner, as a technique of the future.

What exactly is shading?

As we draw short diagonal lines from upper right to lower left, using a black pencil on white paper, we create space for light on the paper. In that space, hidden processes can become visible. Depending on the nature of the lines, various tendencies become evident and forms arise out of the light.

Assja Turgenieff described how she gradually began to understand what Steiner's comments meant in relation to her own work. Steiner said:

> The strokes should never go with the form. They should have nothing to do with the form. In your case, the lines bend, if only slightly, along with the shape. That is wrong. One should learn to shade independently of the form. So, never draw bent lines, otherwise lines are created anyway. The line is a lie in the artistic process. The line can be used for the setup of a drawing, but no more than a builder uses scaffolding to construct a house. When the house is finished, the scaffolding is gone. Therefore you should not start from a line. Eventually all traces of contours should disappear. The strokes should be clearly visible, free, characteristic.

> But the strokes should have character and be as varied as possible; the point is to make them as different as possible—light, fixed, close together or far apart, and so forth. That is what makes it artistic. If you want to obscure an area gradually, you can—as far as I am concerned—also cross through it, but very sharply, never at a right angle. However, it is better to achieve obscuring by putting the strokes closer together or placing new strokes in between the others so that the direction of the lines remains the same. With this you liberate the drawn line, for the line is not beautiful anywhere in art.[6]

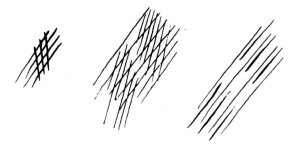

We can now start with the simplest exercises, for example, letting a tree and sunlight appear on a lightly shaded background by gradually shading certain areas darker. The Botany or Parsifal main lessons will provide more material. Working with this technique in eleventh grade is an appropriate introduction to the year in which these young adults discover and learn to deal with their inner development. Shading is therefore appropriate for high school, not elementary school!

Shading with colors is actually painting or embroidering, and thus should not be confused with black and white shading, which stands apart from other drawing techniques.

The following four exercises in the black and white shading technique are related to the painting exercises "Growth processes in the plant world" (see page 243).

1   Darkness traps light that has brilliantly penetrated it (root).

2   Watery, rhythmically repeating forms are created in the meeting of light and darkness (leaf).

3   Surrounded by light, darkness compresses slightly. At several central points, light is condensed into the form of stars. This is where the structure of the light is preserved (flower).

4   Light penetrates darkness. The darkness envelops the light that shines within it (seed).

If such introductory black and white drawings are not a possibility, we could use exercises from seventh and eighth grades; we could also experiment with free shading, and see what kinds of images arise.

4. Sketching

Sketching is practiced in all grades, but particularly in eleventh grade. It is an aid to proper observation, and good observation is needed in all areas of life. Drawing helps us learn to observe in all subjects.

In sketches and line drawings we are emphasizing what is already formed, the lifeless reflection of life, an abstraction. However, in "dynamic drawing" we try to arrive at the form (of an animal, for example) through the dynamic movement of hand and line. In form drawing the line is given its full

From observation to abstract form. (Student, age 17)

value. Both form drawing and dynamic drawing give high school students much material for their development.[7]

In eleventh grade all aspects of drawing can be covered. For example, the students could work on a small scale in sketchbooks they have bound, doing studies at home and outdoors. In class it is preferable to work on a large scale. Drawing plants, animals, people and each other can alternate with assignments inspired more by the imagination. The shading technique, and drawing with other media such as wax crayons, charcoal, Conté crayon and pen and ink, lend themselves well to these assignments.

5   Twelfth grade
   The big picture

The sun shines on the twelfth grade curriculum. Everything unites into a whole. Overviews of History, Philosophy, Religion, Art History, Chemistry, and so forth, create the dwelling; the human race resides within. The twelfth grader, the young eighteen-year-old human being, seeks not only freedom but also self-knowledge, or the initial impulse toward self-knowledge. She becomes aware of the human as a being who plays and creates; she becomes aware of her own task in life.

Usually six or more weeks of painting and an Art History main lesson block provide the framework for an overview of the development of art (using architecture as guide) and aesthetics (Schiller, Beuys) once again. The painting curriculum, placing the human in a central position, can take many different forms. If we emphasize communal art and the development of *Gesamtkunst,* or the totality of cultural expression, painting can contribute to the creation of theatrical sets, book designs, picture books for kindergartners, posters, programs, etc. The teacher can use all kinds of approaches to stimulate the students to transform their ideas into art for the enrichment of culture, for example, as a final project. Alongside this we can place the human being in a central position, for example, in working with portraits.

1. Human beings: head studies

Painting a human head is a special experience in twelfth grade. The activity can be very motivating if the entire class paints together (just as we used to do in elementary school). To begin with, we can examine Steiner's sketch of a face in profile in blue and yellow and his remarks on human flesh colors and the physiognomy of the face, which reflects the essence of a human being. We try to let this essence, which is so difficult to reproduce, stand still for a while so we can capture it in form and color.

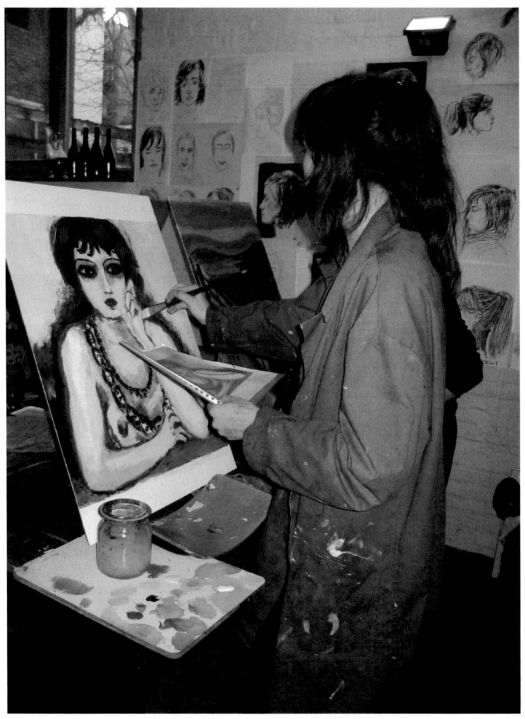

Portrait painting during an Art History main lesson block. (Student, age 17)

In a wet-on-wet painting, we can also start with a light blue base in which space is left blank for the profile. The face can be lightly colored in with yellow. Or we could work with a light ultramarine base and paint the surrounding area with, say, Prussian blue, leaving a space open for the face. Because this is not at all easy, we will immediately do another painting with the same blue-yellow setup, but with the profile facing the other way. (Many conversations about faces will be heard.) The next painting starts with blue and yellow again, but now we let both colors flow together into green in the face, adding a layer of carmine red from the neck over the cheeks to the forehead. For the background we can recall icons: a blushing red, a flower bud, life.

We can examine portraits through the centuries, looking especially at skin colors. We can do a series of paintings in which the color changes: more blue, more red, more yellow. This allows us to change age, temperament and tone, exclusively by means of the painting process. We then start over with different color combinations for backgrounds, hair and clothes, skin color, age, mood, etc. It is best to work in pairs of wet-on-wet paintings, for example "toddler and old man," "melancholy and cheerful" or "blond and

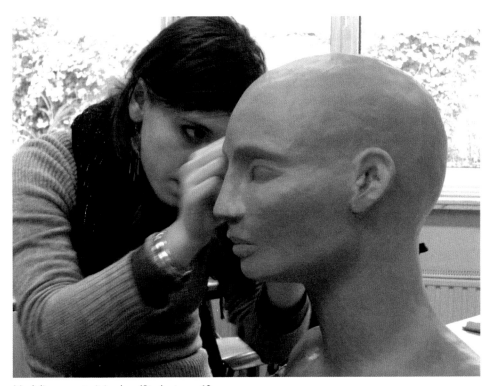

Modeling a portrait in clay. (Student, age 18

dark-haired." We can prepare for these paintings in the previous lesson by doing blackboard sketches of various facial features and adding them to our sketchbooks. As we paint, we leave spaces open for the eyes, nose, mouth and ears, until the color form indicates where they should be; we then add them in a light tertiary color. In this way we continue to paint in terms of color and area and prevent the creation of forms by the placement of shadows.

There will not be time to discuss all the work; sometimes students may do two paintings per class. After each completed assignment a few examples can be chosen to bring to the next lesson, to help introduce the next step of an assignment and motivate the students to practice more self-correction.

2. Continuing the portrait in the veiling technique

For the second half of the block we could start with several techniques. If we choose veiling, preliminary exercises are indispensable; they work with skin tones as harmonious combinations of all the colors and perhaps also as colors that can be painted between black and white (see Part 6 of this book). Faces can also be emphasized in pure color moods; this is a good opportunity to practice the most delicate veiling technique before starting on a face in a larger piece of work.

Further independent work on human figures or faces is better suited to smaller groups; sometimes this can work in the schedule. Smaller groups let us pay attention to individual students when needed. The students can all work fairly independently on the same wet-on-wet assignments, adding variations, and now with the veiling technique as well. Composition, color and form are left up to the individual student.

A sequel to the above can be found in the subject of "mother and child." The teacher can show Madonna icons and later images, up to contemporary masters. Steiner showed how this primordial image can be evoked from the harmony of blue, yellow and pink.[8] Students could also paint portraits of classmates; this requires preparation and composition. Initially we work expressionistically, directly wet-on-wet; then the students receive a lesson in observation. They make sketches, and skin tone, hair, eyes, position and form of the head, clothing and personality are scrutinized.

Only then, in the following lesson, do we start painting. Painting remains "color areas" as long as possible. Introducing the students to the work of Alexej von Jawlensky (1864-1941) at this stage can motivate them to look for the strength in human facial expressions and to appreciate Jawlensky's simplification of faces down to their essentials while avoiding the exaggeration of caricatures.

3. Modern art

There are different ways of allowing the seventeen- or eighteen-year-old to experience the art of our time. In Art History classes as well as in lessons on culture in general, we must travel through the past to be able to understand the present. In particular, the lives of individual artists and their personal oeuvre show how their work influenced, or tried to influence, our times. This is what is interesting for the students.

The students' own creations start to change after intense encounters with authenticity in the works of Andy Warhol (1928-1987) or the expressiveness of Joseph Beuys (1921-1986).

Through their own experiences, and by developing an eye for the individual contributions of each artist and indeed each person (including themselves) to the *Gesamtkunstwerk*, the collective culture, the students can go deeper than the usual superficial level. If they study biographies, these should become immersions to achieve an actual encounter; visits to museums, carefully guided and discussed later in class, can enrich these encounters. The teacher's task, especially in such situations (which may take place in conjunction with the final class trip) is not to avoid personal conversations about art, art observation or the experience of art. Young people can be nurtured for the rest of their lives by thoughts expressed in such discussions; and isn't a conversation a small work of art in and of itself?

The students can now speak as creative human beings, and from their own experience, about devotion and superficiality, honesty and dishonesty in the creative process, human and spiritual creativity, and connections among science, art and religion. As teachers we continually renew our pedagogy in practice from that same creative source; we can thus contribute to the development of freely creative individuals.

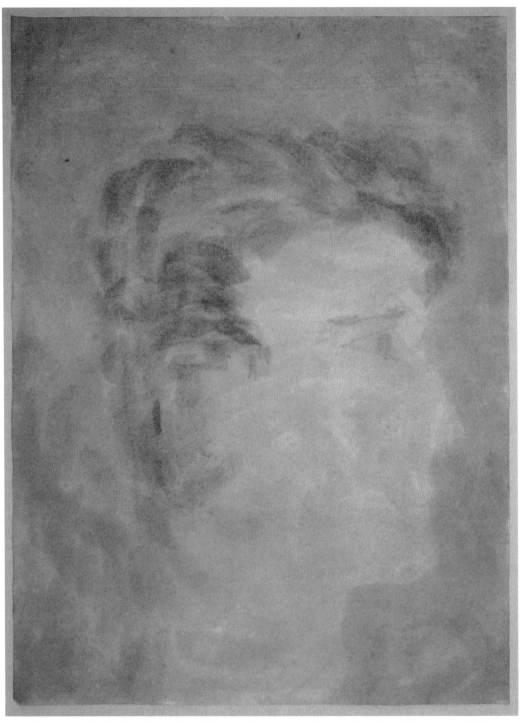

Above and right: Studies of a head on a blue foundation, painted over with yellow. (Students, age 18)

259

Study of a head with red flesh tone. (Student, age 18)

Study of a head created from two color circles. (Student, age 18)

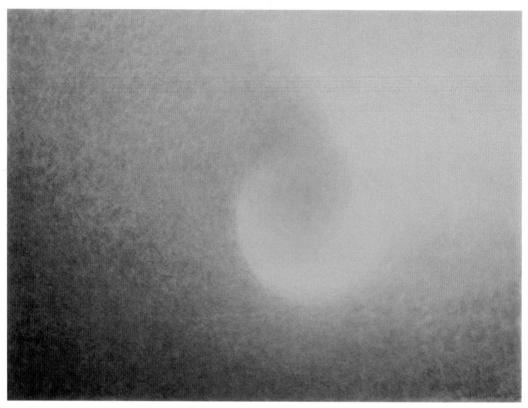

Free color circle between light and darkness, in the veiling technique. (Attie Lichthart)

4. Conclusion: the free color circle

We conclude the curriculum section of this book with an exercise for teachers, students and everyone else that will make use of the book: the "free" color circle. Painting this can be an instructive and inspiring experience for everyone. Attie Lichthart's *Two-Dimensional Painting* accompanied a description of the wet-on-wet technique on page 23; the painting above is a variation, done in the veiling technique.

First put white and black in the corners of the paper—exact precision is not necessary—by leaving the white open and making black by mixing all the colors. Then let them meet in the middle, via red or pink on one side, green on the other. Find your own answers in all the (luster) colors in the center.

Part 6

Color research

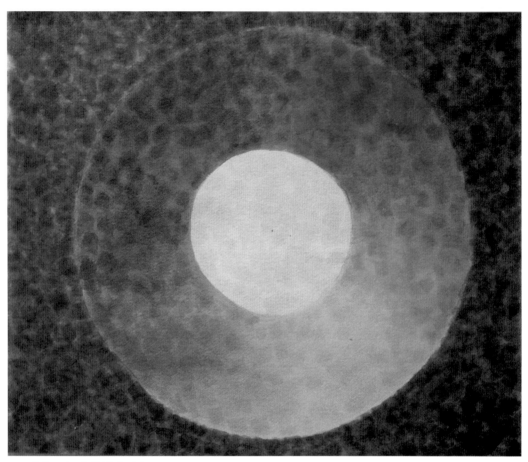

Color wheel. (Dick Bruin)

Only where the senses' knowledge stops
Will we find the gate
That opens up real life
For the world of the soul.
The soul will forge the key
When she grows strong within herself
Through the battle waged by world powers
With human powers
On her own territory;
When she drives out by her own strength
The sleep that shrouds in spirit darkness
The power of knowledge
At the frontier of the senses.
                    – Steiner, Whitsun motto[1]

To further open the door to the worlds of light and color in education, we summarize work by Goethe, Steiner, Hebing and others who have done research on color.

1. Color theory

The term "color theory" suggests a restrictive dogma on color. There are many different color theories; countless books have been written on the subject. Newton's color theories (with many variations) and Goethe's are the best known; Goethe's theory was written in response to Newton's. While Newton splits light to create colors, Goethe demonstrates that colors appear via the interaction of light and darkness. Newton's point of view has had considerable success in science and technology, but for a closer study of color through experimentation, Goethe's approach is important to pedagogy and to art.

Ever since Goethe's theory of color was translated into English, the words and research methods of this scientist/scholar/poet/statesman have been available to teachers with a particular interest in color.[2]

In a chapter on "Physiological Colors," Goethe speaks of afterimages and colored shadows, the phenomena most linked to the eye. In subsequent chapters he does not often mention color as such. He speaks about atmospheric colors (the blue sky, the red of evening) and prismatic colors. Goethe calls these the "physical colors." When covering chemical colors (acids and bases), Goethe stresses the natural law of the dichotomy between the red and blue parts of the spectrum. In the next chapter he brings colors together to form the six-part color circle (see page 75, Basic exercise 2, Mixing colors).

The primordial phenomenon of a division into two polarities and the goal of unity in a third, higher element is described by Goethe as fruitful and related to other disciplines, such as philosophy, physics and painting.

After characterizing each color separately, Goethe gives names to the color combinations that influence each other: the "harmonious"—opposite each other in the color circle, and the "characteristic"—consisting of colors that create a triangle in the color circle, such as yellow, blue and red or purple, orange and green. The "characterless" or "monotone" combinations lie next to each other in the circle (for instance, yellow and green). Steiner's recommendations for the first painting lesson, "Yellow and blue beside yellow and green," and his associated remarks (see the first grade curriculum) can be understood as based on these qualities. Finally, after giving directions for the painter, Goethe provides some explanations of the symbolic value of colors: Purple is majesty, for example.

2. Light in physics

At about the age of twelve, Waldorf students are introduced to the phenomena of light and darkness during the Optics portion of the Physics main lesson block. An overview of what the students encounter in this block follows (see also the sixth grade curriculum description).

- The phenomena that appear when we look at white on black or black on white. A black dot in a white area seems smaller than a same-size white dot in a black area. Light comes toward us, and black gives way.
- Physical colors. The creation of morning or evening red and sky-blue by darkening light and illuminating darkness.

- Afterimages, referred to as "colorful images" by Goethe. If we observe a color at some length, we will see the complementary color wherever we look, though it is actually on our retina.
- Prismatic colors. We perceive these when looking through a prism or another light-refracting medium at a light-dark boundary.
- Colored shadows. Goethe covers these in connection with the phenomenon of afterimages. The experiments that make the colored shadows visible are absolutely fascinating.

(Two sources for these experiments in Optics are *A Phenomena-Based Physics*, three volumes for Grades 6–8 by Manfred von Mackensen, and *Physics for Waldorf Middle Schools* by Robert H. Sonner.)

This sixth-grade introduction to color in Physics consists of observing, experiencing wonder and processing the experience. In twelfth grade, when we revisit color theory as part of the theory of light in Physics, wonder is no longer enough. The teacher now lets the students discover natural laws by way of their own observations, so when they leave school they will have an idea of the lawfulness and wisdom contained in color and light. From sixth grade onward we revisit our color experiences through painting and black and white drawing. In twelfth grade it is interesting to establish connections between color and the laws of physics and to experience the phenomena ourselves through painting.

3. Steiner's lectures on color: luster colors

Both Goethe and Steiner had the needs of the artist as a first priority when developing their theories of color. Goethe establishes the connection between colors and spiritual beings in the last chapter of his *Theory of Color*; he makes sure he cannot be considered "vague," and leaves it at that.

Steiner goes further and describes how we can meet the spiritual being working within each color through intensive observation of and immersion in colors, and that in doing so we will "make important discoveries in the future." He mentions experiences deriving from the intense observation of red, orange, yellow, green and blue in his lecture "Artistic and Moral Experience."[3] For red, he gives the description of "form created from color." The transition from vermilion to carmine red expands into a star shape; we experience the vermilion as an effect of the "wrath of God," and the carmine "makes one learn to pray." "Mercy is there!" This is how Steiner describes inner experiences deriving from external observation. He says these experiences provide the foundations on which the artist can work creatively "out of color" in the future.

Goethe described color perspective, for example blue's tendency to create space and red-yellow to come toward us, from his own experience. Steiner explains how, since the Renaissance, humanity has left behind the use of color perspective, replacing it with linear perspective, and how we can return to it in our time. He also points out the pedagogical value of living in color perspective and fostering sensitivity in the child's soul.[4]

Like Goethe, Steiner puts yellow and blue opposite each other: The space-filling, radiant quality of yellow contrasts with the enclosing, space-creating blue (see page 42). Red stands between these two, the active color resting within itself. Steiner calls these three "luster colors" because of their active character. This is how he relates them to the human being:
   – yellow is the luster of the spirit or the spiritual, of the "I" element;
   – blue is the luster of the soul;
   – red is the luster of life.

Goethe connects these three primary colors by creating a six-part color circle. One can imagine blue and yellow flowing together into green, and on the other side red and blue intensely uniting in purple. The colors are independent beings, but constant movement is created as they blend into one another.

In art in general and painting in particular, we continually encounter both "being" (which is limited) and "becoming" (which is unlimited) through the effects of color. When colors come up against an edge or meet another color, they may intensify or dissolve; they may turn into another color (become enchanted), darken (cool down) or evaporate (heat up).

4. Image colors

An entirely new concept is introduced in Steiner's lectures via his description of image colors. The term "image color" denotes a reflected or shadow color: white, black, green and peach-blossom. These colors differ qualitatively from the luster colors red, blue and yellow. In the case of green and peach-blossom, they form the connection between the two sides of the spectrum: the red-yellow side and the blue side.

These distinctions become particularly meaningful in painting, when the image and luster qualities Steiner describes prove applicable in the depiction of minerals, plants, animals and human beings.

The image color, or image quality of color, can be most clearly observed in plant green. Just as moonlight is an image, a reflection of sunlight, green depicts life, but is itself lifeless. It is the lifeless image of life.

When Steiner describes image colors in terms of the essential aspects of the human being, their relationships to each other become clearer. He refers to green as the "lifeless image of life" (e.g., the color of plants), the peach-blossom color as the "living image of the soul" (e.g., a skin tone), white as the "soul image of the spirit" (e.g., a white cloth, the indication of a purified soul), and black as the "spiritual image of death" (e.g., a black garment to express the impersonal, the unquestionable). From black via green and pink to white, a color movement runs through the realms of nature, from the lifeless (mineral) via the living (plant) to the soul (animal) and the spirit (human being). Each image color is thus described as a reflection of something; every shadow requires a source of light and something to cast the shadow. The image colors can be understood in this way. For black, the source is "lifelessness," and the spirit is the object casting the shadow (although "object" is too physical in this sense). When we see black, we should actually see "lifeless" expressed in the spirit. In other words:
- the shadow of the lifeless in the spirit is black;
- the shadow of life in the lifeless is green;
- the shadow of the soul in the living is peach-blossom;
- the shadow of the spirit in the soul is white.

This is not only about comprehending the essence of colors; Steiner also gave directions for rendering these image colors through painting.

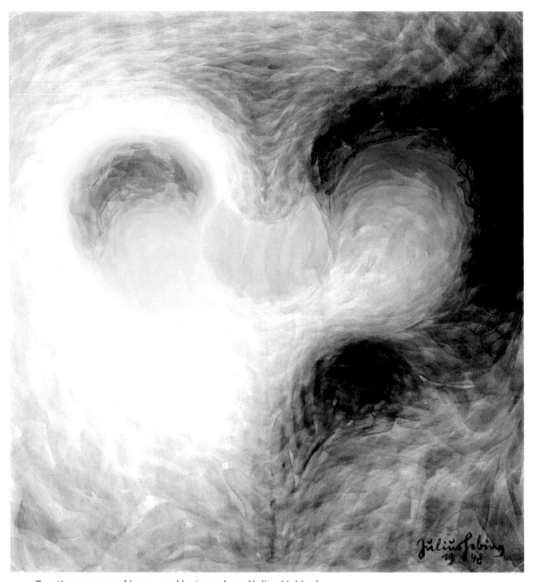

Creation process of image and luster colors. (Julius Hebing)

5. Painting minerals, plants, animals and human beings

Steiner gave useful directions for both teacher and painter when painting minerals, plants, animals and human beings.

When painting plant green, we can emphasize the green's image character by painting it darker than it really is, then applying a yellow-white layer (luster of the spirit), as if enveloping the plant-being in lighted air. These directions can be followed easily, without the need to explain their origins. In practice we can actually see that, rather than being content with the first green we produce, it is better to arouse its "shadow" nature by painting it darker and then going over the whole thing with yellow-white to achieve unity in the painting. If we look at two paintings next to each other, one with and one without a yellow top layer, we can clearly see the difference. These indications for the plant realm also include flowers and fruits; they, too, can be painted darker to emphasize their image character and then covered with a veil of yellow-white.

The mineral world of crystals comes shining toward us with its distinctive forms and colors. The luster of minerals radiates from within; no matter what colors we use, this light or luster character must be evoked in the painting, or the object in question will not have a mineral character. In his third color lecture,[5] Steiner goes on to recommend that the mineral's surface should shine with luster from behind its image, so its essence can be made visible by the white of the page. All colors in the realm of minerals, including image colors, should therefore have a luster character when we paint them, which is why we should always let the white paper shine through when painting minerals.

A quality common to all animals, despite the huge range of differences in their appearance, is their easily aroused inner world. This animation is expressed by blue, the "luster of the soul." In practice this means that we initially paint the animal a little lighter or more yellow-red than it appears and then cover this color with a blue veil. In combination with the plant world, which forms the animal's environment, this requires a finishing touch of yellow-white over the plant green and a blue layer over the animal. When we paint an animal, therefore, we speak of "image luster," a luster that has become image. When we paint plants, the image color is brought to a luster: "luster image."

Human beings are the image of their own essence. The essence of the human being is image. The spiritual pervades the human essence. This is expressed in the peach-blossom color. Everything that is color as regards the human being, including clothing, has an image character. In this case we do not paint white transparent luster, but we subdue the colors, let each color become an image color. For example, when painting people, we take away the radiant force of yellow by painting over it with the complementary color. The color of the face is created from a living encounter between light and darkness, with soft red shining through; this encounter can be translated into yellow and blue, producing green. Green is the result of the meeting of light and dark. From yellow, blue and red, the image color of peach-blossom is created. Through the centuries artists have sought the formula for the living color of human skin. Steiner approaches it in a completely new way: "In the lively weaving of light in darkness, white in black, a soft purple-red shines: living incarnate."[6]

Steiner's lectures on color can thus be seen as a direct continuation of Goethe's work with a completely new approach to color experience, appealing to new skills that can be explored and developed by the contemporary human being.

6. Ongoing color research - the work of Julius Hebing

Painters and scientists and teachers as well, are in charge of continuing color research, which currently includes a vast area of technology. The study of color's effects on people in psychology, therapy and advertising is matched by developments in the arts, where ideas about color influence such things as architecture, stage lighting, fashion and design in general.

For lesson preparation help and a Goethean continuation of the study of color, the work of the painter Julius Hebing is a true treasure trove. His 1950s series of publications *Welt, Farbe und Mensch (World, Color and Human Being)* is the result of painstaking research based on Steiner's color lectures. Entirely in accordance with Goethe's scientific attitude, Hebing converted many phenomena into visible examples of color (see pages 44, 45, 76, 166 and 270). His work in the Stuttgart Waldorf teacher training program and his annual meetings in Ulm, Germany, for teachers who paint with children commanded much respect. The *Welt, Farbe und Mensch* series and his interesting diaries, *Lebenskreise, Farbenkreise (Life Circles, Color Circles)*, are indispensable to any school library. (Unfortunately, they have not yet been translated into English.) The first one is an extensive study reworked by

Hildegard Berthold-Andrae. It is a clear manual that explores the different areas of ongoing color research and makes them accessible by way of experiments. The accompanying color prints are an impressive testimony to the work of this artist, who dedicated his whole life to the study of color.

Hebing's followers, as well as other artists, scientists, teachers, therapists, psychologists, philosophers and others all over the world are involved with this work. Steiner's color lectures provide a basis for ongoing color discovery and research. In Steiner's vision, luster and image colors interact in a living way; Julius Hebing worked on the circle of luster colors and their vivid connections to the image colors in the illustration on page 270, *Creation process of image and luster colors*. It is an image worth frequent study, which can also help us learn to express in words what is happening in the painting.

In his work, Hebing elaborates on Steiner's remark that our experience of color has evolved through the centuries and is still developing.

It is known that the Greeks were not yet able to discern blue; this is evident from their use of language. Steiner states that the Greeks could not see blue because they were still living in the red element; in our time, we are able to discern or experience blue. The colors we can consciously identify and refer to nowadays are not necessarily present for all humanity, however. Hebing describes that, at the time of the rise of colonialism, people were encountered in Africa who had hardly any words in their vocabulary for blue and green; the words they used corresponded more to black and grey. However, they often had an excess of words for the warmer colors. Sheep-herding ethnic groups such as the Herero people had a considerable interest in the colors of their herds. They were able to distinguish between green and blue, but found no need to express this in language. They use twenty-six different expressions for the colors and markings of their herds.

Europeans researching color vocabularies kept running into this phenomenon: indigenous people who had no essential interest in the colors of nature (e.g., blue sky or green trees). Green, blue and violet were interchangeable with colors such as black and grey. One ethnic group had only one word for both green and blue: *enoli*, meaning fresh or raw, similar to what we mean when we say, "He's still green, he's not ready yet." When this group learned about the preparation of indigo as a blue coloring pigment, they called the color *akase*, literally meaning "something that needs to be learned."

This draws our attention to the fact that the eye may initially see, but that conscious observation, the distinction created by giving a color a name, "must be learned"; in other words, it is developing. Julius Hebing gives many examples in *Welt, Farbe und Mensch* and quotes the work of Hugo Magnus, which appeared as early as 1880.

Can we connect color-blindness, which is currently on the rise, to this phenomenon? Hebing developed remarks by Goethe into detailed diagrams, in which insensitivity to red, for example—the most common type of color blindness—becomes evident. Since there is a color-blind child in just about every class, it is important to mention this here. We can give no further information because not enough is known about the phenomenon to enable us to make recommendations for dealing with it in the classroom. Hebing does, however, give us a basis for further research.

7. Steiner's school sketches, explained by Fritz Weitmann

The following is a translation from a chapter from the book *Aus dem Künstlerischen Unterricht der Waldorfschule, Malen und Zeichnen in der Oberstufe (Art Lessons in Waldorf Schools: Painting and Drawing in High School)* by Fritz Weitmann, published by the Pädagogische Forschungsstelle beim Bund der Freien Waldorfschulen, Stuttgart, in 1981.

In this very interesting work, Weitmann not only gives examples from his broad experience as a high school painting and drawing teacher, but also provides an ample overview of quotes by Rudolf Steiner, whose work he consulted. The first section covers the curriculum; the second part is dedicated to "impulses for art and Rudolf Steiner's recommendations for art education." In this part, Weitmann discusses Steiner's paintings, or rather, the indications he supported with painted or drawn sketches, including sketches of the large and small domes of the first Goetheanum. Weitmann provides a concise but very interesting summary of the sketches Steiner made as recommendations for painting lessons. Weitmann writes:

> With the founding of the Freie Waldorfschule in Stuttgart in 1919 and the school for continued education in Dornach in 1921, painting education had to be set up within the framework of these schools. Keeping the age group in mind, the artistic principles

were to correspond with that of living art. In connection with this, Steiner developed a series of pastel sketches as examples to help with the development of education.

The first two sketches, "Sunrise" and "Sunset," were created simultaneously. Both motifs are outwardly similar. They show the rising and setting sun above a flat horizon. Yet the color mood is different. The similarity in the composition invites the spectator to find the difference in the pictorial mood. Of course this was done deliberately. It is in this that the pedagogical, fertile element lies.

If each painting is considered individually, one may be uncertain whether it is a sunrise or sunset. In nature these can look very different; yet each sunrise and sunset have something in common, something typical at their foundation. Rudolf Steiner gave himself the task to develop this in a pictorial way. When we look at the sketches simultaneously, the difference in mood becomes apparent. Yet not everyone can see the difference easily, because the difference is expressed in pure pictorial qualities rather than exaggeration. In the morning mood, the vermilion sun enters through the gates of the day. Blue-green nuances allow us to experience the cool freshness of the morning. Clouds painted in yellow and reddish tones support the rising movement of the sun in both form and gesture. Contrastingly, the evening mood shows warmer, yet more subdued colors. The orange of the sun has a matte quality; it has lost its radiating strength and appears to glow within itself under the descending cloud shapes. While the mood here encourages reflection on the day that has passed, the morning mood evokes action.

The rising and setting of the sun opens and closes the day and places boundaries around the night. In the alternation between day and night, the human being feels part of the great breathing rhythm of the earth. He experiences his link with the cosmos. This relationship between earth and sun is also experienced in the paintings. The vertical rising and falling movement, together with the line of the horizon, can become an invisible hieroglyphic for the viewer, a cross described within the event.

The next two sketches, "Trees in a Sunny Sky" and "Trees in the Storm," were also created simultaneously. They too have similar composition. As regards content, however, they are very different. They have been taken one step further in condensing the image. There is a clear progression from the first to the second sketch. The relationships between cosmos and earth are reinforced on the side of the cosmos, the unusually wide format of the sketch emphasizing the earth's horizon. The movement in the air, gathering into storm clouds, has also been forced into a horizontal direction. The light of heaven is clouded over. Within this stormy landscape one can see a rhythmically positioned group of trees. The green areas of the foliage of the tree, the various directions of the reddish trunks, the shapes of the hill in saturated green together with the way the sky is painted, create a composition out of movement and tension. In "Trees in a Sunny Sky," the soft green of the leaves appears to be floating freely in the clear blue of the sky. The red-brown tree trunks bring cheerful life. The latter, we have been told, was the starting point of the composition, which indicates that the composition aspect was given priority in this case.[7]

The sketch of "Trees in the Storm" is a transformation of the first. Because the atmosphere is condensed through gathering storm clouds, everything else is also condensed: the green of the trees, the color of the trunks and the color of the meadow below. This process of becoming substance results in the stronger formation of palpable reality. The trees are included in the movement of the storm with their dark red trunks bent in one direction. The steely blue of the clouds dominates the obscured earthly green. A dramatically somber mood has been created. The cosmic breathing rhythm of the earth is disturbed by the event, by gales and thunderstorms.

In the first pair of sketches the task is to work out the differences in color; in the second pair, the composition and the intensification of color. The law of polarity and *Steigerung* (intensification) (Goethe) becomes clear.

We now arrive at the third pair of sketches: "Sunlit Tree by a Waterfall" and "Head Study." The difference in subjects belies the fact that these sketches were also made simultaneously. Yet, one and the same motif connects them: the light. For the first time in these series, the external light comes to the fore as a theme. Up until now the colorful mood of the painting was condensed into a tangible content. Now the process of becoming has progressed to such a degree that the objects in the image appear through being lit externally. Yet everything remains purely pictorial.

In the color sketch "Sunlit Tree by a Waterfall," one can see how the yellow light flows toward a tree obliquely creating a play of light and shade, green-yellow-black color nuances. On the other side a blue waterfall contrasts with the yellow flow of light in the composition. Between the tree and the waterfall is a space filled with water vapor and light in which bluish-yellow colors play. A strong brown bottom carries the whole.

This color study is an image for the life of the elements. In all sorts of ways, the elements meet and mingle in a free play of forces and influence the flourishing tree, rooted in the earth. Those who allow this magical mood to act upon them can complete it by imagining fluttering butterflies, humming insects and singing birds. One can think of the activity of elemental beings in nature as they appear in myths and fairy tales and that, for contemplative consciousness, they are especially effective where different elements such as warmth and water, or water and earth, are adjacent to and interact with each other.

According to Marie Groddeck, when demonstrating these sketches, Steiner began with the descending sunlight. He condensed it to a tree of light and flames, in which the earthly green was then woven. The trunk, the most solid part, was the last to appear in contrast with the tree motifs discussed previously, which were begun by first creating the trunks. This sketch is an excellent example of what Steiner means by "bringing the observed interplay of color in relation to the spiritual." The oblique light flowing into the space on the sketch cannot be observed in reality, but it can be felt and experienced inwardly. It becomes visible only where it touches matter. However, what is experienced inwardly is no less real than what can be outwardly observed. Together the visible and invisible provide an image of true reality. If we place inner experience on the Expressionist and reality on the Impressionist side, then we have united both styles in the image as trend. Steiner once said that a future painting style would lie between Expressionism and Impressionism.[8]

"Head Study" takes us away from nature motifs. For the first time a human being becomes the motif. This study is treated in the same way as the tree motif. The subject is the light. A simple profile in yellowish-red nuances contrasts with a blue background. The delicate shadow areas clearly show how the face is connected to the light. Whereas the tree was created by condensing the light, the head space was left open. The blue background was painted, and in it the profile was left open like a negative. The process of becoming was created by the surroundings. In "Sunlit Tree" the process came from within. Subsequently the illuminated head was further developed with yellowish-orange tones.

Steiner once demonstrated in one of his lectures,[9] for those who "live" in the creative force of color, how two color patches, yellow surrounded by blue, are enough to recognize a head and a profile. The way the radiating, fraying yellow and the bordering blue interact gives the impression that nose, eyes, mouth and chin are formed by the color boundary. He called this color setup "the basis for a face in profile." Encouraged by the head study, colorful maps were later made in Geography based on the same principle of color perspective.

The color study "Mother and Child" completes this series and is its climax. It contains a primordial human motif given form out of the color. This study is consequently very important, because Steiner explains every stage of its creation during the painting process. The stages in which the image was created simultaneously show the student's development in painting during the twelve-year school plan: First, experiencing pure color within the soul, in increasingly richer nuances through which the child is guided in the first few years; then slowly forming and condensing color to image quality in the next years; finally, more consciously giving form in painting and developing qualities while painting in the higher classes. The artist Luise van Blommenstein, who attended this lesson, recorded the experience. We borrowed some of the characteristic details from her description.

Steiner had told the students that he wanted to show them a painting done "entirely out of the color," and he applied a blue moon-shaped area with a yellow patch next to it on the stretched white paper. He added: "Do you see, these are two entirely different colors, blue and yellow, but they are very compatible and pleasant to observe. Which other color would fit in?" He mixed a soft pink color out of various pastels and painted a small patch next to the yellow. While turning to face the students, he said: "These three colors together make a triad, as in music. It is a chord, unity within itself. However, now we want to paint the rest of the sheet. For this purpose we need to find a color that does not belong to this triad at all." He applied a soft fresh green around the other colors. The entirety was intensified by a violet, which connected with the blue at the bottom left. Steiner said: "Look, at the bottom right a little patch of white remains. We must now fill up this space with one of the triad colors to keep it all together. Can you feel how this is necessary for the composition?" This was done with soft blue. Then he continued: "Right; now we've finished; the sheet is full. That is a color symphony. Beautiful in its own right. However, now we'll see what can come out of this. We'll paint something in the yellow. But yellow in yellow cannot be seen, so we need to add a little red." Then we are told how Steiner carefully continued working, until eventually a face was created, to which he commented: "The eyes you can just draw." He then drew a small head in the pink. "What else can we make from this? Let's say 'a mother and child,' but then we need a connection between mother and child." This connection was painted with a golden-orange for the arms and hands of mother and child. After some further development and harmonizing of the whole, he applied a shining yellow from top to bottom over the background with broad brush strokes, changing the green into a golden mood. "The light comes from above, it should radiate…"

In Luise van Blommenstein's first description there is a faint echo of this mood during the painting lesson, and of the motif of this image. The painting came about in three clear stages. The first led to an experience in color tone, a triad; the second to the color richness of the composition: a color symphony; the third led to the creation of the image out of the color: the motif. The latter was not a starting point, but a result. From the experience of the color of the soul mood "motherly love," the image of the mother with the child was created. Steiner said later that he wanted to express motherly love. He had intended to execute this pastel study in watercolor, but unfortunately he did not get to do this. A large watercolor with this theme was created out of a different color mood and within a different context.

The motif of motherly love leads to general love of humanity. Steiner had painted it as a central motif in the small dome— it formed itself into an image representative of humankind. The pastel sketch has survived time, but does not belong with the school sketches. This theme would be too demanding for the students.

This is what Weitmann said about the school sketches by Steiner.

Afterword

At the beginning of this book, we started by experiencing color in our direct environment. After our tremendous journey through the multicolored curriculum and our reflections on color, we return to this theme. Have these new insights changed our perception of nature? Have these sense impressions, supported by our all-encompassing thought processes, created a new sense in us, a sense for art? And can we connect this sense with life in such a way that we can speak of an art of life, a healthy way to be in the world?

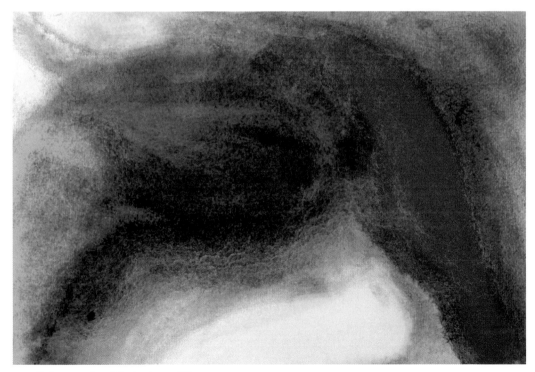

Color exercise. (Student, age 16)

In his lecture "Pädagogik und Kunst" (Pedagogy and Art), Rudolf Steiner reflects on this and says that the force that lies at the basis of this sense of art is love—love for our fellow human beings and the world around us. This is the energy source that we can use when working with children. Love, when fed by insights into humanity and knowledge tested through precise observation, makes all educational "systems" superfluous. Love itself is education. The bonds between teacher and student are the most vitally important factors in the development of the child at school. Thus the science of education becomes the "art" of education.[10]

Our intention has been to place the painting curriculum within this context. It makes no sense to isolate painting lessons or exercises in a world of education that is continually striving for change and renewal. These moments of color become visible within our educational ideal when we see them as colorful beads on a string. The string disappears within the bead and becomes invisible: Strengthened by our experiences, we must suppress the wish to see or expect immediate results.

The night has its special way of working independently of the teacher. We can only pick up the thread the next day to work further on the necklace. At the end of each school year, we try to fasten the ends of the necklace, only to unfasten them again after summer vacation in order to continue working. Thus an ornament for life is created. Whoever wears it travels richly through life and the world, offering a bead where necessary.

We would like to express the wish that this book may contribute to a long string of beads, acquired in childhood and cherished as a precious gem in adults.

Bibliography – A selection of English titles

Works by Rudolf Steiner

Art as Seen in the Light of Mystery Wisdom, London: Rudolf Steiner Press, 1984.

The Arts and Their Mission, New York: Anthroposophic Press, 1964.

The Child's Changing Consciousness, New York: Anthroposophic Press, GA 306, 1996.

Colour, London: Rudolf Steiner Press, GA 623, three lectures, 1971.

Colour, London: Rudolf Steiner Press, GA 291, twelve lectures, 2001.

Conferences with the Teachers of the Waldorf School in Stuttgart, Volumes, 1, 2, 3, 4, Forest Row, UK: Steiner Schools Fellowship Publications, 1989.

The Education of the Child in the Light of Anthroposophy, London: Rudolf Steiner Press, 1965.

The Evolution of the Earth and Man, New York: Anthroposophic Press, 1987.

Four Temperaments, New York: Anthroposophic Press, 1987.

Goethe's Conception of the World, Spring Valley, NY: Mercury Press, GA 6, 1985.

Goethe's Standard of the Soul (includes an English text of *The Green Snake and the Beautiful Lily),* New York: Anthroposophic Press, 1979.

How to Know Higher Worlds: A Modern Path of Initiation, New York: Steiner Press, GA 10, 1993.

Man as Symphony of the Creative Word, London: Rudolf Steiner Press, 1995.

Nature's Open Secret, New York: Anthroposophic Press, GA 1, 2000.

Practical Advice to Teachers, London: Rudolf Steiner Press, 1976.

The Riddle of the Soul, Spring Valley, New York: Mercury Press, GA 170, 1996.

Soul Economy and Waldorf Education, New York: Anthroposophic Press, GA 303, 1986.

The Spiritual Ground of Education, New York: Steiner Books, 2003.

The Study of Man, London: Rudolf Steiner Press, GA 293, 1966. Now published as *The Foundations of Human Experience*, New York: Steiner Books, 1996.

A Theory of Knowledge: Based on Goethe's World Conception, New York: Anthroposophic Press, GA 2, 1968.

Theosophy, New York: Anthroposophic Press, GA 9, 1994.

Ways to a New Style of Architecture, GA 286, manuscript, 1982.

Other Authors

Carlgren, Frans. *Education Towards Freedom*, Edinburgh: Floris Books, 2008.

D'Herbois, L. Collot. *Color I & II*, Driebergen, Netherlands: Stichting Magenta, 1981.

Goethe, Johann Wolfgang von Goethe. *Theory of Colors*, Cambridge, MA: MIT Press, 1976.

Hauschka, Magarethe. *Painting as an Exercise for Breathing*, Anne Stockton, translator, Separate edition of *Der Staedtler Brief* magazine for Art in education. Boll/Göppingen, Germany, 1975.

Kandinsky, Wassily. *Concerning the Spiritual in Art*, New York: Wittenborn Art Books, 1976.

Lissau, Magda. *The Temperaments and the Arts*, Fair Oaks, CA: AWSNA Publications, 2003.

Mayer, Gladys. *Colors, A New Approach to Painting*, Hereford, England: Mercury Arts Group, 1983.

Merry, Eleanor C. *Art: Its Occult Basis and Healing Value*, London: New Knowledge Books, 1961.

Rosenkrantz, Arild. *A New Impulse in Art*, London: New Knowledge Books, 1967.

Schindler, Maria. *Goethe's Theory of Color*, London: New Knowledge Books, 1970.

Stockmeyer, E.A. Karl. *Rudolf Steiner's Curriculum for Waldorf Schools I & II*, London: Rudolf Steiner Press, 1965.

Turgenieff, Assja. *The Imagery of the Goetheanum Windows*, London: Rudolf Steiner Press, 1976.

Notes

Part One

1   Wassily Kandinsky, *Concerning the Spiritual in Art*
2   From Rudolf Steiner's *The Healthy Development of the Human Being*, GA 303, first lecture
3   Rudolf Steiner, *The Education of the Child*, GA 34
4   This time period started at the beginning of the 15th century. See Rudolf Steiner, *An Outline of Esoteric Science*, GA 13, Anthroposophic Press, 1997
5   Rudolf Steiner, *The Nature of Colour*, GA 291, lecture June 2, 1923
6   See Rudolf Steiner, *Architecture, Sculpture and Painting in the First Goetheanum*
7   Rudolf Steiner in *Foundations of Human Experience*, GA 293, Anthroposophic Press 1996, lecture August 21, 1919. Please also see the lectures on December 12, 1914, in *Occult Reading and Occult Hearing*, Rudolf Steiner Press 1975, GA 156, and September 12, 1920, in *Rudolf Steiner on Art*, GA 271, in which the importance of sleep before learning is discussed.
8   Among others: Rudolf Steiner, *Wo und wie findet mann der Geist,* GA 57
9   Ernst Kranich, a.o. *Form Drawing*
10   Rudolf Steiner, *Spiritual Grounds of Education*, Anthroposophic Publishing Co., 1947, GA 305, lecture August 22, 1922. Please also see the last part of the third grade curriculum.
11   Ibid.
12   Rudolf Steiner, *The Nature of Colour*, GA 291
13   Goethe, *Theory of Colors*, paragraph 919
14   Marga Woloschin, *The Green Snake*
15   Edmond Schoorel, *The First Seven Years; Physiology of Childhood*
16   Goethe, *Naturwissenschaftliche Schriften*
17   See Rudolf Steiner, *The Essentials of Education*, GA 308
18   Rudolf Steiner, *Manifestations of Karma*, GA 120 and GA 135, lecture May 26, 1910
19   Rudolf Steiner, *The Nature of Colour,* lecture January 4, 1924 'The Hierarchies and the Rainbow,' GA 291
20   Rudolf Steiner, *Spiritual Grounds of Education*, Anthroposophic Publishing Co., 1947, GA 305, lecture August 23, 1922
21   Ernst Kranich a.o., *Form Drawing*

22   Hedwig Hauck, *Handwork and Handcrafts*
23   See Rudolf Steiner, *Rosicrucianism Renewed*, Steiner Books 2002, GA 284
24   Rudolf Steiner, *The Nature of Colour*, GA 291

Part Two

1   Rudolf Steiner, *The Nature of Colour*, GA 291, lecture May 6, 1921
2   Ibid.
3   Ibid.
4   Ibid.
5   Rudolf Steiner, *The Nature of Colour*, GA 291, lecture January 4, 1924,
      "The Hierarchies and the Rainbow"

Part Three

1   For a comprehensive description see Frans Carlgren, *Education Towards Freedom*
2   Anke-Usche Clausen and Martin Riedel, *Schöpferisches Gestalten mit Farben.*
3   Rudolf Steiner, *Conferences with the Teachers of the Waldorf School 1919 to 1924*,
      GA 300a, b, c, lecture November 16, 1921
4   See Rudolf Steiner, *Conferences with the Teachers of the Waldorf School 1919 to 1924*,
      GA 300a, b, c, lecture November 15, 1920
5   Ibid.
6   See Rudolf Steiner, *An Outline of Esoteric Science*, Anthroposophic Press, 1997,
      GA 13
7   See also Rudolf Steiner, *Secrets of the Biblical Story of Creation,* Kessinger
      Publishing, Whitefish, MT, 2010
8   Rudolf Steiner, *Man as Symphony of the Creative Word*, lecture October 20, 1923,
      GA 230
9   Ibid.
10   Julius Hebing, *Lebenskreise-Farbenkreise*
11   Also see Rudolf Steiner, *The Nature of Colour*, GA 291, lecture May 6, 1921
12   Rudolf Steiner, *Conferences with the Teachers of the Waldorf School 1919 to 1924*,
      GA 300, lecture February 5, 1924
13   Ibid.
14   Anke-Usche Clausen and Martin Riedel, *Schöpferisches Gestalten mit Farben;*
      Günter Meier, *Pflanzenfarben*, Dornach 1994; Let van de Vrande, *Groot plantaardig
      verfboek*, Baarn, 1980; Victoria Finlay, *A Brilliant History of Color in Art*, 2014;
      Monica Rotgans, *Verf. 500.000 jaar verf en schilderkunst*, Warnsveld, 2005

Part Four

1   Rudolf Steiner, *The Nature of Colour*, GA 291, lecture June 2, 1923
2   See Rudolf Steiner, *Practical Advice to Teachers*, GA 295, lecture September 6, 1919

Part Five

1   More about Dürer in Herma Bashin-Hecht's, *Der Mensch als Pilger*
2   Rudolf Steiner, *Practical Advice to Teachers*, GA295
3   Ibid.
4   Rudolf Steiner, *Conferences with the Teachers of the Waldorf School 1919 to 1924*, GA 300 a, b, c, lecture February 5, 1924
5   Margrit Jünemann and Frits Weitmann, *Drawing and Painting in Rudolf Steiner Schools*
6   Assja Turgenieff, *Rudolf Steiners Entwürfe für die Glasfenster des Goetheanums*
7   Anke-Usche Clausen and Martin Riedel, *Zeichnen = Sehen lernen!*
8   Margrit Jünemann and Frits Weitmann, *Drawing and Painting in Rudolf Steiner Schools*

Part Six

1   Rudolf Steiner, *Verses and Meditations Collection*, GA 40
2   Goethe, *Theory of Colors*
3   Rudolf Steiner, *The Nature of Colour*, GA 291
4   See Rudolf Steiner, *The Child's Changing Consciousness as the Basis of Pedagogical Practice*, GA 306. Also see Rudolf Steiner, *The Nature of Colour*, GA 291
5   Rudolf Steiner, *The Nature of Colour*, GA 291, lecture May 8, 1921
6   Ibid.
7   Marie Goddeck, *Die Schilskizzen von Rudolf Steiner*
8   See Rudolf Steiner, *Kunst und Kunsterkenntnis*, GA 271, Rudolf Steiner Verlag 1985
9   See Rudolf Steiner, *Erziehung und Unterricht aus Menschenerkenntnis*, GA 302a, Rudolf Steiner Verlag 1983
10   Rudolf Steiner, *Waldorf Education and Anthroposophy*, GA 304a

Made in the USA
Monee, IL
20 February 2020